Fr.

EUCHARIST
Heaven & Earth Unite

EWTN Publishing, Inc.
Irondale, Alabama

Copyright © 2025 by EWTN Publishing, Inc.

Previously published in 2008 by Fatima Family Apostolate International, Inc. This edition by EWTN Publishing, Inc. contains editorial revisions and deletions to the original text.

Printed in the United States of America. All rights reserved.

Cover design by LUCAS Art & Design, Jenison, MI.

Cover photo by Jacob Bentzinger, Unsplash
(jacob-bentzinger-OrovnGeyG-A-unsplash.jpg).

Unless otherwise noted, biblical references in this book are taken from the Catholic Edition of the Revised Standard Version of the Bible, copyright 1965, 1966 by the Division of Christian Education of the National Council of the Churches of Christ in the United States of America. Used by permission. All rights reserved.

Excerpts from the English translation of the *Catechism of the Catholic Church* for use in the United States of America copyright © 1994, United States Catholic Conference, Inc. — Libreria Editrice Vaticana. English translation of the *Catechism of the Catholic Church: Modifications from the Editio Typica* copyright © 1997, United States Conference of Catholic Bishops — Libreria Editrice Vaticana.

No part of this book may be reproduced, stored in a retrieval system, or transmitted in any form, or by any means, electronic, mechanical, photocopying, or otherwise, without the prior written permission of the publisher, except by a reviewer, who may quote brief passages in a review.

EWTN Publishing, Inc.
5817 Old Leeds Road, Irondale, AL 35210

Distributed by Sophia Institute Press, Box 5284, Manchester, NH 03108.

Paperback ISBN: 978-1-68278-443-3
Ebook ISBN: 978-1-68278-444-0

Library of Congress Control Number: 2025941446

First printing

Eucharist

Author's Dedication

*I dedicate this book on the Eucharist to
Jesus Christ, Mediator,
and to Mary, Mother of God and the Church.*

*Next, I dedicate this labor of love to Mother Angelica,
whose faith and sacrifice have given the world EWTN
and the Shrine of the Most Blessed Sacrament
in Hanceville, Alabama.*

Contents

Foreword by John C. Preiss ix

Introduction 1

1. Biblical Roots of the Eucharist 5
2. "The Church Flows from the Eucharist". 37
3. The Eucharist Unites Members into the Whole Christ. . . . 67
4. Lift Up Your Hearts. 93
5. The Barycenter of Catholic Life 121
6. All the Mysteries of Christ Are in the Eucharist for Transformation in Christ 149
7. Faith in the Eucharist as Sacrifice and Sacrament for Worship and Growth in Sanctifying Grace 179
8. Priesthood and Eucharist Go Together 193
9. Eucharistic Adoration 223
10. The Holy Eucharist and the Holy Angels 253
11. The Church Is Guardian of Eucharistic Faith 271
12. Fire and Spirit — Heaven and Earth Unite 281

About the Author 305

Foreword

AS A CONVERT TO THE CATHOLIC FAITH, I can attest to the profound experience of receiving Jesus and spending time in His True Presence in adoration in my life. I remember driving by a Catholic church, stopping in, and — feeling that something was different — being drawn to Jesus in the Eucharist. Reading *Eucharist: Heaven & Earth Unite* presented to me a beautiful understanding of what really happens in the Consecration and of the sacredness of the altar, where the infinite love of God meets the longing hearts of His people. In this book, Fr. Robert J. Fox invites readers to embark on a transformative journey into the very heart of Holy Mass — unveiling its deepest meaning and the profound reality of Christ's True Presence in the Eucharist.

Fr. Fox, renowned for his devotion to the Blessed Sacrament and his tireless work in spreading the message of Fatima, spent years in prayer, study, and pastoral ministry before authoring this book. His life's mission was to draw souls closer to Jesus through Mary and through the mystery of the Eucharist. Drawing from his experiences at the Shrine of the Most Blessed Sacrament and his global apostolate, he brought to these pages a unique blend of theological insight, pastoral wisdom, and personal devotion.

This book is not merely theological but is a heartfelt invitation to encounter Christ anew. Fr. Fox's writing is both accessible and profound, guiding readers — whether lifelong Catholics or those newly curious — into a deeper understanding of what truly happens at every Mass. Fr. Fox explains how time and eternity intersect in the liturgy and how the sacrifice of Calvary is made present for us, not as a distant memory but as a living reality.

Through thoughtful reflection and clear teaching, Fr. Fox addresses questions that stir in many hearts: What does it mean to say Christ is truly present — Body, Blood, Soul, and Divinity — in the Eucharist? How does the Mass connect us to the worship of Heaven? Why is the Eucharist the "source and summit" of the Christian life? Fr. Fox's answers, rooted in Scripture, Tradition, and the lived Faith of the Church, are both intellectually satisfying and spiritually enriching.

For those who struggle with doubt or distraction at Mass, this book offers clarity and encouragement. Fr. Fox gently leads readers to recognize the hidden glory before them, to see beyond the veil of bread and wine, and to adore the Lord, Who humbles Himself to become our food. Fr. Fox reminds us that every Mass is a miracle, a moment when the eternal Son of God comes to dwell among us, inviting us into communion with Him and with the whole company of Heaven.

This book challenges us to move beyond routine and to embrace the Mass as the greatest treasure of our Faith. It calls us to respond to Christ's gift with adoration, thanksgiving, and a desire to live Eucharistic lives — lives marked by love, sacrifice, and unity with God and neighbor.

May you be drawn ever closer to the Heart of Jesus, present in the Blessed Sacrament, and may your belief in His True Presence be strengthened and renewed. As you journey through these pages, may you echo the words of the disciples at Emmaus: "Did not our hearts burn within us?" (Luke 24:32) — for indeed, the Lord is here, and He calls us to Himself.

John C. Preiss
Director of the Fatima Family Apostolate

Introduction

Our Lord said to St. Francis: "Francis, rebuild my house which, as you see, is falling into ruin." St. Francis found prayer, and especially the Eucharist, to be instrumental in the renewal of the Church.

In our present day, we too are being called by God to repair the Church which Jesus Christ purchased with His own Precious Blood. Pope Benedict XVI emphasized beautifully the Divine Liturgy of the Eucharist and the need of Eucharistic adoration, all for the purpose of upbuilding and renewing the Church.

Recently the Catholic Church celebrated eight hundred years since the conversion of St. Francis. This Saint of Assisi, with his great spirit of joy, love, and faith in the Eucharist, considered so august the reality of what and who the Eucharist is that he did not consider himself worthy to be ordained a priest, to consecrate the bread and wine into Our Living Lord Himself. He felt unworthy to perpetuate Christ's sacrifice as an ordained priest. Thus he remained a permanent deacon until death, two years before which Our Lord gave him the stigmata, His own precious wounds, to remind all of His Sacrifice of the Cross for our redemption.

It was the same St. Francis who is credited with locating the tabernacle front and center in the Catholic church, the house of God. Such centrality of the Eucharist is the effort demonstrated in this book on the Eucharist, uniting heaven and earth. To place the Eucharist first and central in our spiritual lives is crucial to an authentic Christian life.

Eucharist

While the Saint of Assisi did not consider himself worthy of priestly ordination, he would be among the first to encourage all to pray for many holy priests, and that many young men hear and answer Christ's call. No other vocation on this earth can compare with that of the priest, who each day acts in a visible way with visible things (bread, wine, oil) but the effects of which are spiritual and invisible, eternal and heavenly.

> The Eucharist is "the source and summit of the Christian life." "The other sacraments, and indeed all ecclesiastical ministries and works of the apostolate, are bound up with the Eucharist and are oriented toward it. For in the blessed Eucharist is contained the whole spiritual good of the Church, namely Christ himself, our Pasch." (*Catechism of the Catholic Church* [CCC], 1324)

It is my prayer that this book will help many come to know and love Jesus Christ more deeply in the Most Blessed Sacrament. I pray that this book may assist readers to appreciate in awe the infinite profundity of the Sacrifice of the Mass. When repetition occurs, it is to direct the reader to a new dimension of the Eucharist.

As a priest in my fifty-fourth year in Christ's priesthood, I have offered the Sacrifice of the Mass daily these many years. For the past five years I've offered Mass each day at the Shrine of the Most Blessed Sacrament in Hanceville, Alabama. This shrine, under the direction of the Poor Clare Nuns of Perpetual Adoration, Our Lady of the Angels Monastery, was founded by Mother Angelica. She writes the preface to this book. I serve as a priest at this Shrine, where nuns are in adoration of the Real Presence of Our Eucharistic Lord each day and night of the year. They participate gloriously each day in the Divine Liturgy of the Eucharist. During the daylight hours, I meet people who arrive here to adore from throughout the United States and beyond.

Introduction

I encourage you to read this book on the Eucharist in a meditative way so as to appreciate that at Mass "not only the members still here on earth, but also those already *in the glory of heaven*" are united to the offering of Christ (*CCC*, 1370).

It took two years to complete this book. As I proofread the final printed pages, including this introduction, I learned I had bone cancer. That word from the doctor made these pages even more meaningful to me. I ask your prayers that I may participate forever in the heavenly liturgy.

Fr. Robert J. Fox
August 15, 2008
Hanceville, Alabama

1

Biblical Roots of the Eucharist

To get at the biblical roots of the Eucharist, we would have to begin with the first pages of public divine revelation when God creates man in his own image and likeness. To understand the New Testament, we must comprehend it in light of and union with the Old Testament. Through the Fall of man and the various covenants, God calls man back into union with Himself.

God gradually communicates the mystery of Himself in deeds and in words. Already to our first parents God promises salvation (Gen. 3:15) and offers them His covenant. This means God's plan for the Church and the Eucharist, which flows from the Church, is present from the very beginning of the creation of man, man's Fall, and the promise of redemption. The mystery is only gradually unfolded in revelation. The Eucharist is associated with God's promise of redemption, for we will see that the Eucharist contains the very Sacrifice of Redemption and is itself the New Covenant made present now and forever.

Already in Genesis 14, when Abram is returning from his victory in war, he is met by Melchizedek, king of Salem, who "brought out bread and wine; he was priest of God Most High" (Gen. 14:18). To offer bread and wine in a thanksgiving blessing and sacrifice so early in salvation history already prefigures the Eucharist and priesthood, which go together. While explaining His mission, Jesus referred to Psalm 110, which features the priesthood of Melchizedek. The Letter to the Hebrews clearly presents Jesus Christ as God and Melchizedek as a type of Christ, having "neither beginning of days nor end of life, but resembling the Son of God he continues a priest for ever" (Heb. 7:3). "Those who formerly became priests took their office without an oath, but this one was addressed with an oath, 'The Lord has sworn and will not change his mind, "Thou art a priest for ever."'" (Heb. 7:21).

We shall see that Jesus' first public miracle at Cana of changing water into wine anticipates the Eucharist of wine changed into Jesus' Blood. It also marks an anticipation of Jesus' "hour" when He offers Himself in sacrifice on the Cross. Thus His first public miracle ties together the Eucharist and His redeeming sacrifice.

Through prophets, God prepared mankind to accept the salvation He destined for humanity. Again and again, God offers mankind a covenant. Finally God sent his own Divine Son, revealing Himself fully in Jesus Christ and in Him established his covenant forever. We celebrate and participate in that eternal covenant at every Sacrifice of the Mass.

The sacrifice, contained or made present in the Eucharist, was prefigured in Genesis 14:18 and 22:13. It was foretold in Malachi 1:10–14. Such is attested in 1 Corinthians 10:16, 18–21; 11:23–26 and Hebrews 13:10.

As the Passover meal made present for those who participated in it the Exodus event, the Mass, in a complete and true way, makes present what happened at Calvary.

The Passover meal, or Exodus event, is what Christ first celebrated at the Last Supper. After celebrating the old Pasch, to celebrate the memory of the departure from Egypt (Exod. 12), Jesus instituted a new Pasch, namely Himself to be offered by the Church through her priests under visible signs in order to celebrate the memory of His passage from this world to the Father. This new Pasch would make present Jesus Christ in the shedding of His blood, by which He redeemed us. He "delivered us from the dominion of darkness and transferred us to the kingdom" (Col. 1:13).

That eternal covenant, instituted at the Last Supper, was sealed on the Cross, and the acceptance of it was manifested by God in the Resurrection of Jesus Christ on Easter Sunday.

The Hebrew Scriptures of the Old Testament record how under the Old Covenant, sacrifices of lambs, bulls, goats, and other animals were offered in the Temple for the forgiveness of sin. It was no accident that St. John's Gospel relates that Jesus died at the exact time that the Jewish Temple sacrifices were taking place. Jesus is the true Lamb, the true sacrifice who takes away the sins of the world. One near the Temple of Jerusalem could have heard the bleating of the sacrificial lambs as Jesus hung on the Cross and died.

Bl. Anne Catherine Emmerich, in her four-volume *The Life of Jesus Christ and Biblical Revelations*, amazingly follows the Scriptures in her private revelations she received. She thus fills in intimate details of Jesus' birth, public ministry, sufferings, death, and Resurrection. Quotes from volume 3 follow:

> The Pharisees began a violent dispute with Jesus, again bringing forward their charge that he drove out the devil through the power of Beelzebul. Jesus called them children of the father of lies, and told them that God no longer desired bloody [animal] sacrifices. I heard him speaking of the Blood of the Lamb, of the innocent blood that they would soon pour out, and of which the blood of an animal was only a symbol. With the Sacrifice of the Lamb, he continued, their religious rites would come to an end. All they that believed in the Sacrifice of the Lamb, would be reconciled to God, but they to whom he was addressing himself should, as the murderers of the Lamb, be condemned. He warned his disciples in presence of

the Pharisees to beware of them. This so enraged these men that Jesus and his disciples had to withdraw and hurry off into the desert. I saw among the listening crowd, some men with cudgels. Jesus had never before attacked his aggressors so boldly. He and his disciples passed the night in the desert and then went to Corozain....

Crowds of people flocked thither, and laid their sick along the road by which Jesus was to come. On his way to the synagogue, he cured the dropsical, the lame, and the blind.

In spite of the violent attacks of the Pharisees, Jesus spoke in prophetic terms of his future Passion. He alluded to their repeated sacrifices and expiations, notwithstanding which they still remained full of sins and abomination. Then he spoke of the goat which at the Feast of Atonement was driven from Jerusalem into the desert with the sins of the people laid upon it. He said very significantly (and yet they did not understand him) that the time was drawing near when in the same way they would drive out an innocent Man, One that loved them, One that had done everything for them, One that truly bore their sins. They would drive him out, he said, and murder him amid the clash of arms. At these words, a great din and jeering shouts arose among the Pharisees. Jesus left the synagogue and went out into the city. The Pharisees came to him and demanded an explanation of what he had just said, but he replied that they could not now understand it.

In volume 4, Bl. Anne Catherine Emmerich continues her spiritual experiences, which coincide with biblical revelations, giving great details in harmony with St. John the Evangelist, writing: "But there are also many other things which Jesus did; were every one of them to be written, I suppose that the world itself could not contain the books that would be written" (John 21:25). Volume 4 on the death of Jesus follows:

> The hour of the Lord was now come. He was struggling with death, and a cold sweat burst out on every limb. John was standing by the cross and wiping Jesus' feet with his handkerchief. Magdalene, utterly crushed with grief, was leaning at the back of the cross. The Blessed Virgin, supported in the arms of Mary Cleophas and Salome, was standing between Jesus and the cross of the good thief, her gaze fixed upon her dying Son. Jesus spoke: "It is consummated!" and raising his head he cried with a loud voice: "Father, into Thy hands I commend my Spirit!" The sweet, loud cry rang through Heaven and earth. Then he bowed his head and gave up the Spirit....
>
> When Jesus with a loud cry gave up his Spirit into the hands of his Heavenly Father, I saw his soul, like a luminous figure, penetrating the earth at the foot of the cross, accompanied by a band of luminous angels, among whom was Gabriel. I saw a great multitude of evil spirits driven by those angels from the earth into the abyss. Jesus sent many souls from Limbo to reenter their body, in order to frighten and warn the impenitent, as well as to bear witness to himself....
>
> The High Priests in the Temple had recommenced the slaughtering of the lambs, which had been interrupted by the frightful darkness. They were rejoicing triumphantly over the returning light when suddenly the ground began to quake, a hollow rumbling was heard, and the crash of toppling walls, accompanied by the hissing noise made by the rending of the veil, produced for the moment in the vast assemblage speechless terror broken only by an occasional cry of woe. But the crowd was so well-ordered, the immense edifice so

full, the going and coming of the great number engaged in slaughtering so perfectly regulated — the act of slaughtering, the draining of blood, the sprinkling of the altars with it by the long row of countless priests amid the sound of canticles and trumpets — all this was done with so great accord, so great harmony of action, that the fright did not lead to general confusion and dispersion. The Temple was so large, there were so many different halls and apartments, that the sacrifices went on quietly in some, while fright and horror were pervading others, and in others still the priests managed to keep order. It was not till the dead made their appearance in different parts of the Temple that the ceremonies were entirely interrupted and the sacrifices discontinued, as if the Temple had become polluted. Still even this did not come so suddenly upon the multitude as to cause them in their flight to rush precipitously down the numerous steps of the Temple. They dispersed by degrees, hurrying down one group at a time, while in some quarters of the building the priests were able to bring back the frightened worshippers and keep them together. Still, however, the anxiety, the fright of all, though different in degree, was something quite indescribable....

The High Priest Caiaphas and his followers, owing to their desperate insolence, did not lose presence of mind. Like the sagacious magistrate of a seditious city, by threats, by the separation of parties, by persuasion, and all kinds of deceitful arguments, Caiaphas warded off the danger. By his demoniacal obstinacy especially, and his own apparent calmness, he prevented not only a general panic, so destructive in its consequences, but likewise hindered the people from construing those frightful warnings into a testimony of the innocent death of Jesus. The Roman garrison on the fortress

Antonia did all that could be done to maintain order, and although the confusion and consternation were great and caused a discontinuance of the festal ceremonies, yet there was no insurrection....

I remember the following striking incidents: The two great columns at the entrance of the Holy of Holies in the Temple, between which hung a magnificent curtain, fell in opposite directions, the left-hand one to the south, the right-hand to the north. The beam which they supported gave way and the great curtain was, with a hissing noise, rent from top to bottom so that, opening on either side, it fell.... The people could now see into the Holy of Holies. In the northern wall near it was the little cell in which Simeon used to pray. A great stone was hurled upon it, and the roof fell in. In some of the halls the floor sank here and there, beams were displaced, and pillars gave way.

The curtain in the inner chamber of the sanctuary of the Jewish Temple in Jerusalem separated it from the outer chamber. It was reserved for the presence of God and could be entered only by the high priest once a year on the Day of Atonement. Its destruction as Jesus died on the Cross was a sign from God of an end of the Old Covenant, and Jesus' sacrifice on the Cross became the striking of the New Covenant that is eternal and present to us now in the Eucharist.

And behold, the curtain of the temple was torn in two, from top to bottom; and the earth shook, and the rocks were split; the tombs also were opened, and many bodies of the saints who had fallen asleep were raised, and coming out of the tombs after his resurrection they went into the holy city and appeared to many. When the centurion and those who were with him, keeping watch over Jesus, saw the earthquake and what took place, they were filled with awe, and said, "Truly this was the Son of God!" (Matt. 27:51–54).

Jesus Christ gathering the apostles about Him as the first bishops whom he ordained at the Last Supper, the night before He died, instituted then the Holy Eucharist, which perpetuates His New Covenant. Jesus built His Church upon Simon, whom he called Peter or "Rock." Peter was the first to confess Jesus to be the Christ, the Son of the living God (Matt. 16:16–19). Jesus commissioned the total deposit of faith, which He had given to the apostles, to His Church, with Peter as visible head. The faith of the members of the Church has been handed down from the apostles. Peter's mission will be, as the unshakable rock of the Church, to keep this faith from every lapse and to strengthen his brothers and sisters in the fullness of true faith.

While the apostles were given special powers, Jesus entrusted a specific authority to Peter and his successors: "I will give you the keys of the kingdom of heaven, and whatever you bind on earth shall be bound in heaven, and whatever you loose on earth shall be loosed in heaven" (Matt. 16:19).

The Church of Jesus Christ with Her fullness of true faith begins thus to unfold already in the Garden when our first parents fell and God responded with a promise. It will all lead up to the Eucharist, which perpetuates all that God has revealed and has given for our salvation and so that we may have union with the Most Blessed Trinity through Jesus Christ.

From the time Peter confessed that Jesus is the Christ, the Son of the living God, Christ "began to show his disciples that he must go to Jerusalem and suffer many things ... and be killed, and on the third day be raised" (Matt. 16:21). His total ministry led up to that final week of His life, known as Holy Week, when He would institute the Holy

Eucharist. In the Eucharist, Jesus would make present for every age His sacrifice offered sacramentally at the Last Supper, offered physically in a bloody manner on Good Friday. That Eucharist would also make present in the Eucharist His Easter Sunday risen body.

The *breaking of bread* is a scriptural name for the Eucharist. The Lord's Supper, which He took with His apostles on the eve of His Passion and death, anticipated the wedding feast of the Lamb in the heavenly Jerusalem (1 Cor. 11:20; Rev. 19:9).

We are told in the Acts of the Apostles that in the primitive community of Jerusalem, the disciples "devoted themselves to the apostles' teaching and fellowship, to the *breaking of bread* and the prayers.... Day by day, attending the temple together and *breaking bread* in their homes, they partook of food with glad and generous hearts [emphases added]" (2:42, 46).

The *Catechism of the Catholic Church* states:

> In the first community of Jerusalem, believers "devoted themselves to the apostles' teaching and fellowship, to *the breaking of bread*, and the prayers [emphasis added]." (2624).

Breaking of bread was part of a Jewish meal. Jesus, as master of the table, would bless and distribute bread. He did this above all on the eve of His Passion, at the Last Supper (Matt. 26:26; 1 Cor. 11:24). This is how His disciples who were on the way to Emmaus, after his Resurrection, will recognize Him. At first "their eyes were kept from recognizing him" (Luke 24:16).

We are reminded of the liturgy of the Mass in the account of what transpired between Jesus and those two disciples on the way to Emmaus that first Easter Sunday. The disciples had been walking the seven-mile distance from Jerusalem, discussing all that had happened from Holy Thursday evening through Jesus' Crucifixion and rumors of His Resurrection. They were confused.

Eucharist

The first part of the Mass is known as the Liturgy of the Word. This is what Jesus first did for those Emmaus disciples:

> And beginning with Moses and all the prophets, he interpreted to them in all the scriptures the things concerning himself. So they drew near to the village to which they were going. He appeared to be going further, but they constrained him, saying, "Stay with us, for it is toward evening and the day is now far spent." So he went in to stay with them. When he was at table with them, he took the bread and blessed, and broke it, and gave it to them. And their eyes were opened and they recognized him; and he vanished out of their sight. They said to each other, "Did not our hearts burn within us while he talked to us on the road, while he opened to us the scriptures? (Luke 24:27–32)

Notice before the breaking of the bread, Jesus explained all the Scriptures for them, showing that it was necessary that "the Christ should suffer these things and enter into his glory (Luke 24:26). When they recognized Him, Jesus disappeared. His physical presence was no longer needed. It tells us that to remain physically visible would be a hindrance to their faith. At Mass we first have the Liturgy of the Word, then the Liturgy of the Eucharist, in the order that took place with the disciples of Emmaus. Writings of early Church Fathers indicate the basic structure of the Sacrifice of the Mass, just as we have it today.

Thus it is shown in historical studies that the basic structure of the Sacrifice of the Mass is a well-established practice already for the very early Christians. The first Christians had Mass celebrated in their homes. Mass was offered in the catacombs during persecutions of the first centuries. Inscriptions and images remaining still today on the walls in the catacombs in the outlying districts of Rome indicate their faith in the Eucharist as sacrifice. With time, and the end of early persecutions, the Mass was celebrated in public worship places. Always, the fundamental structure of the Mass we know today has remained the same.

Pope Benedict XVI has written of the Mass of 1962 (extraordinary form of the Roman Rite or Missal of Pope St. John XXIII) and that of 1970. Over the many centuries of the Roman Rite, Pope Benedict XVI has written, popes have from time to time made modest changes; changes in some ceremonies of the Divine Liturgy, not in the essence of the essentials of what Jesus gave us at the Last Supper. Pius V did so in 1570, John XXIII did so in 1962, and Paul VI made some greater changes in 1970, the last producing what is called the *Novus Ordo*. "It is not appropriate to speak of these two versions of the Roman Missal [1962 and 1970] as if they were 'two Rites.' Rather, it is a matter of a twofold use of one and the same rite," wrote Benedict XVI. That of Pius V and John XXIII are now known as the *extraordinary form of the Roman Rite*. That of Paul VI of 1970 is called the *ordinary form of the Roman Rite*.

In the history of the liturgy, there is growth and progress, but no rupture. What earlier generations held as sacred remains sacred and great for us too, and it cannot be all of a sudden entirely forbidden or even considered harmful. "It behooves all of us to preserve the riches which have developed in the Church's faith and prayer, and to give them their proper place," we are instructed by Pope Benedict XVI. The Mass has always contained the essentials of what Jesus gave His Church when He instituted the Holy Eucharist.

Some would interpret as only symbolic Jesus' words that He was giving us His Body to eat and His Blood to drink. They point to his words where He called Himself a gate or door (John 10:9), a vine (John 15:1), a lamb (John 1:29), a light (John 8:12), or living water (John 4:14). Christians of the first centuries understood that Jesus was not being merely symbolic in talking about His Real Presence in the Eucharist as His real Body and Blood.

Eucharist

Pope Benedict XVI, in his book *Jesus of Nazareth*, discusses what some scholars claim of St. John's Gospel — that it is the construction of the early community trying to make sense of their experience of Jesus. Pope Benedict cannot accept that. He writes: "The anonymous community is credited with an astonishing level of theological genius — who were the great figures responsible for inventing all this? No, the greatness, the dramatic newness, comes directly from Jesus; within the faith and life of the community it is further developed, but is not created. In fact, the 'community' would not even have emerged and survived at all unless some extraordinary reality has preceded it." That reality is Jesus Christ, true God, true man, the second Person of the Most Blessed Trinity become man.

Pope Benedict XVI informs us that — on question after question — critical biblical scholarship turns out to offer little more than "a graveyard of mutually contradictory hypotheses." He notes that the Good Shepherd text of John 10 does not begin with "I am the good shepherd" but with another image, that of the gate. "Whoever does not enter the sheepfold through the gate but climbs in some other way is a thief and a marauder. The one who enters through the gate is shepherd of the sheep." Then Jesus says, "I am the sheepgate." Pope Benedict writes: "This can only really mean that Jesus is establishing the criterion for those who will shepherd his flock after his ascension to the Father. The proof of a true shepherd is that he enters through Jesus as the door, [or gate]. For in this way it is ultimately Jesus who is the shepherd — the flock 'belongs' to him alone."

Consider Luke 9:18, where one can read: "Now it happened that as he [Jesus] was praying alone the disciples were with him." Benedict says that is a "deliberate paradox." "The disciples are drawn into his solitude, his communion with the Father that is reserved to him alone. They are privileged to see him as the one who ... speaks face-to-face with the Father, person to person. They are privileged to see him in his utterly unique filial being — at the point from which all his words, his deeds, and his powers issue." Benedict is following the pattern of the early Church Fathers. Nothing in the biblical text is accidental or out of place; every passage, every word, has its purpose. Benedict presents us the presupposition of divine direction or inspiration as evident in the biblical narratives.

Read the entire sixth chapter of John slowly and meditatively. Many who do this will discover for the first time how strongly Jesus taught what Catholic dogmas and doctrines teach regarding the Eucharist. When Jesus gave His extended discourse on the Bread of Life and many of the disciples abandoned Him, they knew He was not speaking in mere symbolism. If they had misunderstood Him, misinterpreted Him when they walked away, as the perfect teacher, He would have called them back and made clarifications. He did not. He meant what He said.

Many disciples left Jesus because they knew He was not talking symbolically but meant exactly what He said. Genesis 9:3–4 and Leviticus 17:14 forbade the eating of bloody foods or the drinking of blood. Those abandoning Jesus knew of these teachings from the Old Testament and that Jesus was talking literally. The disciples did not abandon Jesus when He called Himself "door" or "vine" or "Lamb" or "the Son of God." They remained with Jesus when He said He was "the way, and the truth, and the life." They stayed with Him when He said that no one can go to God the Father except through Him (John 14:6). When He forgave sins, they remained. But they left when He spoke of the Real Presence of His Body and Blood in the Eucharist, which He would give us and that we must eat and drink.

Jesus always explained in greater detail whenever there was confusion in understanding. But in John 6, we see Jesus reiterating again and again that He was going to give us Himself to eat and drink and that we could not have eternal life otherwise.

Eucharist

Pope Benedict XVI has noted the liturgical character of St. John's Gospel and its rhythm dictated by Israel's calendar of religious festivals. Early on in John we read of the "Passover of the Jews," a dominant feature, associated with the Temple, and therefore of the Cross and Resurrection (John 2:13–25). There is the healing of the paralytic, the occasion of Jesus' first major public discourse in Jerusalem, connected with a "feast of the Jews" (John 5:1), which is probably the Feast of Weeks, or Pentecost. Then in John 6 there is the multiplication of the loaves of bread and its explanation in Jesus' Bread of Life discourse, the great Eucharistic discourse in John's Gospel, which is presented in the context of the Passover (John 6:4). In John 7:38ff, Jesus gives another major discourse promising "rivers of living water." It is in the setting of the Feast of Tabernacles. Finally Jesus is presented in Jerusalem in wintertime for the Feast of the Dedication of the Temple, Hanukkah (John 10:22).

The life of Jesus in John is completed during His last Passover (John 12:1), when Jesus becomes the true Paschal Lamb who pours out His Precious Blood on the Cross for our salvation. Jesus' great priestly prayer (John 17) is seen, according to Pope Benedict XVI, as containing subtle Eucharistic theology, theology of the sacrifice of the Church, in terms of the theological content of the Feast of the Atonement. St. John is oftentimes seen as the first Christian theologian, as he has years to meditate before writing his Gospel. The Synoptic Gospel writers give historical accounts; John gives theological insights into the life of Jesus Christ, true God and true man; he develops a deeper faith understanding of what Jesus revealed.

In the First Letter of John, which from early Christian tradition is attributed to the Apostle John who wrote the fourth Gospel, we read: "Who is it that overcomes the world but he who believes that Jesus is the Son of God? This is he who came by water and blood, Jesus Christ, not with the water only but with the water and the blood. And the Spirit is the witness, because the Spirit is the truth." (1 John 5:5–7).

St. John, writing at the end of the first century (ca. A.D. 90–100), according to Pope Benedict XVI (*Jesus of Nazareth*), is responding to an early form or interpretation of Christianity that wants only the Word, but not flesh and blood. For such "Christians," Jesus' body and His redeeming death ultimately play no role. That would mean that what is left of this kind of "Christianity" is mere "water" without Jesus' human body and blood, and thus the Word would lose power. Christianity would be mere doctrine, mere moralism, an affair of the intellect, but it would lack flesh and blood. That would be denying the redemptive character of Jesus' blood poured out for us as His human body is crucified, offered in sacrifice for our salvation. The Apostle John in writing of "Jesus Christ it is who came through water and blood — not in water only, but in water and in blood" — as he points to the real body of Jesus offered in sacrifice for our redemption — is pointing at the same time to the sacraments, especially Baptism and the Holy Eucharist.

To appreciate the Eucharist, we have to appreciate and know by proper and full faith who Jesus Christ is. "He is before all things, and in him all things hold together" (Col. 1:17). St. Paul's words about Jesus inspire awe and wonder in our hearts. "He is the image of the invisible God, the first-born of all creation; for in him all things were created, in heaven and on earth, visible and invisible, whether thrones or dominions or principalities or authorities — all things were created through him and for him. He is before all things, and in him all things hold together. He is the head of the body, the church; he is the beginning, the first-born from the dead, that in everything he might be pre-eminent" (Col. 1:15–18).

The Catholic has the infallible and magisterial pronouncements of his Church, which he believes speaks for Jesus Christ, under the guidance and protection of the Holy Spirit. There are many biblical references for the following teachings as to who Jesus is. Here we give but a skeleton summary of Church dogmatic teachings on Our Lord.

On the subject of God the Redeemer, Catholics can know by certain faith that Jesus Christ is true God and true Son of God: John 1:34; John 15:1–11, 24; Phil. 2:5–11; Rom. 9:5; 2 Cor. 11:31; Gal. 1:3–5; Titus 2:13. Christ took to Himself a real body, not a phantom body: Luke 24:39; John 1:14; 2 John 7; Rom. 5:15; 1 Cor. 15:21; 1 Tim. 2:5; 2 Tim. 2:8; Gal. 3:16; Apostles' Creed; Council of Chalcedon (451); Second Council of Lyons (1274); Council of Florence (1438–1445). Jesus Christ was truly generated and born of the Virgin Mary: Gen. 22:18; Matt. 1:1; 9:27; 12:23; 22:42; Rom. 1:3; Gal. 4:4; 2 Tim. 2:8; creeds of the Church. The divine and human natures of Jesus Christ are "hypostatically" united, i.e., joined to each other in one Divine Person, the second Person of the eternal and Most Blessed Trinity: John 8:57–59; Rom. 9:5; 1 Cor. 2:8; Gal. 4:4; Acts 3:15; Council of Ephesus (431); Council of Chalcedon (451); Second Council of Constantinople (553).

In the hypostatic union, each of the two natures of Christ continues unimpaired and unmixed with the other: John 1:14; Phil. 2:6–11; dogmatic writing of Pope Leo the Great (449), Council of Chalcedon (451). Each of the two natures of Christ has its own natural will and its own natural manner of operation: Matt. 26:39; Luke 22:42; John 4:34; 5:30; 6:38; 8:29; 14:31; Phil. 2:8; Rom. 5:19; Heb. 10:9; Isa. 53:7; Third Council of Constantinople (680–681). The hypostatic union of Christ's human nature with the divine Logos, or Word, took place at the moment of conception in the Blessed Virgin Mary: John 1:1; Rom. 1:3; Gal. 4:4; creeds of the Church. The hypostatic union can never cease: Luke 1:33; Heb. 7:24; Council of Constantinople (381).

The hypostatic union was effected by the three Divine Persons acting in common: Matt. 1:18, 20; Luke 1:35; Heb. 10:5; Creed of the

Eleventh Council of Toledo (675); Fourth Lateran Council (1215). Only the second Divine Person assumed to Himself a human nature: John 1:14; 3:16–36; creeds of the Church. Not only as God, but also as man, Jesus Christ is God's natural Son: Matt. 3:17; John 1:14, 18; 3:16; Rom. 8:32; Fathers of the Church, such as St. Augustine. The God-Man, Jesus Christ, is to be worshipped with one single kind of worship, the absolute worship of latria, which is due to God alone: Matt. 28:9, 17; John 5:23; Phil. 2:10; Heb. 1:6; Rev. 5:12; Council of Ephesus (431); Second Council of Constantinople (553).

Christ's divine and human characteristics and actions are to be predicated of the one Word Incarnate: Acts 3:15; 20:28; Rom. 8:32; 1 Cor 2:8; Apostles' Creed; Council of Ephesus (431). Christ was free from all sin, original as well as personal: Matt. 1:18–25; Luke 1:26–35; John 8:29; 8:46; 14:30; 1 Pet. 2:22; 2 Cor. 5:21; Heb. 4:15; 7:26; Council of Florence (1438–1445); Fathers of the Church. The Eternal Son of God became man in order to effect the redemption of men: Isa. 35:4; Matt. 1:21; 9:13; Luke 2:11, 29–32; 19:10; John 3:17; 1 Tim. 1:15; creeds of the Church. Fallen man is incapable of redeeming himself: Ps. 49:7–8; Rom. 3:10–12; Eph. 2:1–5; Council of Trent (1545–1563). The God-Man Jesus Christ is the eternal High Priest: Ps. 110:4; Matt. 22:42–46; Heb. 5:6–10; 7:17–21; Council of Ephesus (431). Christ offered Himself on the Cross for mankind as a true and proper sacrifice: Is. 53:7–12; Matt. 20:28; 26:28; Mark 10:45; Luke 22:19; John 1:29; Heb 8:10; Eph. 5:2; 1 Cor. 5:7; Rom. 3:25; 1 John 2:2; Council of Ephesus (431); Council of Trent (1545–1563).

Christ, by His sacrifice on the Cross, has redeemed mankind and reconciled us with God: Matt. 20:28; Mark 10:45; 1 Cor. 1:30; 1 Tim. 2:6; Rom. 3:24; Eph. 1:7; Col. 1:14; Titus 2:14; Rev. 5:9; Council of Trent (1545–1563). Christ, by His Passion and death, merited reward from God: Isa. 53:10; Phil. 2:9; Heb. 2:9; Council of Trent (1545–1563). After his death, Christ's soul, separated

Eucharist

from his body, descended into the underworld: John 19:40; Acts 2:24; Col. 1:18; Acts 2:31; Ps. 16:10; Rom. 10:6–13; Eph. 4:9; 1 Pet. 3:18–22; Apostles' Creed; Fourth Lateran Council (1215). On the third day after His death, Christ rose gloriously from the dead in His own proper body: Matt. 12:40; 16:21; 17:22; 20:19; 27:63; 28:6; Mark 16:5–6; Luke 24:5–9; John 2:19–20; Acts 1:22; 2:24, 32; 3:15; 13:30–37; 17:3, 18; 26:23; 1 Cor. 15:1–58; Phil. 3:21. The Resurrection of Christ is a basic truth of Christianity and is expressed in all the symbols of faith and all the rules of faith of the Church, both ancient and modern creeds.

Christ ascended body and soul into Heaven, now sits at the right hand of God the Father, and lives on and makes intercession for us: Mark 16:19; Luke 24:51; Acts 1:9, 11; creeds of the Church.

The Jesus Christ mentioned in the dogmatic summary of teachings above is the same Jesus Christ whom we receive in Holy Communion, who is present in the Most Blessed Sacrament. Thus the following statements of faith are also dogmas of faith concerning Jesus in the Eucharist.

The Body and Blood of Christ are truly, really, and substantially present in the Holy Eucharist: John 6:22–71; Matt. 26:26–28; Mark 14:22–26; Luke. 22:15–20; 1 Cor. 11:23–25; Council of Trent (1545–1563).

Jesus Christ becomes present in the Sacrament of the Altar by the transformation of the whole substance of the bread into his Body, and of the whole substance of the wine into His Blood: Council of Trent (1545–1563). The accidents (appearances; everything perceived by the senses) of bread and wine continue after the change of the substance: Council of Trent (1545–1563). The Body and the Blood of Christ together with His Soul and Divinity, and therefore the whole Christ, are truly present in the Eucharist: John 6:54, 56; 1 Cor. 11:27; Council of Trent (1545–1563). The whole Christ is present under either of the two species (of bread or wine): Council of Trent (1545–1563).

When either consecrated species is divided, the whole Christ is present in each part of the species: Council of Trent (1545–1563). After the Consecration has been completed, the Body and Blood are permanently present in the Eucharist: Council of Trent (1545–1563). The worship of adoration (latria) must be given to Christ present in the Holy Eucharist: Matt. 28:9, 17; John 5:23; 20:28; Phil. 2:10; Heb. 1:6; Council of Trent (1545–1563). The Eucharist is a true sacrament instituted by Jesus Christ: Matt. 26:28; Mark 14:24; Luke 22:19; John 6:53–59; 1 Cor. 11:24; Council of Trent (1545–1563).

The matter for the Eucharist is bread and wine: Matt. 26:17; Mark 14:12; Luke 22:7. The form of the Eucharist consists in Christ's words of institution pronounced at the Consecration of the Mass: Council of Trent (1545–1563); Fathers of the Church (St. Irenaeus, *Adversus Haereses*; St. Ambrose, *De Sacramentis*). The reception of the Eucharist is not necessary for salvation for children prior to the age of reason: Mark 16:16; Rom. 8:1; Council of Trent (1545–1563); St. Augustine; St. Thomas Aquinas.

Holy Communion under two forms is not necessary for any individual members of the faithful, either by reason of divine precept, or as a means of eternal salvation: Council of Trent (1545–1563); St. Thomas Aquinas. The power of Consecration can be exercised only by a validly ordained priest: Luke 22:19; 1 Cor. 11:24; Fourth Lateran Council (1215); Council of Trent (1545–1563); St. Justin Martyr; St. Cyprian, St. Thomas Aquinas. The Sacrament of the Eucharist can be validly received by every living and baptized person, including young children: Council of Trent (1545–1563). For the worthy reception of the Eucharist, the state of grace as well as the proper and pious disposition, are necessary: 1 Cor. 11:28–30; Council of Trent (1545–1563); St. Justin Martyr; St. Augustine; St. Thomas Aquinas.

Eucharist

The Mass is a true and proper sacrifice: Gen. 14:18–20; Ps. 110:4; Heb. 5:6; 7:1–28; Mal. 1:10–11; Exod. 24:8; Luke 22:19; 1 Cor. 11:24; Heb. 13:10; 1 Cor. 10:16–21; Council of Trent (1545–1563). In the Sacrifice of the Mass, Christ's Sacrifice of the Cross is made present, its memory is celebrated, and its saving power is applied: 1 Cor. 11:26; Council of Trent (1545–1563); St. Justin Martyr, St. Cyprian. In the Sacrifice of the Mass and in the Sacrifice of the Cross, the sacrificial gift and the primary sacrificing priest are the same; only the nature and the manner of the offering are different: Council of Trent (1545–1563); *Mediator Dei*.

The Sacrifice of the Mass is not merely a sacrifice of praise and thanksgiving, but also a sacrifice of expiation and impetration: Matt. 26:28; Council of Trent (1545–1563); St. Cyril of Jerusalem; St. Augustine. The Church has received from Christ the power of remitting sins committed after Baptism: Matt. 16:19; cf. Eph. 5:5; 1 Cor. 6:9–11; Gal. 5:19; Council of Trent (1545–1563); hence the power to forgive sins is included in the power of the keys: Isa. 22:22; Rev. 1:18; 3:7; John 20:21–23; cf. Matt. 9:2–8; Mark 2:5–12; Luke 7:47–50.

In the spring of 2007, Pope Benedict XVI published a book titled *Jesus of Nazareth*. The book was not an official magisterial teaching of the Church, yet, coming from an author known as the leading theologian in the world even before he became pope, it carried great prestige. It represents a lifetime of scholarship, studying, and meditation on public divine revelation. Few would question that what this book said about Jesus Christ was representative of an authentic Catholic understanding of Our Lord, God, and Savior. Benedict helps us appreciate who Jesus is from the Bible itself.

Jesus of Nazareth is a biblically inspired theological work that brings decades of the personal scholarship and prayer and masterful teaching of Ratzinger–Pope Benedict.

Some have been so bold as to describe Pope Benedict XVI as the best and greatest theologian of all time in the history of Christianity. In this book he reveals a "personal search for the face of the Lord." Pope Benedict states that he "trusts the Gospels" to give us an authentic account of Jesus of Nazareth. The Gospels present Jesus as both a historical man and the Son of God incarnate.

In presenting *Jesus of Nazareth*, Pope Benedict starts with the beginning of revealed revelation in the Old Testament, which is also about Jesus Christ, at least in prophecies and foreshadowing. That is the way the Old Testament of the Bible must be read and interpreted. Belief in the one God of Abraham required an absolute rejection of the many gods and supposed supernatural forces that were so prominent in the religions of the ancient world. There was a distinctive break with all religious traditions when God revealed Himself to the Jews.

The biblical faith of ancient Israel marked a novelty in the world of religion. That novelty, Pope Benedict tells us, comes finally to fulfillment in Jesus Christ, who makes all things new. "In Jesus the promise of a new prophet is fulfilled. What was only imperfect in Moses is now realized fully in him; he lives in the sight of God, not only as a friend but as a Son."

Moses instructed the people of Israel:

> When you come into the land which the Lord your God gives you, you shall not learn to follow the abominable practices of those nations. There shall not be found among you any one who burns his son or his daughter as an offering, any one who practices divination, a soothsayer, or an augur, or a sorcerer, or a charmer, or a medium, or a wizard, or a necromancer.... For these nations, which you are about to dispossess, give heed to soothsayers and to diviners; but as for you, the Lord

your God has not allowed you so to do. "The Lord your God will raise up for you a prophet like me from among you, from your brethren — him you shall heed." (Deut. 18:9–11, 14–15)

Pope Benedict points out that the book of Deuteronomy, as the entire Pentateuch (the first five books of the Hebrew Bible), leads us to a note of unfulfilled hope: "And there has not arisen a prophet since in Israel like Moses, whom the Lord knew face to face" (Deut. 34:10). Moses told the people that all the ancient ways of lifting the veil on the future was abhorrent to God; rather they are to trust in the one true God and his providence.

Israel is promised another prophet who will tell them about God like Moses had, but even more so, because this new prophet will speak to God face to face. Even Moses is lacking in what the new prophet will be. God told Moses: "You cannot see my face.... You shall see my back; but my face shall not be seen" (Exod. 33:20, 23).

What about the future? Will the realm of the supernatural remain always hidden? Will man's destiny be always veiled, so that mankind remains always in a world of shadows and uncertainty regarding ultimate things? Will man never know his final destiny as intended by God? This cannot be — that the one true God who can reveal all things refuses to reveal Himself fully. The revelation that began with Abraham is to end with *Jesus of Nazareth*. As Pope Benedict writes:

> In Jesus the promise of a new prophet is fulfilled. What was only imperfect in Moses is now realized fully in him: he lives in the sight of God, not only as a friend but as a Son; he lives in profound unity with the Father. Only from this point can one truly understand the figure of Jesus that meets us in the New Testament; all that is recorded — the words, deeds, sufferings and the glory of Jesus — has its foundation here.

Jesus Christ does not belong to the world of the ancient superstitions. He is far greater than Abraham or Moses, however privileged and great they were. *Jesus of Nazareth* is entirely new and unique. Jesus Christ is the only begotten Son who fully revealed the face of the Father. He is the Son of the Father, the Word made flesh.

The Gospels inform us that the Prophet, Jesus Christ, exceeds even the greatest expectations of Israel. Pope Benedict thus begins his book with the Baptism of Jesus in the Jordan and concludes with Jesus' own self-revelation in the Transfiguration.

In dealing with the temptations of Jesus Christ, Pope Benedict asks: "What did Jesus actually bring, if not world peace, universal prosperity, and a better world? What has he brought?"

Satan presented the temptation to Jesus to change the stones into bread. There are rocks that look much like loaves of bread in the Holy Land. Doesn't the world need bread? There is so much lacking in justice and peace in our flawed world. Surely the Son of God should turn the stones, perhaps even the mountain, into bread so that all might eat.

Pope Benedict wrote about this temptation: "Is there anything more tragic, is there anything more opposed to belief in the existence of a good God and a Redeemer of mankind, than world hunger? Shouldn't it be the first test of the Redeemer, before the world's gaze and on the world's behalf, to give it bread and to end all hunger?"

In late August 2007, the secular news channels reported what they considered "shocking" news about St. Teresa of Calcutta, founder of the Missionaries of Charity, who in Jesus did so much, and her followers now do so much, to feed and help the poor. They spoke of her lack of faith. Mother obviously wrote about her dark night of the soul and went for years without consolations in her faith, and yet she lived with the greatest charity for the poor throughout the world. She saw Jesus Christ, especially in the poor and the hungry. Mother Teresa, the "Saint of the Gutters" was described in the book *Mother Teresa:*

Eucharist

Come Be My Light, consisting primarily of correspondence between Mother Teresa and her confessors and superiors over a period of sixty-six years. Most of the letters were preserved against her wishes as she had requested that they be destroyed. Her request was overruled after her death; the letters reveal that for nearly the last half century of her life she *felt* no presence of God whatsoever.

The book's editor, Rev. Brian Kolodiejchuk, writes of this dryness, or *dark night of the soul*. Mother Teresa experienced the presence of God "neither in her heart nor in the Eucharist."

The absence seems to have started at almost precisely the time she began tending the poor and dying in Calcutta. Although she radiated in public peace, love, and cheerfulness, her letters tell that she lived in a state of deep and abiding spiritual pain. She bemoaned the "dryness," "darkness," "loneliness," and "torture" she underwent. She compared the experience to Hell and at one point says it has driven her to doubt the existence of Heaven and even of God.

The extent of it all, for me, was a cause for even greater admiration for Mother Teresa of Calcutta. She was indeed heroic in the face of such a dark night of the soul. For years I sensed the guidance of the Holy Spirit in the concise answers and comments she would make on critical problems or questions put to her. Always there was a presence about her that radiated joy, peace, and the presence of God. She rose above her feelings and persevered and worked tirelessly, guided and strengthened by the Holy Spirit, the grace within her. She believed without feeling it. God chose not to give her consolations after she heard that initial voice and call to serve the poor of the world.

Mother Teresa wrote her director that Jesus loved him, "[but] as for me — the silence and the emptiness is so great that I look and do not see, listen and do not hear. — The tongue moves but does not speak.... I want you to pray for me — that I let Him have [a] free hand."

Years ago, a young priest of my acquaintance related to me that he sat beside Mother Teresa on an airplane from Rome to New York. "What was it like sitting beside her?" I asked. The young priest replied in certain words the following: "She radiated to me a spirit as if she had never left her chapel. It was as if she was at prayer, at adoration in her chapel." That same priest, Fr. Joseph Langford, later became with Mother Teresa a founder of her Missionary priests of Charity.

I have often asked God not to permit that I be tested with such dark nights of the soul, such as St. John of the Cross described, such as St. Thérèse of Lisieux, the Little Flower, and Mother Teresa endured. God knows how weak I am. I fear I could not endure.

I think the Holy Spirit was always working in Mother Teresa of Calcutta wherever she went. Jesus was always there, sending with the Father the Holy Spirit upon her as she worked, instructed, and responded to the world, and, above all, in her work for the poor.

It seems to me God willed this dryness, this spiritual dark night of the soul for forty-plus years for Mother Teresa, and it was so that she would continue to seek Jesus especially in the poor. It kept her humble for the humble poor people.

One year as the Christmas season approached, she said that the upcoming Christmas holidays should remind the world "that radiating joy is real" because Christ is everywhere — "Christ in our hearts, Christ in the poor we meet, Christ in the smile we give and in the smile that we receive."

Even during her daily Holy Hour and Mass Mother Teresa experienced emptiness — sensibly nothing in that which she required of her sisters before the Most Blessed Sacrament each morning before going out to minister to the poor. She would say that her sisters could not meet Jesus in the poor without first meeting Jesus Christ in the Eucharist and the Holy Hour of prayer.

Mother Teresa will without doubt go down as the greatest saint of the twentieth century, along with St. Padre Pio, who radiated, especially at the Sacrifice of the Mass, Christ Crucified in the Eucharist, and St. Faustina for Divine Mercy.

Return now to what Pope Benedict wrote about the temptation of Christ: "Is there anything more tragic, is there anything more opposed to belief in the existence of a good God and a Redeemer of mankind, than world hunger? Shouldn't it be the first test of the Redeemer, before the world's gaze and on the world's behalf, to give it bread and to end all hunger?"

Ah! Yes. And in our own time God gave us Mother Teresa of Calcutta as a figure of Jesus Christ feeding, clothing, housing the poor. He gave us St. Padre Pio as a living crucifix offering the Sacrifice of the Mass, visibly expressing what the Eucharist is. He gave us St. Faustina to express His mercy.

Pope Benedict explained that Satan's temptations are inspired by the logic of: "What use is Jesus if he did not bring a solution to our pressing human problems?" The temptations that Satan offers are from a mere human point of view; a matter of solving human problems and satisfying human ambitions. This type of logic does not consider salvation of the soul — our eternal destiny.

God does not exist, and His Son did not become man, in order to fulfill every human need and desire in this world. That kind of God is not the true God. It is an attempt to make God in the image of man, whereas God made man in His own image and likeness. Jesus came so that we could be made more and more into the image and likeness of God with eternal divine life.

Jesus did not bring a man-made god to us. He brought God as He truly is. So Jesus is replying to the temptations of Satan — that God does not conform Himself to the image of this world. As Benedict writes, "He has brought God, and now we know his face, now we can call upon him. Now we know the path that we human beings have to take in this world. Jesus has brought God and with God the truth about our origin and destiny: faith, hope, and love. It is only because of our hardness of heart that we think this is too little."

Satan is appealing to the reasonableness of human thinking — he is asking that we judge God by our standards of efficiency. This, however, doesn't work. As Pope Benedict writes: "To the tempter's lying divination of power and prosperity ... he [Jesus] responds with the fact that God is God, that God is man's true Good.... The fundamental commandment of Israel is also the fundamental commandment for Christians: God alone is to be worshiped." Jesus came to bring this true God to us, and Jesus identified with our suffering, our distress, and even feelings of despair. Even this flawed and sinful world is in the hands of God.

Pope Benedict devoted his longest chapter of *Jesus of Nazareth* to Jesus' Sermon on the Mount, which is found in chapters 5 to 7 in St. Matthew's Gospel. Benedict saw that sermon as a "biography" of Jesus Himself, as well as a program of life for the Christian disciple to follow. The three parts of the Sermon on the Mount reveal the Person of Jesus Christ, the incarnate Son of the Father, the Word made flesh.

First part: we are given the Beatitudes, which tell who Jesus is — the all-powerful One who empties Himself out of love and mercy.

Second part: Jesus gives a new "Torah" in which Jesus presents Himself with a greater authority than that of the Mosaic tradition. Repeatedly Jesus says: "You have heard that it was said, but I say to you."

Finally, Jesus speaks of His own relationship to God the Father as the model for prayer in the Our Father. "Pray then like this" (Matt. 6:9–13).

The Sermon on the Mount, in addition to an updated, higher moral code, reveals who Jesus is. Because He is the Son of God, equal to the Father, He can and does give us the program for Christian discipleship. Only because Jesus is God does He have the authority to place Himself above the Torah and at the heart of true religious life. We can see then why St. Matthew ends the Sermon on the Mount with these words: "And when Jesus finished these sayings, the crowds were astonished at his teaching, for he taught them as one who had authority, and not as their scribes" (Matt. 7:28–29).

According to Pope Benedict, the saints give us the clearest "interpretation" of the Christ life — of living the Beatitudes, of which Christ is at the center. In fact, the lives of the saints provide a hermeneutic through which *all* of Scripture can be interpreted. This is because, according to Pope Benedict, Scripture is not a "purely historical affair," something that can be comprehended and interpreted purely through academic methods. Rather, Scripture is best interpreted by looking at the lives of the saints, those who imitated Christ in their virtue, in their application of the Beatitudes, especially in the face of suffering. In this sense, "The saints are the true interpreters of Holy Scripture," in the words of Pope Benedict.

The Torah of Moses had given the heart of the Jewish faith and the foundation of the Jewish social order. Jesus in the Sermon on the Mount now places Himself as the fulfillment of both.

Pope Benedict writes of a Jewish theologian, Jacob Neusner, author of *A Rabbi Talks with Jesus*. Benedict sees this book as a sympathetic and respectful examination of the preaching of Jesus. Yet, Neusner cannot bring himself to become a Christian because he concludes that Jesus is adding something new to the salvation history of "eternal Israel." What is Jesus adding? He is adding Himself. Benedict writes that Neusner read the message of Jesus in its full depth. Jesus is "the way, and the truth, and the life" (John 14:6). In openness to the Holy Spirit, we can and should believe Jesus Christ is true God and true man.

The Sermon on the Mount is much more than a code of morality. It reveals the full truth that Jesus is God, and salvation is only in and through Him. Faith in this truth requires an entirely new way of living and thinking.

How should we pray? According to Pope Benedict, we must be weary of the kind of prayer that Jesus Himself warns about: vain, repetitive prayer. Still, Jesus taught the apostles the Lord's Prayer. They understood it was a prayer to be repeated. It expressed a perfect way of praying so as to transform and open up our lives.

As St. Benedict taught, *mens nostra concordet voci nostrae* — our mind must be in accord with our voice. In accord with this teaching, Pope Benedict wrote that in the Our Father prayery, God "provides the words of our prayer and teaches us to pray." When we pray the Our Father, we are praying to God with words given by God. It is an encounter with the Spirit of God in the word that goes ahead of us. This is because the words of the Our Father are not our words, but God's words.

Pope Benedict XVI has written that the essence of Heaven is that it is where the will of God is unswervingly done. The very essence of Heaven will be — already is — oneness with God's will. Earth becomes Heaven when God's will is done there. Thus when we say the Our Father, we pray that God's will may be done on earth as it is in Heaven. We pray that earth may become Heaven. The Our Father is contained in the Mass as the Eucharistic Divine Liturgy unites Heaven and earth. As Jesus did the will of the Father in His Sacrifice of the Cross, so He does in the Sacrifice of the Mass, which is the same sacrifice.

In teaching us how to pray by praying the Our Father, Jesus obviously had the Eucharist in mind as well. Jesus Himself is to be our daily bread. Jesus spoke extensively about the Bread of Life and even called himself the Bread of Life. This Bread, Jesus' own Flesh and Blood, is necessary for salvation: "This is the bread which came down from heaven, not such as the fathers ate and died; he who eats this bread will live for ever" (John 6:58). Jesus explained to the people the petitions of the Our Father, and also the Beatitudes. To live the Sermon on the Mount, we must learn to really pray the Our Father, live the Beatitudes, appreciate the depth of the Eucharistic mystery, and live the Mass. This explains why the Our Father is included in every Eucharistic celebration.

"No one takes [my life] from me, but I lay it down of my own accord" (John 10:18). St. Maximus the Confessor explained that the obedience of Jesus' human will is inserted into or part of the everlasting "yes and Will of the Son in relationship to the Father. In giving himself to be crucified, Jesus gave his human existence into the great action of love for the Father and all his human brothers and sisters. His Body is 'given for you.'"

The real interior act of Jesus giving Himself unto and into crucifixion *once* transcends time, and again and again can be brought into time. St. Bernard of Clairvaux put it this way: the true "once" (*semel*) bears within itself the "always" (*semper*). The Mass perpetuates the sacrifice of the death of Jesus Christ, and what is perpetual takes place in what happens only once and comes into our time now and reaches into Heaven.

Pope Benedict XVI's *Jesus of Nazareth* examines two "milestones" of the entire revelation of who Jesus is in the Paschal Mystery. The three Synoptic Gospels connect the events of Peter's confession of faith and the Transfiguration. In John's Gospel, Peter's confession comes during the Bread of Life discourse: "Jesus said to the twelve, 'Will you also go away?' Simon Peter answered him, 'Lord, to whom shall we go? You have the words of eternal life; and we have believed, and have come to know, that you are the Holy One of God.'" (John 6:67–69). Note, that profession came after He multiplied bread to feed thousands, just as His Body will be fed to millions through the centuries, without the supply running out. It came after Jesus walked on the water, demonstrating His authority over the elements. And finally, it came after His great discourse on the Eucharist as related in John 6.

Jesus asks the apostles about His identity. Then at the Transfiguration He allows His true identity to shine forth like the sun. This took place at a critical moment in the life of Jesus. His great preaching in Galilee is over, and Jesus is on the way to Jerusalem knowing He is going to His Passion and death. It is important that the apostles know who Jesus is. And that for two reasons: If they realize that He is God become man, they can know that His sacrificial death on the Cross is for the redemption of the world. Also, if they do not know who He is, His Crucifixion unto death will prove too much for them.

First Jesus asked the apostles who the "people" say that He is. They reply that the people consider Him to be John the Baptist or Elijah or Jeremiah — or one of the great prophets. There is a hint of truth in this misconception of who Jesus is. The "people" are right in that Jesus is a prophet, but He is not simply another prophet, he is *the prophet*. They make the same mistake as the people of today who, according to Pope Benedict, have not had an encounter with the Person of Christ, but rather have interpreted who Jesus is "in terms of the predictable and the possible, not in terms of himself, his uniqueness." It is not enough that the people know *about* Jesus. It is necessary for all of us to *know Jesus*. The disciples know Jesus because He has chosen them to receive His intimate revelation.

The long history of revelation given to the patriarchs, to the Chosen People, to the contemporaries of Jesus will reach its most transparent moment in the *Transfiguration*. The unity of revelation is seen with the eye of faith from Abraham and Melchizedek — from Mount Moriah and the sacrifice of Isaac; to Tabor and the transfigured Jesus, preparing the apostles for Calvary's Sacrifice of the Cross; to the Resurrection and Ascension and the descent of the Holy Spirit. All is really present and re-presented in the Divine Liturgy of the Eucharist — where

Jesus reveals Himself anew, and the Jesus of Heaven and salvation history becomes present to us now in the Eucharist — in union with His eternal presence in Heaven.

In the next two chapters we shall meditate on *Sacramentum Caritatis* (*SC*), issued by Pope Benedict XVI, February 22, 2007.

2

"The Church Flows from the Eucharist"

In the Holy Eucharist, Jesus Christ has so completely made the gift of Himself to us that He not only gives us His Precious Body to eat and His Precious Blood to drink in Holy Communion, He actually gives us the very sacrifice of Himself on the Cross to offer at each Holy Mass. The Apostle John tells us that Jesus loved us "to the end" (John 13:1), as He was led to "lay down his life for his friends" (John 15:13).

We were all created in the image and likeness of God (Gen. 1:27). God loves each one of us, even after we have failed Him by serious sin. He welcomes us back to the Banquet of His own Body and Blood when we repent and are sacramentally absolved. Jesus Christ is Truth (John 14:6). Our souls passionately desire the truth. Many, even most men and women, do not realize that in their passionate desire for truth they are really desiring Jesus Christ.

If only the desire of our human hearts for truth could be lifted up to appreciate passionately the great action of the infinite worship Jesus offers in the Sacrifice of the Mass. Jesus foretold that when He was lifted up, He would draw all things to Himself. At each Mass, as we lift up our hearts, we are first lifting up Jesus Christ to God the Father. It is a divine reality. "'And I, when I am lifted up from the earth, will draw all men to myself.' He said this to show by what death he was to die" (John 12:32–33).

Eucharist

As a priest, celebrating the Eucharist for over fifty years, my heart yearns to appreciate and experience more deeply what my faith knows to be true. In the Sacrament of the Eucharist, Jesus manifests in particular the truth about both His divine and human love, the divine love that is the very essence of the reality of God.

Every Sacrifice of the Mass proclaims with visible and audible qualities: GOD IS LOVE. As a priest, I know that the Eucharist is the very center of my life as it is the life of the Church. The Eucharist is the reason I have existed in the world for more than fifty years as a Catholic priest. My heart is pained if I realize some want a rushed Mass. If only they would listen to the "still small voice" (1 Kings 19:12) speaking within them. My heart is pained in myself when I know that I too am restless at times, a restlessness more for self than for the Lord. And yet, with St. Augustine, who said that our hearts are restless, I do believe that my heart will be restless until I rest in Jesus, my Lord.

From time to time, I stop to think that during the years I have striven to live the priestly life of Jesus Christ, I have celebrated the Sacrifice of the Mass considerably more than twenty thousand times. But the wonder is not in the number of times. The infinite wonder is that any one Mass is of infinite value, giving infinite worship and glory to the Father in the power and unity of the Holy Spirit. The daily Sacrifice of the Mass perpetuates the Paschal Mystery of Jesus Christ.

In 1987, Pope St. John Paul II, to prepare for the Great Jubilee introducing the third millennium of Christianity, called the universal Church to the Marian Year. Later, the same pope declared the Year of the Eucharist from October 2004 to October 2005. But in reality, every year that is lived with the fullness of true Christianity is a Marian year. Every year lived in true faith is a Eucharistic year. In divine providence, as God ordained it, we would not have Jesus Christ except through Mary responding to the will of God in answering *fiat* to the archangel Gabriel. She answers that *fiat* yet to every grace the children of the Church receive, the children of the Church of which Mary is Mother. Through the Eucharist until the end of time, mankind will have Jesus Christ, and His infinite sacrifice will be perpetuated daily. Every year is thus Marian. Every year is Eucharistic. Every authentically Christian life is Marian and Eucharistic.

When I was a relatively young priest, a good, holy nun, hearing that I frequently spoke with fervor about our Blessed Mother, wrote to ask me if I would organize in the diocese a Marian Conference like the one she had attended in another state. She wrote: "I heard you are a Marian priest." She felt I was a priest who could accomplish this. I had never previously heard such an expression, "a Marian priest." Upon reading her letter, my immediate thought was: "Isn't every priest Marian? How could one be a priest and not be Marian?" To me, it was like saying, "I hear you are a Eucharistic priest," or "a priest of the Eucharist" or "a priest of the Catholic Church." They all fit together as one Church. So, I believe every baptized member of the Catholic Church should have a spirituality that is both Marian and Eucharistic.

"Fr. Réginald Garrigou-Lagrange, O. P., is the greatest living theologian today," I was told by the seminary rector when I was a seminarian a half century ago. He still appeals to me. And this is what that theologian wrote about Mary's power of intercession:

> Mary's mediation ... has as purpose to obtain for us the application at the appropriate time of Jesus' merits and hers, acquired during their life on earth and especially on Calvary.... Even during her life on earth, Mary appears in the gospels as distributing graces. Jesus sanctifies the precursor through her when she comes to visit her cousin Elizabeth. Through her He confirms the faith of his disciples at Cana.... Through her He confirms John's faith on Calvary, saying: "Son, behold thy mother." Through her finally the Holy Spirit gave himself to the Apostles,

for we read in the Acts (Acts 1:14) that she prayed with them in the Cenacle while they prepared themselves for the apostolate and for the light and strength and graces of Pentecost.

With still greater reason is Mary powerful in her intercession now that she has entered heaven and has been lifted up above the choirs of the angels. The Christian sense of the faith assures us that a mother in heaven knows the spiritual needs of the children she has left behind her on earth.... It is universal for the faithful to recommend themselves to the prayers of the saints in heaven. As St. Thomas says, when the saints were on earth, their charity led them to pray for their neighbor. With still greater reason do we say that in heaven they pray for their neighbor since when their charity is inflamed by the beatific vision it is greater than it was on earth.

With these truths about Mary and the saints expressed, can we not see their role and participation with us in the Divine Liturgy of the Eucharist on earth as they constantly engage in the heavenly liturgy? Can we not sense their presence at Mass? Since the Eucharist is the chief source of grace for us and Mary is the dispenser of heavenly graces, surely she has a role with Jesus in the Eucharistic celebration and the dispensing of grace of which her Son is the source.

The entire Blessed Trinity is present in the Holy Eucharist. It is not only Jesus Christ, true God and true man, as God the Son incarnate who is present. The entire Trinity is present. There is contained in this mystery of God Himself, the trinitarian love of God the Father, Son, and Holy Spirit. God is one. He cannot be divided. Where one Person of the Blessed Trinity is, in a special way through the incarnate Lord Jesus, God become man, all three Persons must exist.

In the Holy Eucharist, God, the Blessed Trinity, infinite Divine Love itself, becomes totally a part of our human condition. God

"The Church Flows from the Eucharist"

became man so that man may become one with God in Jesus Christ. We, God's children, made in His image and likeness, are given an increase in the life of God, which is often called sanctifying grace, through the Eucharist which is the God-Man Himself. Jesus Christ is living among us in a sacramental presence, a Real Presence, so we can adore the entire Blessed Trinity through Jesus Christ.

If we understand the Holy Eucharist in any depth, that understanding entails the revelation of God's loving plan through all of salvation history (Eph. 1:10; 3:8–11). The triune God, who is love (1 John 4:7–8), has become fully human while remaining God the Son. Thousands of years of salvation history unfolds gradually to reveal the reality that is the Eucharistic Sacrifice and the Real Presence. Under the appearances of bread and wine, Jesus Christ, Our Lord, God, and Savior, offers Himself in sacrifice and gives Himself to us in the Paschal meal (Luke 22:14–20; 1 Cor. 11:23–26). God shares His own life with us through the Eucharist. For this reason, Pope Benedict wrote that the Faith of the Church is "a eucharistic faith," because it is "nourished at the table of the Eucharist" (*Sacramentum Caritatis*, 6).

Between the Father, Son, and Holy Spirit there is a perfect communion of love. Jesus Christ, "through the eternal Spirit offered Himself without blemish to God" (Heb. 9:14). Jesus makes that same offering present today through the Eucharist whereby God gives us His own divine life ever increasingly. The "mystery of faith" that the priest proclaims after the Consecration is a mystery of trinitarian love. It is a mystery that "renews history and the whole cosmos" (*SC*, 10). We are called to participate in that infinite mystery of the Lord's sacrifice perpetuated where He feeds us Himself for eternal life. The Eucharist is Heaven on earth. We become one with the heavenly Divine Liturgy through the Eucharistic Sacrifice of the Mass on earth.

The Church Fathers of early centuries were explicit that the foreshadowings in Old Testament salvation history gave way to truth itself:

Eucharist

Jesus Christ, the incarnate Son of God has come to earth to redeem us. The Fathers taught that His Sacrifice of the Cross is perpetuated in the Sacrifice of the Mass, and His Real Presence is made present here and now at Mass. In the celebration of the Eucharist, Christ's perfect gift is not mere repetition of the Last Supper. There is always a radical newness of Christian worship. We enter into Christ's "hour" and are drawn into Jesus' act of self-oblation and participate properly, actively, and more fully when we offer ourselves in union with Jesus' offering of Himself in His Sacrifice of the Cross. We are not limited in Jesus' sacrifice, His actions and presence on earth having happened two thousand years ago. In the Eucharistic celebration, we participate *now* in all that Jesus did then. Celebrating the Eucharist is not a matter of repeating Jesus' sacrifice. It is a matter of making present now his Sacrifice of Redemption. Through the action of the Holy Spirit, Jesus Christ is present and active in the Church today, beginning with the Church's vital center, the Holy Eucharist.

The Holy Spirit acts in the Eucharistic celebration particularly at the moment of *transubstantiation*. St. Cyril of Jerusalem wrote that we "call upon God in his mercy to send his Holy Spirit upon the offerings before us, to transform the bread into the body of Christ and the wine into the blood of Christ. Whatever the Holy Spirit touches is sanctified and completely transformed" (Catechesis 23, 7: *PG* 33, 1114ff.). St. John Chrysostom also noted that the priest invokes the Holy Spirit when he celebrates the sacrifice. Invoking the Holy Spirit by the priest celebrant of the Mass is known as the *epiclesis*. Petition is made to the Father to send down the gift of the Spirit so that the bread and wine offered will now become the Body and Blood of Jesus Christ. The Holy Spirit is also involved so that the community of faith as a whole will become ever more the Body of Christ. The Church is the Mystical Body of Christ. Christ is Her Head. The Holy Spirit is Her Soul. We are Her members. Thus, the faithful become a spiritual offering pleasing to the Father.

"The Church Flows from the Eucharist"

Every time the Holy Eucharist is celebrated we profess our faith in the primacy of Jesus Christ's gift to us, namely Himself in His supreme sacrifice. Jesus Christ loved His Father from all eternity as the second Person of the Blessed Trinity. Now He loves Him as God-Man and loves us in the process, as we are his brothers and sisters. Jesus shares our human nature; He wants us to share His divine nature. "I came that they may have life"(John 10:10). In celebrating the Eucharist, He is drawing us into His eternal love, into His eternal life.

Jesus draws us also into His "hour" and invites all to be bonded to Himself in one Church, His Mystical Body. Jesus loved us on Calvary with a love greater than any human love. His love was first for the Father, and now Jesus makes the same supreme act of love for the Father and for us in one act that is present in our time as the offering is eternally present in the heavenly liturgy. The Eucharist makes present Christ's redeeming sacrifice of love, and it is Christ Himself who gives Himself to us to build up His Body, the Church, for the glory of His Father. Truly, it is a question of redeeming the time. It is a matter of redeeming our time and presenting our time and the entire cosmos to be sanctified in Jesus' infinite act of redemption that is made present on our altars as it is present forever in Heaven in infinite mystery.

The cosmos? Yes. God became man in Jesus Christ, but never did He become an angel, not even the greatest angel, whereas our human nature is a little less than the angels. Man is both spirit and matter. The Son of God was made flesh, became hypostatically one with a soul created for Jesus and a body provided by Mary. He is of the spiritual world and the material universe by God's power and design and man's cooperation through the Virgin Mother Mary. God, thus, in becoming man, became one with all aspects of His creation, the spiritual and material. There is evidence that Satan's revolt was when he was given that knowledge that God would become man but never an angel. Consider this in light of the Letter to the Hebrews:

In many and various ways God spoke of old to our fathers by the prophets; but in these last days he has spoken to us by a Son, whom he appointed the heir of all things, through whom also he created the world. He reflects the glory of God and bears the very stamp of his nature, upholding the universe by his word of power. When he had made purification for sins, he sat down at the right hand of the Majesty on high, having become as much superior to angels as the name he has obtained is more excellent than theirs. For to what angel did God ever say, "Thou art my Son, today I have begotten thee"? Or again, "I will be to him a father, and he shall be to me a son"? And again, when he brings the first-born into the world, he says, "Let all God's angels worship him." Of the angels he says, "Who makes his angels winds, and his servants flames of fire." But of the Son he says, "Thy throne, O God, is for ever and ever, the righteous scepter is the scepter of thy kingdom.... But to what angel has he ever said, "Sit at my right hand, till I make thy enemies a stool for thy feet"? Are they not all ministering spirits sent forth to serve, for the sake of those who are to obtain salvation? (Heb. 1:1–8, 13–14)

In the Letter to the Hebrews, the writer, under divine inspiration, complains of people who have had the Word of God presented to them but "have become dull of hearing": "For though by this time you ought to be teachers, you need some one to teach you again the first principles of God's word. You need milk, not solid food; for every one who lives on milk is unskilled in the word of righteousness, for he is a child. But solid food is for the mature, for those who have their faculties trained by practice to distinguish good from evil" (5:11–14). Cannot such words apply to one who supposedly has the fullness of true faith but does not appreciate it, does not meditate with it, does not digest it? Such is the case with the "Catholic" who does not appreciate the reality of what the Sacrifice of the Mass is. Some do not appreciate that Jesus Christ is truly present, that His sacrifice of infinite value is made present at the altar, that the mysteries of Christ come to us now.

The offering of Jesus Christ is forever. It is not renewed, changed, repeated. It is eternal:

> Thus it was necessary for the copies of the heavenly things to be purified with these rites, but the heavenly things themselves with better sacrifices than these. For Christ has entered, not into a sanctuary made with hands, a copy of the true one, but into heaven itself, now to appear in the presence of God on our behalf. Nor was it to offer himself repeatedly, as the high priest enters the Holy Place yearly with blood not his own; for then he would have had to suffer repeatedly since the foundation of the world. But as it is, he has appeared once for all at the end of the age to put away sin by the sacrifice of himself. And just as it is appointed for men to die once, and after that comes judgment, so Christ, having been offered once to bear the sins of many, will appear a second time, not to deal with sin but to save those who are eagerly waiting for him.... But when Christ had offered for all time a single sacrifice for sins, he sat down at the right hand of God, then to wait until his enemies should be made a stool for his feet. For by a single offering he has perfected for all time those who are sanctified. (Heb. 9:23–28; 10:10–14)

The priest who is in the line of apostolic succession has been validly ordained, and, at the Sacrifice of the Mass on earth, he offers the same eternal Sacrifice of Jesus Christ that Christ offered on Calvary and presents to the Father in Heaven. This is because he offers *in persona*

Christi (in the Person of Christ). But Jesus Christ is in Heaven. So, He is on our altars and acts through the priest. As it were, the Sacrifice of the Cross, perpetuated on our altars on earth, tunes into the sacrifice of Christ — to His risen body with the glorified wound marks beside the Father — and it reaches across the barriers of time and space. Thus there is made present the sacrifice, the same sacrifice of Christ once offered on Calvary, now offered in Heaven. This infinite act of the New and Eternal Covenant is made present. We tune into the heavenly liturgy — to the eternal Sacrifice of Jesus Christ.

At every Holy Mass, we are at Calvary's Cross of Good Friday, at the Resurrection of Easter Sunday, as well as the Ascension of Jesus Christ into Heaven, and are blessed with the power of the Holy Spirit of that first Pentecost Sunday. The Eucharist brings together Good Friday, Easter Sunday, and Pentecost. For all eternity, Jesus remains the one who loves us first in obedient love to His Father. In our time, as in the eternal heavenly liturgy, Jesus loves us. At the Sacrifice of the Mass, Jesus comes from Heaven to earth so we may go from earth to Heaven. Thus is continued the eternal embrace of Jesus loving us.

It is Our Eucharistic Lord that makes up the very essence and essential activity of the Church. The Church flows from the Eucharist. From Christian antiquity the words, *Corpus Christi* were used to describe three aspects of the existence of Jesus Christ: First, Christ's Body is that born of the Virgin Mary, conceived of the Holy Spirit. Second, Christ's Body is also His ecclesial Body, that is the Mystical Body we call the Church. Third, Christ's Body is also His Eucharistic Body, that is, His Real Presence under the appearance of bread and wine that have been transubstantiated into Himself. We then eat His Body and drink His Blood for eternal life, the very life of God, by which we will live in Heaven and live now in grace upon earth.

Jesus Christ is inseparable from His Church. In offering Himself on the Cross in sacrifice for us, this gift of self pointed to the mystery of the Church. The Eucharist is directed to the unity of all the faithful within ecclesial communion. If we receive Jesus with faith and love, in the state of sanctifying grace, it builds up the unity of the Church.

In celebrating the Eucharist, individual members of the faithful come into one in Jesus' Body, that is, in His Church. Thus ecclesial communion is catholic, that is universal, by its very nature. This tells us why divisions among Christians is so painful to Our Lord and contrary to His divine nature and the purpose for which Christ instituted the Holy Eucharist. We can understand, then, why Jesus at the Last Supper, the first Eucharist, spoke of the vine and the branches. He spoke of the Holy Spirit, the role of the Advocate, the Advocate who is the Spirit of love, truth and unity.

At the Last Supper when Jesus instituted the Holy Eucharist, He prayed his high priestly prayer for unity: "And now I am no more in the world, but they are in the world, and I am coming to thee. Holy Father, keep them in thy name, which thou hast given me, that they may be one, even as we are one" (John 17:11). Yes, we are in the world now. Jesus is in the world in a physical manner no more, but sacramentally, yes, so that we may be one in Him as He is one with the Father in heavenly glory. The Eucharist is indeed Heaven on earth.

The Second Vatican Council instructed us:

> The other sacraments, as well as with every ministry of the Church and every work of the apostolate, are tied together with the Eucharist and are directed toward it. The Most Blessed Eucharist contains the entire spiritual boon of the Church, that is, Christ himself, our Pasch and Living Bread, by the action of the Holy Spirit through his very flesh vital and vitalizing, giving life to men who are thus invited and encouraged to offer themselves, their labors and all created things, together with him. (*Presbyterorum Ordinis*, 5)

The Church Is the Great Sacrament

We can appreciate this relationship of the Holy Eucharist with the other six sacraments if we consider the mystery of the Church herself as the Great Sacrament. The Church is not an eighth sacrament, but she is visible, a great visible sign that gives glory to God and grace to man. The Church does this through and under seven special visible and audible sounds and signs as instituted by Jesus Christ.

The Second Vatican Council stated that "the Church is in Christ like a sacrament or as a sign and instrument both of a very closely knit union with God and of the unity of the whole human race" (*Lumen Gentium*, 1). The Church not only *receives* but *expresses* what she herself is in the seven sacraments. The sacraments affecting the lives of the faithful make possible that our whole existence, all we are and do, becomes an act of worship pleasing to God. This is how Jesus Christ, through the Spirit, reaches out to touch our lives individually in every detail and the Church universally.

Since the Eucharist is the source and summit of the Church's life and mission, the summit of its worship, we must both celebrate and receive this sacrament in faith, hope, and love frequently throughout our lives. It is the way of true religion, true worship, ordained by the incarnate Lord. Ideally, if possible, we should join in celebrating it daily.

Baptism and Confirmation Are Ordered to the Eucharist

We were first incorporated into the Mystical Body of Christ, His Church, through Baptism, which is the first sacrament received and is required to receive other sacraments validly. The Sacrament of Confirmation, through the bestowing of the gifts of the Holy Spirit, is for the building up of Christ's Body (1 Cor. 12:1–31). By the gifts of the Spirit received in Confirmation, we are to give ever greater witness to Jesus, to His gospel in the world. In fact, the Holy Eucharist brings our Christian initiation, started with Baptism and Confirmation, to completion. The Holy Eucharist represents the center and goal of all sacramental life in our pilgrimage toward Heaven, which we reach already by faith, hope, and love in sacramental worship upon earth, joining us to the heavenly liturgy.

Eucharist and Reconciliation Go Together

When we have sound faith and truly love the Eucharist, that is, love Jesus Himself living and acting sacramentally on this earth, on our altars, in our tabernacles, present not in a passive way, but present and acting in a dynamic way, then we love the Sacrament of Reconciliation as well. Why? If we appreciate in awe the infinite God incarnate, present and perpetuating His infinite act of love, worship, sacrifice, offered even in the glory of Heaven, as evidenced by the wound marks of crucifixion that His risen and ascended body retained, then we will appreciate the need for purification to prepare us for the Eucharistic celebration and reception upon earth. There can be no authentic and complete catechesis on the Eucharist unless there is also catechesis on the Sacrament of Reconciliation.

> For as often as you eat this bread and drink the cup, you proclaim the Lord's death until he comes. Whoever, therefore, eats the bread or drinks the cup of the Lord in an unworthy manner will be guilty of profaning the body and blood of the Lord. Let a man examine himself, and so eat of the bread and drink of the cup. For any one who eats and drinks without discerning the body eats and drinks judgment upon himself. (1 Cor. 11:26–29)

No one is teaching the gospel and Church teachings on the Eucharist fully and properly if the Sacrament of Reconciliation is ignored.

When we have sinned, serious sin in particular, individual absolution by the priest is the ordinary form intended by Jesus Christ and His Church to readmit us to the Eucharist.

The *Catechism of the Catholic Church* reminds us that the priest in the administration of the Sacrament of Pardon and of Reconciliation acts as "the sign and the instrument of God's merciful love for the sinner" (1465). Pope Benedict XVI spoke of this during an address he gave as part of a course on the Sacrament of Penance:

> What takes place in this Sacrament, therefore, is especially a mystery of love, a work of the merciful love of the Lord. "God is love" (I Jn 4:16)....
>
> The priest in the Sacrament of Confession is the instrument of this merciful love of God, whom he invokes in the formula of the absolution of sins.
>
> The priest, minister of the Sacrament of Reconciliation, must always consider it his duty to make transpire, in words and in drawing near to the penitent, the merciful love of God. Like the father in the parable of the prodigal son, to welcome the penitent sinner, to help him rise again from sin, to encourage him to amend himself, never making pacts with evil but always taking up again the way of evangelical perfection.

The proper understanding of *indulgences* helps us understand that by our own power and efforts alone, we are not able to make reparation for the wrong we have done. The sins of each individual harm the whole Mystical Body of Christ. Indulgences involve not only Christ's infinite merits, but the super-abundant merits of our Blessed Mother and the saints, whose merits from Jesus Christ have gone beyond their own needs for salvation and entrance into Heaven. That tells us how closely we are united to each other in Jesus Christ. It tells us too how the supernatural life of each helps others. The conditions for gaining plenary indulgences include receiving the Sacrament of Confession, Holy Communion, and having a detachment to sin. They again remind us of the centrality of the Eucharist in Christian life and our union with Heaven.

Anointing of the Sick and the Holy Eucharist

The Holy Eucharist is also related to the Sacrament of the Anointing of the Sick. Jesus' Eucharistic Body administered to the seriously sick is known as *Viaticum* (food for the journey). Jesus instituted a special sacrament for those seriously sick (James 5:14–16). While the Eucharist shows that Christ's sufferings and death have been transformed into love and what He offered for us remains with us and is offered in our worship, the Anointing of the Sick unites the sick person's sufferings with Christ's self-offering and sufferings. Anointing of the Sick joined with Viaticum, these two sacraments prepare one for entrance into the Communion of Saints in Heaven. This draws the sick person into the perfect love of Jesus Christ for souls.

The Eucharist and Anointing perfects one's journey to the Heavenly Father. Viaticum thus gives the sick person a glimpse and participation into the fullness of the Paschal Mastery. Jesus Christ died to save us. The person anointed has his sufferings sacramentally united to the sufferings and death of Jesus Christ. He then partakes in Viaticum with the same Jesus Christ in Heaven, where He is always making intercession for us, always offering His Body, Blood, Soul, one in divinity with the Trinity, to the Father in the Holy Spirit on our behalf. But the Sacraments of Viaticum and Anointing have Jesus particularizing His Paschal Mystery and His self-offering for this one person here and now.

Holy Orders Related to Holy Eucharist

It is relatively easy for the informed Catholic to see how the Holy Eucharist relates to the Sacrament of Holy Orders. We cannot have the Holy Eucharist unless there are men ordained by Holy Orders to consecrate bread and wine into Our Lord's own Body and Blood, while perpetuating Jesus' Sacrifice of the Cross. The relationship of these two sacraments is evidenced in Jesus' words in the Upper Room: "Do this in remembrance of me" (Luke 22:19). On the night before He died, Jesus instituted the Sacrament of the Eucharist and Holy Orders, or priesthood of the New Covenant, at one and the same time.

Jesus as both priest and victim in the altar of His Sacred Body is the mediator between God the Father and His people (Heb. 5:5–10). Jesus is the victim of atonement (1 John 2:2; 4:10) who offered Himself on the altar of the Cross and perpetuates that sacrifice now in the Eucharist. The priest at Holy Mass, in saying "This is my body" and "This is the cup of my blood," acts in the *Person of Christ*, who is the one High Priest of the New and Eternal Covenant (Heb. 8–9).

The Catholic Church teaches that priestly ordination in a line of apostolic succession through bishops who have the fullness of Christ's priesthood is the indispensable condition for the valid celebration of the Eucharist. The ordained bishop or priest makes Christ Himself present to His Church as Head of His Body, Shepherd of His flock, High Priest of the redemptive sacrifice perpetuated on our altars today. The ordained priest acts "in the name of the whole Church when presenting to God the prayer of the Church, and above all when offering the Eucharistic sacrifice" (CCC, 1552). From this, priests must realize that they are never to put themselves or their personal opinions in first place. Always, they must present Jesus Christ, first and last.

A priest who would act as if on stage, making himself the center of the liturgical action, is contradicting his very identity as a priest of Jesus Christ and the reality that is the Eucharist. The priest as the servant of others is to work to be a sign pointing to Jesus Christ, an instrument of Christ's heart and hands. This calls for humility, obedience to the prescribed rites of the Church, a union of himself in mind and heart with Jesus, and His oneness with His Church. To give emphasis to his own personality during the Divine Liturgy is improper when the priest is to give emphasis to the Person of Jesus Christ, true God and true man. The Divine Liturgy is the office of the Good Shepherd, who offers His life for His sheep (John 10:14–15).

The holy priesthood bestowed through ordination in the Sacrament of Holy Orders calls for complete configuration to Jesus Christ. Jesus Christ was celibate, and priestly celibacy is a priceless treasure. There is a reason why the Eastern practice chooses only bishops from the ranks of the celibate. The priest's personal choice of celibacy expresses in a special way the dedication that conforms him to Christ and his exclusive offering of himself for the Kingdom of God. Jesus Christ, the eternal High Priest, lived His mission, even to the Sacrifice of the Cross, in the state of virginity. This is a certain point of reference to understanding the Latin Church tradition of the celibate priesthood. For the priest, celibacy is a special way of conforming himself to Christ's own way of life.

Personally, as a Catholic priest, from the time I was ordained as a young priest and through more than fifty years active in the holy priesthood of Jesus Christ, I have always considered myself as married to the Church, Christ's Mystical Body. This choice of the priest has first and foremost a nuptial meaning. It is a profound identification with the heart of Jesus Christ, the Bridegroom who gives his life for his Bride. The priestly life lived in celibacy is a sign expressing total and exclusive devotion to Jesus Christ, to the Church, and to the Kingdom of God. Priestly celibacy, lived with maturity, joy, dedication, brings immense blessings for the Church and society itself.

Holy Eucharist and Holy Matrimony

Since the Eucharist is the Sacrament of Charity, it has a particular relationship with man and woman united in Holy Matrimony. The entire Christian life bears the mark of the spousal love of Jesus Christ for His Church. Baptism introduces one to the nuptial mystery of Christ's Mystical Body and precedes the wedding feast, the Eucharist. Frequent and reverent participation in and reception of the Eucharist strengthens the union of each member of the Church with Jesus Christ. So too does the worthy celebration and reception of the Eucharist inexhaustibly strengthen the indissoluble unity and love of two persons united in sacramental Christian marriage.

At the Sacrifice of the Mass, both husband and wife participate in the perpetuation of the New Covenant struck on Calvary, the greatest act of love ever offered by man, and that man on the Cross of Calvary two thousand years ago was and is the God-Man, Jesus Christ. Union in Holy Matrimony for husband and wife is strengthened and nourished by the worthy reception of Jesus' Body and Blood, Soul and Divinity in Holy Communion. St. Paul spoke of this when he compared the union of love between husband and wife to that of Christ's love and union with His Church. "This is a great mystery, and I mean in reference to Christ and the church" (Eph. 5:31–32).

For St. Paul, conjugal love is a sacramental sign of Christ's love for His Church — Christ's love culminated on the Cross. It was the supreme expression of His "marriage" with humanity. It was also the origin and heart of the Eucharist, and it still is. Both the Cross and Resurrection of Christ are present realities that attract us to His love. The family — the domestic Church — is the primary sphere of the Church's life. The family is a miniature Mystical Body of Christ. The husband as head represents Christ in a special way. The wife and mother represent the Body of Christ, the Mystical Body of Christ's Church, whereas the children are the members. Marriage and motherhood represent essential realities that must always be held in high esteem.

Jesus Christ can never be separated from His Church. As there is an indissoluble, exclusive, and faithful bond between Christ and the Church, which has sacramental expression and reality in the Eucharist, from which the Church flows, all this corresponds to the basic fact that God intends one man to be united to one woman in marriage for life. This is so much the nature of true marriage that the Church, based on Sacred Scripture (Mark 10:2–12), does not admit the divorced and so-called "remarried" to the sacraments. This is because their state in life contradicts "the loving union of Christ and the Church signified and made present in the Eucharist" (*SC*, 29). This does not mean that the Church turns her back on those who are divorced and remarried. As Pope Benedict acknowledged, the Church's pastors must "discern different situations carefully, in order to be able to offer appropriate spiritual guidance to the faithful involved" (*SC*, 29). This is because the marriage bond between a man and a woman — like the bond between Christ and His Church — is indissoluble.

The Eucharist and Entrance to Eternity

In the liturgy of the Eucharist, known as the Sacrifice of the Mass, we are given a real foretaste of the eschatological fulfillment for which each one of us and all creation are destined by God (Rom. 8:19–25). Each of us was created by God with His plan in view that we will spend eternity with God in Heaven. Only God's love can give us that ultimate and final gift. He gives that gift in the Eucharist. We must be open to that gift and disposed by faith, hope, and love. We are in fact "aliens and exiles" while yet in this world (1 Peter 2:11), but through our supernatural virtue of faith, we share now in the fullness of risen life. The Risen Christ is present in the Eucharist and unites Himself to us in Holy Communion so that we may live forever, not only in our souls but also in our bodies, which will be resurrected and glorified to live eternally in Heaven. Jesus has told us:

> For this is the will of my Father, that every one who sees the Son and believes in him should have eternal life; and I will raise him up at the last day.... This is the bread which comes down from heaven, that a man may eat of it and not die. I am the living bread which came down from heaven; if any one eats of this bread, he will live for ever; and the bread which I shall give for the life of the world is my flesh.... Truly, truly, I say to you, unless you eat the flesh of the Son of man and drink his blood, you have no life in you; he who eats my flesh and drinks my blood has eternal life, and I will raise him up at the last day. For my flesh is food indeed, and my blood is drink indeed. He who eats my flesh and drinks my blood abides in me, and I in him. As the living Father sent me, and I live because of the Father, so he who eats me will live because of me. This is the bread which came down from heaven, not such as the fathers ate and died; he who eats this bread will live for ever. (John 6:40, 50–51, 53–58)

Jesus' coming fulfilled an expectation present already among God's people in Old Testament times, present in the people of Israel. Jesus came so that we could have eternal life with God in Heaven, sharing in the very life of God. "I came that they may have life, and have it abundantly" (John 10:10). That life and its increase comes, after Baptism, chiefly through the Eucharist. By His teaching, by His self-gift, Jesus inaugurated the eschatological age. This is to say, in opening the gates of Heaven for fallen mankind, by bridging the relationship between God and man, by bringing God and man into union with each other, Jesus has assured us, promised us, eternal life in Heaven. This promise applies to both body and soul, if we are true to His New Covenant. Jesus, by dying for all, brought together the dispersed children of God. Thus Jesus brought to fulfillment the promises made by God to the fathers of old (Jer. 23:3; Luke 1:55, 70).

Jesus established the New Covenant; in fact, He is the New Covenant. For continuing the New Covenant among people still in this world, Jesus called the twelve apostles, the counterpart of the twelve tribes of Israel under the Old Covenant. To the Twelve He gave the command at the Last Supper, which was just before His redemptive Passion and death, to celebrate His memorial, just as He did that Holy Thursday night. It was already Good Friday when Jesus instituted the Holy Eucharist, for the Jews recognized a new day at sunset, not at midnight. The Sacrifice of the Mass was thus established by Jesus on the same day as His sacrificial death on the Cross. The apostles and their successors would be able to make present through the centuries what Jesus offered in the gift of Himself in sacramental sacrifice at the Last Supper. Thus, under the New Covenant, the People of God would be brought together in unity. The Eucharist is the great sacrament of the Mystical Body that brings about the Great Sacrament, the Church Herself. It is why we call it the *Most* Blessed Sacrament. The Eucharist would be the sign and instrument of the eschatological gathering of God's people. The Eucharistic banquet is a real foretaste of the final and heavenly banquet, foretold by the prophets (Isa. 25:6–9). It is described in the New Testament as "the marriage supper of the Lamb" (Rev. 19:7–9). It is forever celebrated in the joy of the Communion of Saints in Heaven, the heavenly liturgy. It is the New and Eternal Covenant. For all eternity, Jesus, with His glorified body with its glorified wounds, is offering to the Father in the unity of the Holy Spirit what He offered on Calvary. The Eucharist is Heaven on earth.

It has always been the practice of the Church, already from the time of the Sacrifice of the Mass offered in the catacombs, to offer the

Eucharist for the souls of the dead. This is so that, once purified, they can enter into the Beatific Vision of God. The Eucharist we celebrate and receive looks forward to our bodily resurrection. Again we are reminded: "He who eats my flesh and drinks my blood has eternal life, and I will raise him up at the last day" (John 6:54). That surely establishes the eschatological dimension of the Eucharist, celebrated, received, and adored. It will strengthen us on our journey to Heaven.

Mother of the Church and the Eucharist

God's gifts to us find their perfect fulfillment in the Virgin Mary, Mother of God and Mother of the Church. The Eucharist directed to the resurrection of the body, the salvation of the soul, is reflected in the Assumption of Mary, body and soul into Heaven. Her Assumption is a sign of certain hope for us. If the celebration and worthy reception of Jesus Christ in the Eucharist is a promise of our future resurrection, Mary, who gave us the body of Jesus, nourished Him, intermingled her blood with His, is seen in the faith of the Church as not having to wait for the end of the world. Her blessed body is already in Heaven, assumed there. Our bodies too will be resurrected and taken to Heaven on the last day.

She who is the Lady of the Eucharist did not have to undergo the corruption of the grave. Mary, most holy, images the perfect fulfillment of the "sacramental" way that God comes down to have union with His children, made in God's own image and likeness, and lifts them up, body and soul, to Heaven. The Eucharist is indeed a foretaste of heavenly glory and already unites us to Jesus in Heaven while we live by faith in grace still upon earth.

Mary always lived in obedient faith. Mary was always open and responsive to God's Word. She always lived in harmony with the divine will. She treasured in her Immaculate Heart the words and the will that came to her from God, the Word made flesh. She ever understood the Word of God more deeply (Luke 2:19, 51).

Mary, the great woman of faith, always placed herself in God's hands with total confidence. She always abandoned herself to His will. The mystery of the union of the hearts of Jesus and Mary is seen as she ever more deeply became involved in the redemptive mission of Jesus. She is seen as Co-Redemptrix, that is, together with Christ as the head and source of all grace, Mary cooperated perfectly, so much so, that she became the Mother of us all, the Mother of the Church.

Mary was associated in her heart with the Sacrifice of Jesus as He redeemed the world. Mary lovingly consented to the immolation of her victim Son, born of her, giving Him up to the Father in union with her Son's will. She who gave us Jesus Christ was given to all of us as our Mother as Jesus was dying on the Cross: "Woman, behold, your son" (John 19:26).

Mary wholeheartedly received the Word from the time of the Annunciation to His death on the Cross. Jesus loved His own "to the end" (John 13:1). Mary loved in union with her Son, taking His dead body into her arms, the same body she conceived of the Holy Spirit and nourished so that we "may have life, and have it abundantly" (John 10:10).

Mary received and offered Christ's sacrifice in union with Him. Mary is the perfect model of everything that the Church is and hopes to become. Thus Mary inaugurated the participation of the Church in the sacrifice of the Redeemer. The Immaculata is associated with Christ's work of salvation from the beginning to the end. She is present at all the major moments of Christ's life in salvation history as He redeemed us. She is present, too, at the completion or birthday of the Church, when She received Her Soul, that is, when, after the Ascension, Jesus united with the Father sent the Holy Spirit upon the Church on Pentecost Sunday.

Eucharist

Pope Benedict XVI articulated the Church doctrine of Our Lady's coredemption in his Post-Synodal Exhortation, *Sacramentum Caritatis*. Pope Benedict referenced the Second Vatican Council's principal teaching on Marian Coredemption, found in *Lumen Gentium*, and confirmed that our Mother was "completely involved in the redemptive mission of Jesus" (*SC*, 33):

> The Blessed Virgin advanced in her pilgrimage of faith, and faithfully persevered in her union with her Son unto the cross, where she stood, in keeping with the divine plan, grieving exceedingly with her only begotten Son, uniting herself with a maternal heart with His sacrifice, and lovingly consenting to the immolation of this Victim which she herself had brought forth. Finally, she was given by the same Christ Jesus dying on the cross as a mother to His disciple with these words: "Woman, behold thy son." (*Lumen Gentium*, 58)

If we believe that the Mass is a re-presentation of the Sacrifice of the Cross, we can understand, then, the position that every celebration of the Eucharist brings a certain presence of Mary, Mother of God, Co-Redemptrix.

Eucharist as the Mystery of Faith Celebrated

The Eucharist is experienced by believing, devout Catholics as the mystery of faith. It is the mystery of faith celebrated. Our Catholic Faith and the Eucharistic liturgy have their source in the Paschal Mystery, which Jesus lived and instituted during the first Holy Week, that is, His last week on earth. The Paschal Mystery first lived becomes present today through the Eucharist.

The liturgy is by its very nature, that is, the reality it expresses in sign, linked to beauty. The Divine Liturgy of the Eucharist is a radiant expression of the Paschal Mystery wherein Jesus Christ draws us to Himself and invites us to union with Himself in a holy communion. It is the means to keep the Mystical Body alive and united in Jesus Christ. It is why the reception of the Eucharist is called "Holy Communion."

What Jesus Christ did that first Holy Week, and what He gave us, is made present in the celebration of the Eucharist today. That is why Pope Benedict XVI wrote: "The liturgy is a radiant expression of the paschal mystery, in which Christ draws us to himself and calls us to communion" (*SC*, 35). As St. Bonaventure would say, in Jesus, we contemplate beauty and splendor at their source. This is no mere asceticism, but the concrete way in which the truth of God's love in Christ encounters us, attracts us, and delights us, enabling us to emerge from ourselves and drawing us towards our true vocation, which is love. God allows Himself to be glimpsed first in creation, in the beauty and harmony of the cosmos (Wisd. 13:5; Rom. 1:19–20).

The Eucharist and the Whole Christ

It was St. Augustine who referred to the Church, the Mystical Body of Jesus Christ, as the "whole Christ." The Head, Jesus Christ, His members, those baptized into the Church, together make up the "whole Christ." Jesus Christ used the example of the vine and branches (John 15: 5) to demonstrate this mystery of faith that is our union with Christ the Head in the *divine organism* that we call the Church or the Mystical Body of Christ. He did this at the Last Supper when He instituted the Holy Eucharist. We see here again how the Church flows from the Eucharist.

To quote the words of the great Bishop of Hippo: "The bread you see on the altar, sanctified by the word of God, is the Blood of Christ. In these signs, Christ the Lord willed to entrust to us His Body and the Blood which He shed for the forgiveness of our sins. If you have received them properly, you yourselves have become Christ Himself" (*In Johannis Evangelium Tractatus*, 21, 8: *PL* 35, 1568). And again, "One should not believe that Christ is in the head but not in the body; rather He is complete in the head and in the body" (Ibid., 28, 1: *PL* 35, 1622).

The Eucharistic liturgy is the act of God. It draws us into Jesus Christ through the Holy Spirit. Its basic structure is not something an individual priest or bishop, or the universal Church Herself, has the power to change. It is the act of Jesus Christ, the God-Man extended in time and space. Its structure can never be determined by the latest trends. It is timeless in its essence, which is the Paschal Mystery of Jesus Christ, extending across time and space and into eternity, where the heavenly liturgy is forever. What St. Paul wrote under the inspiration of the Holy Spirit applies here: "For no other foundation can any one lay than that which is laid, which is Jesus Christ" (1 Cor. 3:11). The celebration of the Eucharist involves the living Tradition inaugurated by Jesus Christ who is "the same yesterday and today and for ever" (Heb. 13:8).

The Church obeys Jesus Christ's command in celebrating the Eucharistic Sacrifice. The Church has experienced the Risen Lord and the outpouring of the Holy Spirit for two thousand years and will thus continue Jesus' sacrifice that also brings the Risen Lord. From the very beginning of the Christian era, the Christian community has gathered for the breaking of the bread, that is, for the celebration of the Eucharist on the Lord's Day, Sunday, the very day Jesus rose from the dead. The early Church had but one feast, that of Easter, or the Resurrection, and every Sunday was seen as a little Easter, or living memorial and presence of the crucified and Risen Christ. Jesus rose from the dead on Sunday, the first day of the week, the day that the tradition of the Old Testament saw as the beginning of God's work of Creation. Sunday, the day of Creation has become the day of the

"The Church Flows from the Eucharist"

"new creation," when the believer experiences liberation and is able to say as the Apostle Thomas finally did, "My Lord and my God!" (John 20:28). Each Sunday the Catholic Christian who practices and lives his faith is made a new creature as we commemorate Jesus Christ who died and rose again. Each Eucharist in which we participate, and each Sunday especially, is the day to experience the joy of the Resurrection.

The primary way to elicit the full participation of the faithful in the sacred rite of the Eucharist is to celebrate the rite properly as approved by the Church. For two thousand years, the proper celebration of the Eucharist, adhering to the approved liturgical norms in all their richness, has sustained the faith life of believers. The faithful are called to take part in the celebration as they participate in a royal priesthood, a holy nation (1 Peter 2:4–10). The faithful need the ordained priesthood of Holy Orders for perpetuating the Sacrifice of the Cross and the Real Presence of Jesus in the Most Blessed Sacrament — but they participate in the priesthood of the faithful, of the baptized: "But you are a chosen race, a royal priesthood, a holy nation, God's own people, that you may declare the wonderful deeds of him who called you out of darkness into his marvelous light. Once you were no people but now you are God's people; once you had not received mercy but now you have received mercy" (1 Pet. 2:9–10).

The *General Instruction of the Roman Missal* — along with the Second Vatican Council and other official documents of the Magisterium — reminds us that the "the diocesan Bishop, the chief steward of the mysteries of God in the particular Church entrusted to his care, is the moderator, promoter, and guardian of the whole of its liturgical life" (22). Bishops, priests, and deacons, according to each one's proper rank, have a role in the celebration of the Divine Liturgy, and it is their principal duty. Communion with the bishop is required for the lawfulness of every celebration within his territory. This union with the bishop is required because he is the celebrant par excellence within his diocese. It is the bishop's responsibility to ensure unity and harmony in the celebrations taking place in his diocese.

The proper respect for the liturgical books and the richness of signs in the celebration of the liturgy — all should foster a sense of the sacred. The use of outward signs established by Jesus Christ in the institution of the sacraments and in the liturgy approved by the Church have as their purpose to help cultivate faith, love for God, adoration of God through Jesus Christ, reverence, and unity among believers. Everything associated with the celebration of the Divine Liturgy — liturgical vestments, the furnishings, and the sacred space — all is directed to the same end. This is because the liturgy engages "the whole human person," and so even the physical signs must direct the Church to the proper worship of God. Remaining true to the prescribed rubrics also leads to a "recognition of the nature of Eucharist as a gift," rather than something owed (*SC*, 40).

St. Augustine in a famous sermon said that "the new man sings a new song. Singing is an expression of joy, and, if we consider the matter, an expression of love" (Sermon 34, 1: *PL* 38, 210). Again, "he who sings well prays twice." For two thousand years, the Church has continued to create music and songs representative of a rich patrimony of faith and love. Gregorian chant is esteemed by the Church as the chant proper to the Roman liturgy.

There are many instances of young people manifesting a love for Gregorian chant. It speaks of reverence in song.

Having taught in religion classrooms for forty-eight and a half years, I think it is unfortunate that some parishes move children from the congregation to another area other than the sacred space of worship in order to present them catechesis apart from the celebration of the Liturgy of the Word of God, including the homily. There is intrinsic unity in the liturgical action of the celebration of the Eucharist.

"The Church Flows from the Eucharist"

The Church has made it clear: the Liturgy of the Word and the Eucharistic Liturgy, with the rites of introduction and conclusion, "are so closely interconnected that they form but one single act of worship" (*General Instruction of the Roman Missal, 28*; *Sacrosanctum Concilium*, 56). There is not merely a juxtaposition. There is an intrinsic bond between the Word of God and the Eucharist. Faith is born and strengthened in listening to the Word of God (Rom. 10:17). It is from the two tables of the Word of God and the Body of Christ that the Church both receives and gives to the faithful the Bread of Life. There is a presence of Jesus Christ in both the Word of God read and explained in Church and the Consecration of the Eucharist. While the mode of Christ's presence is different in the manner of presence, it must be kept in mind that the Word of God in the Divine Liturgy leads to the Eucharist as its end.

> To accomplish so great a work, Christ is always present in His Church, especially in her liturgical celebrations. He is present in the sacrifice of the Mass, not only in the person of His minister, "the same now offering, through the ministry of priests, who formerly offered himself on the cross," but especially under the Eucharistic species. By his power He is present in the sacraments, so that when a man baptizes it is really Christ Himself who baptizes. He is present in His word, since it is He Himself who speaks when the holy scriptures are read in the Church. He is present, lastly, when the Church prays and sings, for He promised: "Where two or three are gathered together in my name, there am I in the midst of them" (Matt. 18:20)....
>
> In the earthly liturgy, by way of foretaste, we share in that heavenly liturgy which is celebrated in the holy city of Jerusalem toward which we journey as pilgrims, and in which Christ

is sitting at the right hand of God, a minister of the sanctuary and of the true tabernacle [Rev. 21:2; Col. 3:1; Heb. 8:2]; we sing a hymn to the Lord's glory with all the warriors of the heavenly army; venerating the memory of the saints, we hope for some part and fellowship with them: we eagerly await the Savior, our Lord Jesus Christ, until He, our life, shall appear and we too will appear with Him in glory [Phil. 3:20; Col. 3:4] [emphasis added]. (*Sacrosanctum Concilium*, 7–8)

The Eucharistic Prayer of the Mass is "the center and summit of the entire celebration" (*General Instruction of the Roman Missal*, 78). The different Eucharistic Prayers have been handed down to us through the centuries by the Church's living Tradition. There is a profound unity between the invocation of the Holy Spirit and the institution narrative where "the sacrifice is carried out which Christ himself instituted at the Last Supper" (*General Instruction of the Roman Missal*, 79d).

The Second Vatican Council rightly emphasized the active, full, and fruitful participation of all Catholics in the Eucharistic celebration (*Sacrosanctum Concilium*, 14–20; 30ff.). Pope Benedict XVI echoed this sentiment in *Sacramentum Caritatis* and commented that what we understand to be active participation needs to be reoriented to what the Council Fathers intended. Namely, that active participation "must be understood in more substantial terms, on the basis of a greater awareness of the mystery being celebrated and its relationship to daily life." Pope Benedict urged the faithful to make an offering of themselves in union with the priest who is offering the "immaculate Victim" (*SC*, 52). There must be a greater awareness of what is happening at Holy Mass so that the faithful might more fruitfully participate in the sacrifice of their redemption.

3

The Eucharist Unites Members into the Whole Christ

ACTIVE PARTICIPATION IN THE EUCHARISTIC CELEBRATION is essentially in our hearts, in our minds, our wills, our spirits. It is essential that we understand and realize that sacramentally the Eucharist is perpetuating the Paschal Mystery. While only the priest of Holy Orders can consecrate, we join within ourselves in offering the Victim, Jesus Christ, to God the Father. The priest makes present the Victim. We all join in the offering. As we should offer our very selves in union with Jesus Christ as we offer Him to the Father.

We participate actively when we listen to the Scriptures read during Mass — when we ask the Holy Spirit to reveal Jesus to us through the Scriptures. We can ask the Holy Spirit to show us how the readings at Mass are related to each other, how they are related to our lives.

We should ask the Holy Spirit to help us see Jesus in others at Mass, even in those who naturally do not appeal to us.

When the priest holds up the paten with the unconsecrated bread upon it, at the offertory of the Mass, we can place ourselves spiritually also on that paten, our entire day, our week, our very life. Place all on the paten, where is the bread to be transformed into the Body of Jesus Christ, and desire to be transformed more and more into the likeness of Jesus Christ.

When we receive Holy Communion, we can look at the crucifix and ponder how Jesus offered His physical body and blood for us in sacrifice. We can recall in faith and love that it is the same Jesus we are receiving when we come to the altar. It is the same Jesus who wants to open our eyes as He finally did the two disciples on the way to Emmaus.

Active participation is not accomplished if one approaches the Eucharist in a superficial manner, without an examination of one's life. This inner disposition of heart is to be fostered by recollection, by silence at least for a short time before the beginning of the liturgy. Fasting before celebrating the Divine Liturgy and making a sacramental Confession, which is required if serious sin has been committed, are also involved in what the Church means by "active participation."

It is clear that full participation in the Eucharist takes place when the faithful approach the altar in person to receive Jesus in Holy Communion with faith and love. The mere fact that one is present in church during the liturgy does not automatically give anyone the right or even an obligation to approach the table of the Eucharist. Even if one is in serious sin and is not able to receive Holy Communion, he or she still has the obligation of participating in the liturgy insofar as possible. Such people should, through the practice of spiritual communion, express within their hearts the desire to be united to Jesus.

The Eucharist manifests not only our personal communion with Jesus Christ our Head, but implies full communion with the whole Church. However sad, this is the reason why the Church asks Christians who are not Catholic to understand and respect the Church's conviction, which is grounded in the Bible and Tradition. It is this: only Catholics in full communion, and in the state of sanctifying grace, are to approach the altar to receive Holy Communion.

Interior participation of the faithful, corresponding to the gestures and words at the Mass, is required so that they don't risk falling into a certain ritualism. Going through the actions by habit without realizing what one is doing, without an interior realization within the mind and heart that the perpetuating of the Paschal Mystery, the very Sacrifice of the Cross, is taking place, without that conscious realization, one is lacking in full and active participation. One's faith must be activated and come alive at Mass, and by faith, we behold the Real Presence of Jesus Christ coming onto the altar. It happens in the very act of transubstantiating bread and wine into the Lord's Body, Blood, Soul, and Divinity. Each communicant, after examining his or her conscience, must express love for Our Lord and Savior coming into our bodies and souls in this sacrament. A time of *fervent thanksgiving* within one's heart after receiving Our Divine Lord is also required for full participation.

Faith in the mystery of God present among us is expressed by showing concrete outward signs of reverence for the Eucharist. Silence in the presence of the Most Blessed Sacrament; making a genuflection upon entering the church where the Eucharist is present; always genuflecting whenever passing before the altar; kneeling before the Most Blessed Sacrament and during the central moments of the Eucharistic Prayer; making the Sign of the Cross or bowing before approaching to receive Our Lord in Holy Communion; these are all expressions of the sense of faith in the mystery of God present among us.

There is an intrinsic relationship between Eucharistic celebration and Eucharistic adoration. St. Augustine wrote: "No one eats that flesh [of Jesus Christ] without first adoring it; we should sin were we not to adore it." In a similar vein, Pope Benedict XVI understood Eucharistic adoration as the "natural consequence of the Eucharistic celebration" (*SC*, 66). The faithful who engage in Eucharistic adoration will experience more fully and more fruitfully the reality of what is the liturgical celebration of the Eucharist. The Sacrifice of the Mass will be more meaningful to them, more effectively will they experience the awe of the mystery of God present and acting among us. Young children, especially from the time they begin to prepare for First Holy Communion, should be taught the meaning and the beauty of spending time with Jesus. From preschool days, they should be helped to cultivate a sense of awe before Jesus' presence in the Eucharist. Little children entering church can be taught the use of holy water, the making of the Sign of the Cross, and to genuflect, so as to adore God as they go to their place in church.

Sincere and informed Catholics believe in eternal life. It is not merely a matter of "afterlife," for even pagans have often had some belief in that. We, however, believe in something different. We believe that in Jesus Christ, through sanctifying grace, we are able to share in eternal life by being made "partakers of the divine nature" (2 Pet. 1:4). "This 'eternal life' begins in us even now, thanks to the transformation effected in us by the gift of the Eucharist" (*SC*, 70). The Eucharistic food is not changed into us. Rather, we are mysteriously transformed by receiving Jesus Christ, who nourishes us by uniting us to Himself. Jesus draws us into Himself.

The Church bids us to live the Mass, to live the Eucharist. "As the living Father sent me, and I live because of the Father, so he who eats me will live because of me" (John 6:57). St. Paul's exhortation is a call and description of how the Eucharist makes our whole life a spiritual worship pleasing to God: "I appeal to you therefore, brethren, by the mercies of God, to present your bodies as a living sacrifice, holy and acceptable to God, which is your spiritual worship" (Rom. 12:1). The apostle insists on the offering of our bodies to God in Jesus Christ. The body of Christ was resurrected. He ate with the apostles after He appeared to them following His death and Resurrection. This was to demonstrate He was not simply an apparition or something disassociated from the body that lived among them, taught them, and died on the Cross. It was not merely a spirit but the real body of Jesus. This same resurrected body unites Himself to us. St. Augustine wrote: "This is the sacrifice of Christians; that we, though many, are one body in Christ. The Church celebrates this mystery in the sacrament of the altar, as the faithful know, and there she shows them clearly that in what is offered, she herself is offered" (*De Civitate Dei*, 10, 6: *PL* 41, 284).

> *The Eucharist is also the sacrifice of the Church.* The Church which is the Body of Christ participates in the offering of her Head. With him, she herself is offered whole and entire. She unites herself to his intercession with the Father for all men. In the Eucharist the sacrifice of Christ becomes also the sacrifice of the members of his Body. The lives of the faithful, their praise, sufferings, prayer, and work, are united with those of Christ and with his total offering, and so acquire a new value. Christ's sacrifice present on the altar makes it possible for all generations of Christians to be united with his offering. (*CCC*, 1368)

Offering and living the Eucharist is a new worship of the New Covenant, the gift from the Father of His Son incarnate, which includes and transfigures every aspect of life: "Whether you eat or drink, or whatever you do, do all to the glory of God" (1 Cor. 10:31). In all our actions we are called to offer true worship to God. In this way the intrinsically Eucharistic nature of Christian life begins to take shape. Everyday existence, our work and experiences, are embraced by the Eucharist, that thus, day by day, there is a progressive transfiguration of all those called by grace to reflect the image of the Son of God (Rom. 8:29) and grow ever more into His likeness. As Pope Benedict XVI explains, the worship that is pleasing to God "becomes a new way of living our whole life … since it is lived as part of a relationship with Christ and as an offering to God" (*SC*, 71).

Such is what it will be for each of us in glory in Heaven, ultimately with both body and soul. We shall have eternal life in body and soul because of the Eucharist in our lives upon earth, where we encountered heaven in, with, and through Jesus Christ in the unity of and by the power of the Holy Spirit.

From the beginning of Christianity, baptized Christians were clearly aware of this radical newness that the Holy Eucharist brings to our human life upon earth. From the first, the faithful perceived the profound influence of the Eucharistic celebration on their manner of daily life. St. Ignatius of Antioch said it this way in speaking of Christians as "those who have attained a new hope," and he described them as "those living in accordance with the Lord's Day," *iuxta dominicam viventes* (Letter to the Magnesians, 9, 1: *PG* 5, 670). Christians experienced this day as the first day of the week, since it commemorates the radical newness of life brought by Jesus Christ. Sunday became thus the day when Christians rediscover the Eucharistic form that their lives are meant to have. Hence, truly honoring the Lord's Day means living one's life "in the awareness of the liberation brought by Christ" (*SC*, 72).

Christians living a life of purity in thought, word, and deed, conscious of their bodies as temples of the Holy Spirit, realizing their union in Jesus Christ for each Sunday, often each day — such they knew was the effect of the Holy Eucharist. Their bodies and souls became in real living union with the very resurrected body and soul of Jesus Christ, who once was crucified for them. (see *SC*, 73).

While the Church views the celebration for all the faithful as the "Sunday obligation," yet for those of sincere and deep faith, it is a Sunday fulfillment of joy and love of the Father who is one with Jesus in the unity of the Holy Spirit. Then, rather than seem as an "obligation," which it is for us as children of God indebted to our Heavenly Father, missing the Eucharistic celebration on the Lord's Day should be viewed most painfully by those prevented by circumstances of life, such as lack of a priest, or being confined by an illness.

What is a joy is not a burden. The very life of faith is seriously endangered when one loses the desire to share in the celebration of the Eucharist, which commemorates Christ's paschal victory.

The Eucharist Unites Members into the Whole Christ

Participating in the Sunday liturgical assembly with others with whom we form one Body in Jesus Christ, is not only demanded by a rightly formed Christian conscience, but it is at the same time the source that forms a correct conscience. Those who deliberately do not fulfill the Sunday obligation do not find freedom. They lose an authentic sense of Christian freedom, freedom of the children of God. Sunday is the Day of the Lord. It is the Lord's Day, not our day.

Pope St. John Paul II, called "the Great" in his own time, issued an apostolic letter, *Dies Domini*, telling us the day of the Lord with regard to the work of Creation, is *Dies Christi*, the "day of Christ." It is the day on which the Christian community gathers for the celebration, and *dies hominis*, the day of mankind, as it is the day of joy, rest, and fraternal charity. Jesus Christ rose from the dead on Sunday. With the Father, He sent the Holy Spirit upon the Church on Sunday. Sunday has become the primordial day, when all believers can become heralds and guardians of the true meaning of time. A new meaning of life and the experience of time is experienced when one recognizes the Lord's Day and adores God in a special way on that day, which occurs each week as the first day.

Sunday is also a day of rest from work. Civil society, unfortunately, in recent decades, often treats Sundays as another weekday. Sunday, from the time of the meaning of the Sabbath in Jewish tradition, has been seen as the Lord's Day, a day of rest from daily exertions. Work is for man, not man for work. While work is of fundamental importance to the fulfillment of the human being and the development of society, it must be carried out with full respect to human dignity. It should always serve the common good. People must not be enslaved by work or idolize it as if it is the ultimate and definitive meaning of life in itself. Sunday is the day consecrated to God and gives meaning to our lives and to our work for time and eternity. There is dignity to human labor. Jesus Christ Himself was a carpenter before beginning

His public ministry. The Eucharist is essential for that realization and for the sanctification of work. It is the day to bring members of Christ's Mystical Body together in worship and also a special day for individual families, in their homes, to unite and express and appreciate their union in love.

Each Sunday, the Catholic Christian affirms and experiences the communal dimension of his life as one of many who has been redeemed by Jesus Christ. Participating in the Divine Liturgy and receiving the Body and Blood of our Redeemer, Jesus Christ, intensifies our union to the one who died for us (1 Cor. 6:19–20; 7:23). It intensifies our union with Jesus Christ, the Head, and also affirms and intensifies our union with the whole Christ as well. Participation in this Eucharistic mystery helps us to understand more profoundly the meaning of the Communion of Saints, to whom we are ever more intensely united already on this earth through the Eucharistic celebration and its fruitful reception.

The effects of celebrating and participating in the Eucharist have both a vertical and horizontal sense. *Vertical* because we direct our adoration toward God the Father through Jesus Christ in the power of the Holy Spirit; the vertical dimension is present as we offer God the Father the Sacrifice of Jesus Christ. The *horizontal* is realized in our union with our brothers and sisters in the Church as the grace of the Eucharist gives all of us a greater sharing in the life of God and we worship in union with the Church. As in Christ's own example of the vine and branches, the sap in the vine is the same as the sap in branches, thus uniting them as one, so it is in the Church. In the Church all have the indelible mark or character of Jesus Christ from Baptism on their souls and share in the divine life when in the state of grace. The Eucharist keeps the members alive in Christ and ever more abundantly.

This is how Pope Benedict XVI expressed the above in a General Audience, March 29, 2006: "Wherever communion with God, which is communion with the Father, the Son and the Holy Spirit, is destroyed, the root and source of our communion with one another is destroyed. And wherever we do not live [in] communion among ourselves, communion with the Trinitarian God is not alive and true either."

We are called to be members of Jesus Christ and thus members of one another in the Mystical Body of Christ (1 Cor. 12:27). We are a divine organism as members of the Church united to the Head with the Holy Spirit as Soul. This membership originates from and is grounded ontologically in Baptism. It is nourished by the Eucharist. This divine organism is a supernatural reality that requires visible expression. God became man and visible in Jesus Christ; the Church, which is both human and divine, requires human, visible expressions. This is accomplished in visible ways in the signs and words that are essential to the Eucharist in which is the hidden Jesus and wherein He acts with the same infinite majesty and power as He acted on Calvary. God the Father sees the same Paschal Mystery accomplished in both, the liturgy and Calvary. The sacraments in general are acts of Jesus Christ extended in time and space.

Eucharistic spirituality is more than participation in the Sacrifice of the Mass and devotion to the Real Presence in the Most Blessed Sacrament. It involves the whole of our lives. The Christ life for the authentic Christian involves every aspect of living; sanctifying every moment, movement, activity. Living a Eucharistic spirituality is most important today, when God is being removed from the consciousness of society.

Secularization, with its inherent emphasis on individualism, has its greatest negative effects on those who are thus isolated and lack a sense of belonging. From the time of Christ's death and Resurrection, and His sending together with the Father the Holy Spirit upon the Church, Christian life has meant fellowship. That union or fellowship is not merely a natural network of relationships; it is a supernatural communion, strengthened by hearing God's Word and sharing in the Eucharist. This is Divine Liturgy enlivened by the Holy Spirit. It touches Heaven as Heaven touches participants.

It is sometimes heard that fellowship is stronger among Evangelical Protestant communities. However valuable and good it is for them, the believing, practicing Catholic experiences the highest and greatest fellowship possible in the Eucharist. And for that he needs a valid priesthood of Christ in men. At the Eucharist, he participates, in virtue of Baptism and the indelible character of Christ on his soul, in the sacrifice made possible by Jesus Christ through the instrumentality of the ordained priest of Holy Orders. He offers to the Father, too, the victim Christ that the Consecration of the ordained priest brings about in the Eucharistic Sacrifice. Then, together with his fellow Catholic Christians, he receives the living Body, Blood, Soul, and Divinity of Our Lord and Redeemer in Holy Communion. This is fellowship at its highest, its greatest potential. It is a communion with Christ that is holy. It is a union with others who receive Jesus. It is why it is called "Holy Communion."

What the Gospel and Church means by saying, "God became man in Jesus Christ," is a concrete reality, not a mere private conviction or an abstract idea. Jesus Christ is a real person, the second Person of the Most Blessed Trinity, who has become man. God in becoming man became part of human history, and Jesus Christ is capable of renewing the life of every man and woman. Thus the Church teaches that the Eucharist is the source and summit of the Church's life and mission. This faith reality must be translated into the spirituality, into the life of each Catholic Christian and thus lived "according to the Spirit" (Rom. 8:4; see Gal. 5:16, 25). As God stepped into human history and time in the Incarnation, so through the Eucharist, we step, as it were, into Heaven. Heaven and earth unite.

St. Paul, whose conversion from persecuting the first Christians led him to Jesus living and acting in the Eucharist, wrote: "I appeal to you therefore, brethren, by the mercies of God, to present your bodies as a living sacrifice, holy and acceptable to God, which is your spiritual worship. Do not be conformed to this world but be transformed by the renewal of your mind, that you may prove what is the will of God, what is good and acceptable and perfect" (Rom. 12:1–2). The Apostle to the Gentiles thus emphasized the link between the spiritual worship and the need for a new way of understanding and living one's life. It is accomplished in Christ when we worship through the Eucharist and go forth from Holy Mass on a mission to live Christ and take Him into our bodies and minds and to every aspect of life. A new way of thinking and acting for the Christian is an integral part of Christian life. "Have this mind among yourselves, which was in Christ Jesus" (Phil. 2:5).

Jesus has gone to His Father. Now, we can indeed, touch the resurrected and ascended Lord Jesus through the Holy Eucharist. Like the Apostle Thomas, at the time of Consecration, we can behold the Body of the Lord as we see the species of bread in the Host, but know by faith it is really the Lord, we can look up, adore, as the priest elevates the Host, and whisper, "My Lord and My God." Jesus in Heaven at the Father's side has come to earth, to our altar, He is before us. And then again as the priest elevates the chalice with the Precious Blood of Jesus Christ, we can look up again, adore, and whisper, "My Lord and My God." We are present at the Eucharist: Heaven on earth.

This touching, this communion with the Risen Lord Jesus is far superior to what Mary Magdalene sought when she saw the Risen Savior. We do not touch Jesus apart from His Cross, for the celebration of the Eucharist perpetuates the Sacrifice of Calvary. We find Jesus both crucified and risen through the Eucharist.

The crisis today is seen in the secularization of culture. The West has been losing its Christian culture and mentality. This is why there are so many who do not practice any religion. Many have not been

Eucharist

able to survive with the mind of Christ in today's cultural wars. We can see too often within the same family, one practices the Faith with devotion, another is indifferent to its practice; one may even have lost faith in God. Our prayers for the nonpracticing individuals are important; more so, is our example.

The Eucharistic mystery puts us in dialogue with various cultures and in some way challenges them. St. Paul in his First Letter to the Thessalonians wrote: "Test everything; hold fast what is good" (5:21) The gospel can permeate every culture. The presence of Jesus Christ and the outpouring of the Holy Spirit can engage every cultural reality. This is the mission of members of the Church.

The celebration of the Eucharistic Sacrifice and the reception of Jesus in Holy Communion nourishes and increases within us all that we already first received at Baptism when we were then called to holiness. It was an individual call that placed us in the community of Christ's Body. It was individual, for each one is individually baptized. Our individual lives must be deeply affected in the way we live when we worship in faith through the celebration of the Eucharist within the community of the Church and receive in love the Lord Jesus. Our daily lives thus sanctified become a worship pleasing to God, and the living of our daily lives is a vocation from God carried out. We then do everything for the glory of God.

The world is "the field" (Matt. 13:38) in which God has planted each one of us, His children through Baptism, as good seed. The Eucharist strengthens that seed now sprouting into a healthy plant. Each one is called in our various vocations to live out the Christ life in a radical newness. Each one of us thus reflects Jesus Christ in a special way. Each one is promised to be able to draw the needed strength from Jesus in the Eucharist regardless of where they find themselves.

The Eucharist should strengthen the love between man and woman, cause them as parents to be open to life, to the raising of children; these are privileged spheres in which the Eucharist reveals its power to transform life and give it its full meaning. When I was a young priest, I became very conscious of young adults who struggled for purity and then, after marriage instructions, finally entered the state of Holy Matrimony. I then became conscious of the goodness and relationship of Holy Matrimony and Holy Eucharist in their lives.

Married couples should remember that God so loved the world that He gave it His Son made flesh, become man, to die on the Cross, to become its salvation (John 3:16). With God loving us to this extent, surely the believing husband and wife will want to live in grace and stay in grace by frequenting the sacraments.

The life of the ordained priest above all must be a life of Eucharistic spirituality. There can be no authentic priestly spirituality aside from being intrinsically Eucharistic. The bishop expresses this during the liturgy of ordination: "Receive the oblation of the holy people to be offered to God. Understand what you do, imitate what you celebrate, and conform your life to the mystery of the Lord's Cross."

The priest should make his spiritual life his highest priority. I remember well the rector of the seminary I attended saying: "Do you want to know what kind of priest you will be? You will be the same kind of priest that you are a seminarian." The priest must make his Eucharistic spiritual life his highest priority. He must seek God tirelessly. He must do this while serving the concerns of his people and leading them to Our Eucharistic Lord. There are dark and difficult hours in everyone's life, and the priest is no exception, just as there were such hours in the life of Jesus Christ. He must be both priest and victim.

The priest through Eucharistic spirituality will grow into ever closer union with Jesus Christ. Possessed by God's love, bearing witness to God's love at all times and occasions, the dark moments, the festive moments, however difficult in hours when the weight of the cross is especially felt, such is an essential part of a true priestly life.

Eucharist

The Eucharist is the essence of his life. The priest with an authentic Eucharistic spirituality will celebrate the Sacrifice of the Mass daily, even if the faithful cannot be present. It will be a great pain for him should he ever not be able to celebrate Mass.

I remember during the weeks of recuperation in the hospital after a terrible automobile accident when I was seventy-seven years old, wherein my neck was broken among other various complications, how painful it was not to be able to celebrate the Holy Sacrifice of the Mass each day. I was most grateful when a priest came and offered the Holy Mass at the hospital as I participated from a wheelchair. When, finally, I arrived home in a neck brace and foot cast, on entering my home near the Monastery of Our Lady of the Angels and Shrine of the Most Blessed Sacrament (Hanceville, Alabama), as I entered the house with difficulty, I said: "Get my Mass vestments from the closet upstairs. I want to offer Mass now." I was very weak, but that celebration of the Eucharistic Sacrifice was glorious for me and more glorious, I believe, for God. Priesthood lived, I believe, must be Eucharistic and Marian. Mary is Our Lady of the Eucharist. The life of every true Catholic, lay and religious, should be Eucharistic and Marian, but this is true especially for the priest. My first Mass back home was in honor of the Immaculate Conception.

Every celebration of the Eucharist is *objectively of infinite value* in the heart of God the Father as it perpetuates Christ in His redeeming sacrificial death and makes present the Risen Jesus Christ, our Savior. The Mass is thus spiritually most fruitful, and there is no comparison in any other prayer or act of worship. When the Mass is celebrated in a loving, faith-filled, and attentive way, it is formative in the deepest and highest sense of the word. It fosters the priest's configuration to Jesus Christ and transformation into Christ, the Priest. It strengthens his priestly vocation.

There are various approved ecclesial vocations. Each one is noble. To each such vocation in the Church there is seen in a vivid way "the prophetic witness of consecrated men and women, who find in the celebration of the Eucharist and in the Eucharistic Adoration the strength necessary for the radical following of Christ, obedient, poor and chaste" (Synod on the Eucharist, prop. 39). The Church blesses all the many special works in the lives of such consecrated Church members. Still, the principal purpose of their lives is "the contemplation of divine things and assiduous union with God in prayer" (*Code of Canon Law*, can. 663, §1).

St. Mother Teresa of Calcutta noted that besides morning Mass, her nuns must spend a Holy Hour in union with Jesus, in Eucharistic adoration, before beginning their day of service to the poor. It is the only way, the saintly nun felt, that her Missionary Sisters of Charity would receive strength to serve the poor.

The reverent and loving celebration of the Eucharist and its devout reception provides the moral energy to live the authentic freedom of the children of God. In his encyclical letter *Veritatis Splendor* (*The Splendor of Truth*), Pope St. John Paul II stated that the moral life "has the value of a 'spiritual worship' (Rom. 12:1; Phil. 3:3), flowing from and nourished by that inexhaustible source of holiness and glorification of God which is found in the sacraments, especially in the Eucharist; by sharing in the sacrifice of the Cross, the Christian partakes of Christ's self-giving love and is equipped and committed to live this same charity in all his thoughts and deeds" (107). Pope Benedict XVI added: "'Worship' itself, Eucharistic Communion, includes the reality both of being loved and of loving others in turn. A participation in the Eucharist which does not pass over into the concrete practice of love is intrinsically fragmented" (*Deus Caritas Est*, 14).

The Eucharist is most important in giving spiritual help and strength to those who witness the life of virginity. The life of priestly celibacy is associated with the Eucharist. The Eucharistic mystery has an intrinsic relationship to consecrated virginity. The Church accepts Jesus Christ as her Bridegroom. Consecrated life is an objective sign and foreshadowing of the "marriage supper of the Lamb" (Rev. 19:7–9), which is the very goal of all salvation history.

When one lives a Eucharistic spirituality, a moral transformation will take place in his or her life. This is true for every vocation in life: single, married, religious. Jesus Christ intends to nourish every baptized member of the Church with His own Body and Blood, the Eucharist. Our moral life must flow from and be nourished by that inexhaustible source of holiness and glorification of God, which is found in the sacraments, especially the Eucharist. By sharing in the Sacrifice of the Cross, which we do at every Holy Mass, one partakes of Christ's self-giving love and is equipped and committed to live this same charity in every thought and deed.

When we consciously invite Jesus Christ into our lives and know and believe that we are participating in the perpetuation of Christ's own redeeming Sacrifice of the Cross at Mass and receiving the resurrected Jesus Christ in Holy Communion, then we truly find freedom as sons and daughters of God. This fills the heart with joy in the Holy Spirit. It is a joy from God at the discovery of the love of God at work in the hearts and souls of those who are open to the Lord's supreme gift of Himself in sharing His divine life with us. In abandoning ourselves to Him, we thus find true freedom.

There must be a *Eucharistic consistency* between the way we worship and the way we live. We must take Jesus Christ into every walk of life, according to each one's vocation. Worship pleasing to God is never a purely private matter. It is a community matter. We worship as members of the Mystical Body of Jesus Christ. And the worship at its highest point, as ordained by God Himself for His Mystical Body, the Church, is the celebration of the Eucharist. We are called to worship as a community, in union with others, in, with, and through Jesus Christ, our Head.

We must work, as the fruit of our communion with the Lord Jesus in the Eucharist, so as to reflect the life of Jesus Christ in our union with others. This is true whether it be in the life of marriage, in the family, in the workplace, in social endeavors, in the life of religious, or politicians and legislators, whatever, one must be conscious of grave responsibility at all levels. This responsibility before society includes the immediate family, the local community, and the larger communities that together make up a nation.

The love that we celebrate in the Eucharist is not something we can keep to ourselves. The Eucharist is never private by its nature. The very nature of the Eucharist is that Jesus is to be shared with all, and we all share Jesus together. The Eucharist is thus the source and summit of the Church's life. The Eucharist is also the mission of the Church. We are to lead others to Our Eucharistic Lord. "That which we have seen and heard we proclaim also to you, so that you may have fellowship with us" (1 John 1:3).

The most beautiful work in the world is to know Jesus Christ and to make Him known to others. The institution of the Holy Eucharist was at the very heart of Jesus' mission upon earth, which makes possible the perpetuation of the Paschal Mystery until the end of the world. He was sent by the Father for the redemption of the world (John 3:16–17). His entire life led up to the Eucharist. At the Last Supper, Jesus entrusted to His apostles the sacrament that makes present His self-sacrifice for the salvation of us all. He did this in obedience to the Father.

When Jesus said, "It is finished" just before He "bowed his head and gave up his spirit," those words, "knowing that all was now finished" (John 19:28–30), included especially His work of the institution of the Eucharist the evening before. He knew the Eucharist would perpetuate His Sacrifice of the Cross that He was now undergoing to redeem the world. The wounds in His hands, feet, and side once risen from the dead, would remain in His glorified body, always present at the right hand of His Father in Heaven to make intercession for us.

> This makes Jesus the surety of a better covenant. The former priests were many in number, because they were prevented by death from continuing in office; but he holds his priesthood permanently, because he continues for ever. Consequently he is able for all time to save those who draw near to God through him, since he always lives to make intercession for them. (Heb. 7:22–25)

In the heavenly liturgy, the Risen Savior, once crucified, but now risen and glorified, with His wounds and marks of crucifixion still in His body to remain for all eternity, is always forever interceding by presenting to God the Father His sacrifice for His brothers and sisters. His sacrifice is not repeated but perpetuated in the power of the Holy Spirit. The Eucharist does not involve a new or additional sacrifice. The Eucharistic Sacrifice is the same sacrifice as that of the Cross. It is the same sacrifice of the heavenly liturgy. "For we know that Christ being raised from the dead will never die again; death no longer has dominion over him. The death he died he died to sin, once for all, but the life he lives he lives to God" (Rom. 6:9–10). "For Christ also died for sins once for all, the righteous for the unrighteous, that he might bring us to God, being put to death in the flesh but made alive in the spirit" (1 Pet. 3:18).

When in faith and love we celebrate the sacred mysteries, that is, the Eucharist especially, we are given the spiritual strength, vision, wisdom, desire, and ability through grace to bear witness to Christ in our daily lives. While the priest at ordination, as already stated, is told: "Understand what you do, imitate what you celebrate, and conform your life to the mystery of the Lord's Cross," all the faithful should also understand what they do or should do at the Eucharistic celebration in their full and active participation. Then they conform their lives to the mystery of the Lord's Cross. St. Paul spoke of himself as dying daily. As we live the Mass conformed to Christ and the mystery of His Cross, we will be living out a martyr's spirit.

We are to become witnesses of God's love in Jesus Christ. We become witnesses to Christ when Christ Jesus is made present through our actions, words, and way of being. Witness to Christ is "the means by which the truth of God's love comes to men and women in history." This is most true in the case of martyrdom because martyrs, through their suffering and death, reflect the Passion and death of Christ on the Cross, that which is made present at the Mass. In this sense, martyrdom itself is Eucharistic (see SC, 85).

I worked as a pastor and parish priest for forty-eight years and taught children and youth religion classes, grades one through twelve during all those years. I did not hesitate to teach children that their faith in Jesus Christ and the Catholic Church, which Our Lord founded, must be so strong that each one of them must be willing to die a martyr rather than ever deny Jesus and His Church. I think that must be an essential part of the catechesis in which we form children in the fullness of true Catholic Faith.

If anyone of us has not shared the truth of the love of Jesus Christ with his brothers and sisters, he has not yet given what is his mission, the mission of all members of the Church. The Eucharist understood in faith reminds us both of the union we must have with others in Jesus Christ and the salvation that He won for us by His Precious Blood.

As a parish priest, and now as one retired, still offering daily Mass at the Shrine of the Most Blessed Sacrament founded by Mother Angelica near Hanceville, Alabama, it has always been my practice to preach in an ever new way the same dogma of faith as to the reality of the Eucharist. It seems to me at least one-third of my sermons as a pastor, if not more, referred explicitly to the reality of the Eucharist.

Eucharist

I still preach directly on the Eucharist. As members of the Church, although we should be concerned about the physical welfare of others, we were created to know, love, and serve God and to be happy with Him forever in Heaven. The Eucharist, after Baptism, is the principal means to obtain that end in Heaven, for which we were created. While all the sacraments are essential to the total life of the whole Christ, Head and members, it is the Eucharist that makes sacramentally present the gift that the crucified Lord made of His life, for us and for the whole world. With good reason, then, do we call it the *Most* Blessed Sacrament.

The Eucharistic mystery offered in our hearts gives rise to the service of charity toward others. To love everyone, known and unknown, even those toward whom I am not emotionally attracted in my feelings, is the fruit of an intimate encounter with God, an encounter that enables one to conquer even one's feelings. The Eucharist enables one to look at other persons, not only with one's physical eyes and feelings, but from the perspective of Jesus Christ Himself. Then I can see in all others, brothers or sisters in Christ, for whom the Lord Jesus gave His life, loving them "to the end" (John 13:1).

The Christian community must be conscious, ever more so, that when it celebrates the Eucharist, that sacrifice is for all, no one excluded. Each Catholic who participates in the celebration of the Eucharist should subsequently become personally engaged for others, to bring others to Christ. "You give them something to eat" (Matt. 14:16), as Jesus Christ said to His disciples in the multiplication of the loaves and fishes. It is an invitation to us to be instruments in leading others to the Eucharistic Christ.

Sin is social. If one sins, especially serious sin, it is harmful to the entire Mystical Body of Christ, His Church. "If one members suffers, all the members suffer with it; if one member is honored, all rejoice together (1 Cor. 12:26).

The good news is that grace in the Mystical Body of Christ is also social. There are social implications to the Eucharistic mystery. The union with Jesus Christ that is brought about by the Eucharist also brings a newness to our social relations, thus: "This sacramental 'mysticism' is social in character" (*Deus Caritas Est*, 14). When we are united to Jesus Christ, we are at the same time united with all those to whom He gives Himself. While it is true that each one of us should have a personal relationship with Our Lord and Savior, Jesus Christ, yet, I can never possess Jesus Christ just for myself alone. I can belong to Jesus only in union with all those who have become, or will become, His own. Pope Benedict XVI pointed this out in his encyclical letter *Deus Caritas Est*.

The Eucharist is the sacrament of communion between brothers and sisters of all cultures and nationalities who open themselves to be reconciled in Jesus Christ. We read in Ephesians how Jews and pagans became one people:

> Remember that you were at that time separated from Christ, alienated from the commonwealth of Israel, and strangers to the covenants of promise, having no hope and without God in the world. But now in Christ Jesus you who once were far off have been brought near in the blood of Christ. For he is our peace, who has made us both one, and has broken down the dividing wall of hostility, by abolishing in his flesh the law of commandments and ordinances, that he might create in himself one new man in place of the two, so making peace, and might reconcile us both to God in one body through the cross, thereby bringing the hostility to an end. And he came and preached peace to you who were far off and peace to those who were near; for through him we both have access in one Spirit to the Father. (Eph. 2:12–18)

Commenting on Ephesians 2:14, Pope Benedict wrote: "Only this constant impulse towards reconciliation enables us to partake worthily of the Body and Blood of Christ (Mat. 5:23–24)." (*SC*, 89).

Even for those who are living a good Christian Catholic life, avoiding serious sin, the Sacrament of Reconciliation, (Confession) should be frequent, at least once a month.

Because we enter into and partake of the Paschal Mystery, which transforms us, we must denounce the evils so prevalent in our time, such as terrorism, economic corruption, sexual promiscuity and exploitation, disunity of family life, and the like. No superficial solution to such problems is possible. Jesus Christ shed His blood for all; there is an inestimable value to each person of the human race for whom Christ shed His blood. We all have the mission to bring others to understand in greater depth the profundity of the Sacrifice and Sacrament of the Holy Eucharist. The task is gigantic, of course. Jesus started with twelve lowly fishermen.

Millions of human beings, made in the image and likeness of God, and for whom Jesus shed His blood, are displaced, live in poverty, in hunger. Hundreds of thousands even live in huge camps throughout the world in such conditions. The Lord Jesus, who is the Bread of Eternal Life, calls us to concern about the millions in extreme poverty. Less than half of the amount spent each year in the world on armaments would more than suffice to free the great portion of humanity living in such destitution. Peoples in such large numbers living below the poverty line are in such conditions not because there are no means possible to alleviate these conditions, but the cause has to do with international, political, commercial, and cultural relations. The very mystery we celebrate obliges us to concern.

Those who truly live a Eucharistic spirituality are given strength and courage from on high to work for a civilization of love, not only in our community but for the nation and the world. The very first

Christians shared their love and their goods (Acts 4:32) and helped the poor (Rom. 15:26).

The true Eucharistic spirituality and its practice can foster a real change in the way we view and approach history and the entire world. An honest presentation of two thousand years of history reveals how the Catholic Church opened minds to many scientific explorations and discoveries. The true Catholic mind, which is one with the mind of Jesus Christ, aware of the transcendence and awesomeness of God, has through the centuries produced multiple masterpieces of art and magnificent architecture for cathedrals and basilicas. The awareness of the Real Presence of the God-Man in the Eucharist and the Sacrifice of Jesus Christ that redeemed the world perpetuated at Catholic altars, such has challenged the best that man can create in art and architecture to express that faith.

In a profound Eucharistic spirituality, Christian people should be aware that in giving thanks to God through the Eucharist, they do so in the name of all creation, aspiring to the sanctification of the world. Man was the crowning achievement of God's creation as after God had created the universe, He created man in His own image and likeness and then rested. That seventh day of rest is Eucharistic in a special way as each Sunday of the year is a little Easter, celebrating the Resurrection through celebrating the Eucharist that brings the resurrected Christ.

The authentic Christian life, nourished by the Eucharist, gives us a glimpse of the "new creation" inaugurated in the Resurrection of Jesus Christ, whom the Church Fathers considered the New Adam. By virtue of our Baptism, we enter the new creation established by Jesus Christ:

> And you were buried with him in baptism, in which you were also raised with him through faith in the working of God, who

Eucharist

raised him from the dead. And you, who were dead in trespasses and the uncircumcision of your flesh, God made alive together with him, having forgiven us all our trespasses.... If then you have been raised with Christ, seek the things that are above, where Christ is, seated at the right hand of God. Set your minds on things that are above, not on things that are on earth. For you have died [to sin], and your life is hid with Christ in God. When Christ who is our life appears, then you also will appear with him in glory. (Col. 2:12–13; 3:1–4)

The celebration and reception of the Eucharist is an encounter with the Risen Christ now in Heaven. We should desire to live every day in the newness of life that Jesus Christ brought us in the mystery of the Eucharist. The beauty of the heavenly liturgy must be reflected in our Eucharistic assemblies on earth. The liturgy celebrated with faith and reverence is the efficacious sign of the infinite beauty of the holy mystery of God. In the Eucharist, we discover Jesus Christ, risen from the dead, the same who ascended into Heaven, the same who is now seated at the right hand of God the Father.

The book of Revelation, the last book of the Bible, has John relating to us a vision of heavenly worship. It reminds us that we touch Heaven today in celebrating the Eucharistic Sacrifice. At each Sacrifice of the Mass Heaven comes to earth, and we are lifted to Heaven while still on earth. The third chapter of Revelation ends with: "Behold, I stand at the door and knock; if any one hears my voice and opens the door, I will come in to him and eat with him, and he with me. He who conquers, I will grant him to sit with me on my throne, as I myself conquered and sat down with my Father on his throne" (vv. 20–21). Christ Jesus is inviting all men to the messianic banquet in Heaven (Luke 14:12–14; 22:30).

The fourth chapter of Revelation begins: "After this I looked, and lo, in heaven an open door! And the first voice, which I had heard speaking to me like a trumpet, said, 'Come up hither, and I will show you what must take place after this.' At once I was in the Spirit, and lo, a throne stood in heaven, with one seated on the throne!" (vv. 1–2). John then writes of the symbols of the four Evangelists who wrote the Gospels of the New Testament: lion (Mark); ox (Luke); face of a man (Matthew); eagle in flight (John the Apostle, whose height and depth of the good news is singular and profound). "Day and night they never cease to sing, 'Holy, holy, holy, is the Lord God Almighty, who was and is and is to come!'" (v. 8).

Revelation 4 continues:

> And whenever the living creatures give glory and honor and thanks to him who is seated on the throne, who lives for ever and ever, the twenty-four elders fall down before him who is seated on the throne and worship him who lives for ever and ever; they cast their crowns before the throne, singing, "Worthy art thou, our Lord and God, to receive glory and honor and power, for thou didst create all things, and by thy will they existed and were created." [Twenty-four elders here represent the twelve tribes of Israel in the Old Testament or Covenant and the twelve apostles who replaced them in the New Covenant.] (vv. 9–11; see 21:12–14)

In the fifth chapter of Revelation:

> And between the throne and the four living creatures and among the elders, I saw a Lamb standing, as though it had been slain.... The four living creatures and the twenty-four elders fell down before the Lamb, each holding a harp, and with golden bowls full of incense, which are the prayers of the saints; and they sang a new song, saying "… for thou wast slain and by thy blood didst ransom men for God from

every tribe and tongue and people and nation, and hast made them a kingdom and priests to our God, and they shall reign on earth." Then I looked, and I heard around the throne and the living creatures and the elders the voice of many angels, numbering myriads of myriads and thousands of thousands, saying with a loud voice, "Worthy is the Lamb who was slain, to receive power and wealth and wisdom and might and honor and glory and blessing!" And I heard every creature in heaven and on earth and under the earth and in the sea, and all therein, saying, "To him who sits upon the throne and to the Lamb be blessing and honor and glory and might for ever and ever!" And the four living creatures said, "Amen!" and the elders fell down and worshiped. (vv. 6, 8–14)

We do indeed join the angels of Heaven during the *Sanctus* of every Holy Mass. For, "Holy, Holy, Holy" is the prayer of the angels always before the throne of God. We borrow the "Holy, Holy, Holy" from them. It is inserted into the Liturgy of the Mass, where we join Heaven and Heaven joins us. The Book of Revelation describes for us the heavenly liturgy to which we are joined in the Eucharistic liturgy in Christ's Church on earth. When we celebrate the Eucharist, we do indeed act in Jesus Christ on behalf of all creation.

4

Lift Up Your Hearts

The book of Revelation, or the *Apocalypse*, is the very last book of the Bible. It has much symbolic language. The author of the book calls himself John (1:1; 22:8). Many of the early Church Fathers identified the author with the Apostle John. There are definite linguistic and theological affinities to the Gospel of St. John.

This final book of the Bible mentions angels and saints, the woman and the dragon, and especially the sacrificial Lamb. There is the altar, there is sacrifice. There are references to the *Parousia*, the Second Coming of Jesus Christ, as noted also in 1 Corinthians 15:23. It is about end times. But it is also about a presence of Jesus right now. Jesus Christ will not come back at the end of the world with any more glory or presence than He has in the Holy Eucharist now.

The book among other things is a prophetical work, describing in anticipation the many trials of the followers of Jesus Christ. It tells of their eventual triumph over Satan and forces of evil. It is eschatological, describing the glories of the heavenly Jerusalem in the City on High.

The book of Revelation is the most image-laden book of the New Testament. It is rich in allegory and subject to numerous, legitimate interpretations. An interpretation too often overlooked is that this book has to do with the divine Eucharistic liturgical celebrations.

The Book of Revelation is a mystery. But mystery is exactly what the Eucharist is. Many writers have attempted explanations of the last book of the bible that are wrong. The mystical number 666 in

Revelation — the beast, the whore of Babylon, who is it? Prejudiced writers have even attempted to make these represent the Catholic Church. Fact is, we don't know. Some say that the book of Revelation tells all future events, or, just for the first century. Some have interpreted the book to be God's history in code.

In this book there occurs repeatedly the covenant of man with God in Christ, man's fall from the covenant (sin), then repentance, a renewing of man with the covenant in Jesus. It concerns man's struggle to attain salvation.

The book of Revelation made no sense to the first century Christians apart from the Sacrifice of the Mass. When John the Apostle describes his first vision, he writes: "I was in the Spirit on the Lord's day, and I heard behind me a loud voice like a trumpet saying, 'Write what you see in a book and send it to the seven churches'" (Rev. 1:10–11). John is speaking of Sunday, the primary Eucharistic day of worship in the week. When John turned to see, what did he see? He saw the temple, the heavenly Jerusalem, where Jesus Christ is the one essential mediator between Heaven and earth, who is the Eternal One. He sees Jesus Christ, the eternal High Priest, who is immutable, who speaks with divine authority. He sees that "from his mouth issued a sharp two-edged sword, and his face was like the sun shining in full strength" (Rev. 1:16). The Word of God, made flesh, the second Person of the Trinity, who became a man in all things except sin, resides now in Heaven and on earth. Jesus Christ, the Word, lives and acts both in Heaven and on earth in His Church. His Word resides on earth as well, and, as Vatican II taught, when the Word of God, the Scriptures, are read and explained in Church, there is a presence of Jesus Christ. This is because Jesus Christ Himself is the one who speaks during the Liturgy of the Word, for "He Himself ... speaks when the holy scriptures are read in the church" (*Sacrosanctum Concilium*, 7).

In the book *Benedictus: Day by Day with Pope Benedict XVI*, this is how Pope Benedict XVI has explained Christ's Divine Person and Eucharistic Sacrifice and priesthood: "The Eucharistic sacrifice facilitates *communio* with the divinity, and men receive back the divinity's gift in and from the sacrifice.... It is God *who gives himself*, taking man up into his action and enabling him to be both gift and recipient."

John wrote the book of Revelation twenty-five years after the destruction of the Temple of Jerusalem. The Jews were devastated by the destruction of the Temple. It had been considered the most beautiful building in the world even by some non-Jews. It was the center of their worship and the dwelling of God — the focus of Jewish life. Remember how Jesus had told the people not to get carried away in admiring the beauty of the building of the Temple.

John in the book of Revelation is saying that you now have the true Temple, which is Jesus Christ, Himself, the Lamb.

In chapter 4 of Revelation, he describes his vision of heavenly worship:

> After this I looked, and lo, in heaven an open door! And the first voice, which I had heard speaking to me like a trumpet, said, "Come up hither, and I will show you what must take place after this." At once I was in the Spirit, and lo, a throne stood in heaven, with one seated on the throne! And he who sat there appeared like jasper and carnelian, and round the throne was a rainbow that looked like an emerald. Round the throne were twenty-four thrones, and seated on the thrones were twenty-four elders, clad in white garments, with golden crowns upon their heads. From the throne issue flashes of lightning, and voices and peals of thunder, and before the throne burn seven torches of fire, which are the seven spirits of God; and before the throne there is as it were a sea of glass, like crystal.

And round the throne, on each side of the throne, are four living creatures, full of eyes in front and behind: the first living creature like a lion, the second living creature like an ox, the third living creature with the face of a man, and the fourth living creature like a flying eagle [this represents the four evangelists of the four Gospels, Mark, Luke, Matthew and John]. And the four living creatures, each of them with six wings, are full of eyes all round and within, and day and night they never cease to sing, "Holy, holy, holy, is the Lord God Almighty, who was and is and is to come!"

And whenever the living creatures give glory and honor and thanks to him who is seated on the throne, who lives for ever and ever, the twenty-four elders fall down before him who is seated on the throne and worship him who lives for ever and ever; they cast their crowns before the throne, singing, "Worthy art thou, our Lord and God, to receive glory and honor and power, for thou didst create all things, and by thy will they existed and were created." (vv. 1–11)

In the book of Revelation, John describes seven lamps, four living creatures, twenty-four elders (priests). John saw a sea of glass, which some interpret as water. In the center of the heavenly temple was the Ark of the Covenant. John sees men worshipping with the angels. At our Sacrifice of the Mass upon earth, we say or chant the *Sanctus*, or "Holy, holy, holy," which is the song of the angels. We borrow it from them. It is sung in Heaven.

In John's vision, the One worshipped is shared in by men and angels. John turned and saw the new heavenly temple, and the earth lifted up to that temple. The Lamb is the central character. The Lamb is standing as slain. "And between the throne and the four living creatures and among the elders, I saw a Lamb standing, as though it had been slain" (Rev. 5:6). Notice that Jesus Christ is the Lamb who was slain, crucified, yet He is living, standing in the heavenly Jerusalem, or temple. The Ark of the Old Testament was taken and hidden and never found again. But in the heavenly temple there is found the true Ark of the New and Eternal Covenant.

Revelation chapter 12 reveals the woman and the dragon: "And a great portent appeared in heaven, a woman clothed with the sun, with the moon under her feet, and on her head a crown of twelve stars" (v. 1). This is a symbol both of the Church and of Mary, Mother of the Church, the twelve stars represent the twelve tribes of Israel, which under the New Covenant in Jesus Christ become the twelve apostles. Mary herself is the Ark of the New Covenant. She was the first tabernacle of Jesus Christ. She gave us Jesus, who is the New Covenant. The battle that goes on between the children of Mary, the members of the Church, and the dragon, Satan and his agents, is ongoing through the centuries, as Pope St. John Paul II pointed out.

The Church will always be under attack, as Jesus foretold: "Be of good cheer, I have overcome the world" (John 16:33). Where do you go for strength and defense? You go to the Sacrifice of the Mass. You call upon the good holy angels who join you in adoring and fighting the evil spirits. The battle today is not essentially between man and evil spirits but between the good, holy angels and the fallen angels, and it is over us that they do battle. The good angels adore the Lamb, Jesus Christ their King, in Heaven. They are present at every Holy Mass, and we worship together, especially at the *Sanctus* of the Mass.

The first beast (Rev. 13) that arose from the sea, some see as the Gentiles, the pagan Roman Empire. The dragon seeks to destroy and pervert the will of God. In chapter 14, John sees the Lamb standing on Mount Zion, Jerusalem. He sees companions of the Lamb, and he hears the melody of harpists, and the singing of a new hymn before the throne of God. He witnesses angels calling to worship and to give

God honor and glory. "Worship him who made heaven and earth" (v. 7). He witnesses angels and the harvest of the earth. To the Jewish mentality — and the apostles and first Christians were Jewish — lamb meant sacrifice. Unfortunately, Jewish leaders rejected the Lamb and were influenced by the beast.

John sees robed priests in Heaven, worshipping with the angels. Revelation directs God's will to end the corrupt practices of some religious leaders and leaders of governments. The angel in chapter 17 reveals that in the battle with the beast "the Lamb will conquer … for he is Lord of lords and King of kings, and those with him are called and chosen and faithful" (v. 14).

The martyrs under the altar crying out for vengeance (Rev. 9–10) that John saw is symbolic. The blood of sacrifices in the Old Covenant gather under the altar. It has been traditional to offer the Sacrifice of the Mass with relics of martyrs within the altar. Early Christians in the catacombs offered Mass over tombs of martyrs. Having relics in the altar says that Mass is a sacrifice. John saw priests dressed like priests in the Old Testament Temple offering sacrifice. But priests of the New Covenant perpetuate the true sacrifice of the Lamb, Who is Jesus Christ.

What is obvious in the book of Revelation is that the struggle against evil forces goes on through all times. But also, obvious in the presentation of the altar, priests, sacrifice, angels, and Mary, is the reality of what the Mass is. There was no other Christian church when John wrote, for Jesus Christ founded only the Catholic Church. John saw a New Heaven and a New Earth, and the former had passed away. The temple had come down on Mt. Zion — where Jesus instituted the Eucharist and where Pentecost took place.

In the heavenly Church, the new Jerusalem, the spiritual Bride of Christ, the liturgy sees an image of Mary, Mother of the Church, as in Revelation chapters 21 and 22:

Then I saw a new heaven and a new earth; for the first heaven and the first earth had passed away, and the sea was no more. And I saw the holy city, new Jerusalem, coming down out of heaven from God, prepared as a bride adorned for her husband; and I heard a great voice from the throne saying, "Behold, the dwelling of God is with men. He will dwell with them, and they shall be his people, and God himself will be with them; he will wipe away every tear from their eyes, and death shall be no more, neither shall there be mourning nor crying nor pain any more, for the former things have passed away."

And he who sat upon the throne said, "Behold, I make all things new." . . .

Then came one of the seven angels who had the seven bowls full of the seven last plagues, and spoke to me, saying, "Come, I will show you the Bride, the wife of the Lamb." And in the Spirit he carried me away to a great, high mountain, and showed me the holy city Jerusalem coming down out of heaven from God, having the glory of God, its radiance like a most rare jewel, like a jasper, clear as crystal. It had a great, high wall, with twelve gates, and at the gates twelve angels, and on the gates the names of the twelve tribes of the sons of Israel were inscribed; on the east three gates, on the north three gates, on the south three gates, and on the west three gates. And the wall of the city had twelve foundations, and on them the twelve names of the twelve apostles of the Lamb. . . .

And I saw no temple in the city, for its temple is the Lord God the Almighty and the Lamb. And the city has no need of sun or moon to shine upon it, for the glory of God is its light, and its lamp is the Lamb. By its light shall the nations walk; and the kings of the earth shall bring their glory into it, and its gates shall never be shut by day — and there shall be no night there; they shall bring into it the glory and the honor of the nations. But nothing unclean shall enter it, nor any one who practices abomination or falsehood, but only those who are written in the Lamb's book of life....

"Behold, I am coming soon, bringing my recompense, to repay every one for what he has done. I am the Alpha and the Omega, the first and the last, the beginning and the end."

Blessed are those who wash their robes, that they may have the right to the tree of life and that they may enter the city by the gates....

"I Jesus have sent my angel to you with this testimony for the churches. I am the root and the offspring of David, the bright morning star."

The Spirit and the Bride say, "Come." And let him who hears say, "Come." And let him who is thirsty come, let him who desires take the water of life without price. (21:1-5, 9-14, 22-27; 22:12-14, 16-17)

New Heaven and New Earth is a description of God's eternal kingdom in Heaven under the symbols of new heavens and a new earth. (Isa. 65:17-25; 66:22). The new Jerusalem and Bride is a symbol of the Church (Gal. 4:26). The wedding day of the Lamb is a symbol of God's reign about to begin (Rev. 21:1-22). Christ's Bride is the Church (2 Cor. 11:2; Eph. 5:22-27).

When at the Sacrifice of the Mass the priest says, "Lift up your hearts," we should be lifted up like John was. For the Eucharist is Heaven on earth.

I am reminded of my own experience on a jet plane as I was flying over Greenland. Greenland is a vast island of snow, mostly in the Arctic Circle. It's less than 5 percent habitable and has a population of about fifty-six thousand people. Flying across Greenland on a clear day, looking down from my plane window, I was in awe of seeing nothing but whiteness, glistening in the sun, and for endless miles.

During the sixteenth century, there was a religious persecution in Greenland, and all priests were killed or banished. So for fifty years there was no Mass at all in Greenland. After fifty years there were still some scattered Catholics left. They used to meet every year for a Christmas celebration in a lonely house almost covered with snow.

On one such Christmas night, they all gathered together in the house. First they said some prayers. Then an old man arose, went to a bureau, and took from it what used to be a white cloth, like a big, square napkin. Now it was yellowed with age and tattered. It was a corporal, that linen cloth at the center of the altar the priest places there from the burse as he begins the Liturgy of the Eucharist. On it, during Holy Mass, rests the Body and Blood of Jesus Christ, the consecrated Host and chalice with wine consecrated into the Precious Blood of Our Lord.

The old man reverently held the linen cloth for all to see, and said: "Brethren, fifty years ago Mass was last said in this country. I served that last Mass. Let us kneel down and thank God for this precious relic, on which rested the Body and Blood of Jesus Christ. And let us pray that God may send us priests to offer the Holy Sacrifice in our midst again. Tears streamed from all eyes as they knelt to pray, in the presence of the tattered corporal upon which the Body of Christ had lain.

This account, when I first learned of it years ago, of the priestless people of Greenland, who had been deprived of their priests and therefore the Eucharist, touched me deeply and with a certain sense of shame. We stand before the altar of God, ashamed, because we are surrounded by Catholic churches, where Mass is frequently offered, and too often we do not value enough the blessed privileges that are ours.

As a priest, I must never forget, nor let people forget, that under the Eucharistic species of bread and wine is found the very substance of Christ — Body, Blood, Soul, and Divinity — the same Lord who is present in Heaven. He is present in Heaven this moment, reigning at the right hand of God the Father. He reigns upon our altar sacramentally as the gift of his Most Sacred Heart.

The eternal Son of God made man, the second Person of the Most Blessed Trinity, dwelling in the tabernacles of our Catholic churches, is the same Jesus whom we receive in Holy Communion. In the Eucharist, it is the same Jesus who dwelt at Nazareth, who preached to the Jews of Palestine. It is Jesus who told us of the good Samaritan. It is He who healed the sick, delivered Magdalene from the devil, and raised Lazarus from the dead. It is He who, when wearied in the boat, slept as the storm raged. It is He who was crushed by anguish in the Garden of Gethsemane. It is He who was transfigured on Mt. Tabor, where His face did shine as the sun and whose garments became as white as snow glistening under the sun, such as I saw flying over Greenland. It is He who was crucified upon Calvary. It is the mysterious pilgrim joining the two disciples on the way to Emmaus, who made Himself known "in the breaking of bread" (Luke 24:35). It is He who ascended to Heaven to the Father's right hand. He is the eternal High Priest, ever living, who never ceases to make intercession for us, and who is the guest of our souls at the Sacrifice of the Mass through our reception of Holy Communion. It is the Son of God incarnate whom the priest holds in his hands and then elevates on high for all to see and adore. "Things into which angels long to look" (1 Pet. 1:12).

Not least among the sufferings of Jesus during His Passion was the realization, as His mind penetrated the centuries, of the ingratitude of men for the Holy Eucharist, His Body in sacramental form. He had looked forward with a great desire to the night of the Last Supper, when He would institute the Holy Eucharist. Jesus had prepared the minds of the apostles for the great mystery of giving us His Body to eat and His Precious Blood to drink as this Paschal Mystery would be made present during the centuries until time is no more.

Already in the Old Testament there were foreshadowings of the Eucharist: Melchizedek offering bread and wine in sacrifice as well as the manna in the dessert, to name two. In the New Testament, Christ multiplied the loaves of bread. Finally, the night of the first Holy Mass arrived, the Last Supper.

And when the hour came, he sat at table, and the apostles with him. And he said to them, "I have earnestly desired to eat this passover with you before I suffer."... And he took a cup, and when he had given thanks he said, "Take this, and divide it among yourselves."... And he took bread, and when he had given thanks he broke it and gave it to them, saying, "This is my body which is given for you. Do this in remembrance of me." And likewise the cup after supper, saying, "This cup which is poured out for you is the new covenant in my blood. (Luke 22:14–15, 17, 19–20)

It was the mission of Christ to bring all men into union with God, and it was the plan of the Father that men would be brought into union with God by becoming united to the human nature of His Son. It was to be a union with His Son, not based purely on affections or emotions, but a union so intimate that the human mind could not grasp its full significance and the splendor of the mystery. The incarnate Son of God was to come into the souls of men — Body, Blood, Soul, and Divinity — and there pour forth His divine life; a union so close that it would no longer be Christ and us but we would become one in Christ.

The mystery of the Real Presence of Jesus Christ in the Eucharist, which brings us a union so intimate that the human mind cannot grasp its full significance and the splendor of this mystery, nonetheless leaves theologians trying to explain that there is no contradiction.

Our senses behold but bread and wine and see no change after the words of Consecration at the Sacrifice of the Mass.

Yet, the Church teaches that the substance of the bread changes, and that means the deepest reality of the bread, its very *substance* changes and becomes the Body of Christ. The accidents, or appearances, only remain; the same color, texture, taste, etc. are the same. *Substance*, explained philosophically, is *being* in itself, whereas appearances can only be *in* something. In the *substantial* change, the accidents of both bread and wine remain the same. On the deepest level of the *being* of these elements there is a change, so that the *substance* of bread and wine no longer remain, but only Jesus: Body and Blood, Soul and Divinity.

The Second Vatican Council had the wonderful vision of the Divine Liturgy that links earth to Heaven, the worship of the Mystical Body of Christ. The Second Vatican Council gave a universal call to holiness. Such is required to transform our secularized society. A deeper and personal spirituality, a union with the merciful Heart of Our Lord Jesus Christ rooted in the sacred liturgy of the Church, is the essential requirement for holiness. Full participation in the Divine Liturgy of the Eucharist consists in there being interior participation in offering the Sacrifice of the Cross, which the Mass perpetuates, and also in receiving Jesus Christ in Holy Communion. Such participants in the Divine and Eucharistic Liturgy are linked to Heaven even while dwelling upon earth.

In the Lord's Prayer we pray: "Thy Kingdom come, Thy will be done on earth as it is in Heaven." Pope Benedict XVI pointed out that the petition that asks for our daily bread serves as the hinge between the three petitions that pertain to the Kingdom of God and the three last petitions that have to do with our needs. We pray for bread for today. That is for daily physical nourishment and needs but also for heavenly food, which we receive in the Eucharist. We pray that God's kingdom will come and earth will become like Heaven. "With the Eucharist ... Heaven comes down to earth, the future of God enters the present and it is as though time were embraced by divine eternity," said Pope Benedict XVI during a homily on the feast of Corpus Christi, June 11, 2009.

"Do not lay up for yourselves treasures on earth ... but lay up for yourselves treasures in heaven" (Matt. 6:19–20). Earthly treasures do not give true happiness. They can destroy the spirit. They fade away. Heavenly treasures will last forever. They bring true happiness even on this earth as they give us glimpses of Heaven. When we are in earnest to store up treasures in Heaven, we have freedom from despairing guilt. We have power over persistent sin. Already in our earthly life we develop a dynamic, personal relationship with the Creator of the universe and see signs of His beauty everywhere. We have a clarity and purpose in our lives and are able to develop deep friendships with brothers and sisters in Jesus Christ. We are happy in the conviction of knowing the truth and have clarity about what is right and wrong, the ability to forgive, and spiritual strength in our own weakness. We know peace in times of trial, knowing ultimately where we are going as we have joy in the knowledge of salvation, divine wisdom, and hope for our eternal future. Such are glimpses of Heaven.

St. Paul was content with his many trials and persecutions. He wrote, "When I am weak, then I am strong" (2 Cor. 12:10). This brilliant teacher and zealous apostle was lifted up so as to be given a special glimpse of Heaven; he was shown heavenly mysteries he could not describe (2 Cor. 12:4). He wrote beautifully about the reality of the Eucharist.

We come face to face with Jesus when we celebrate the Eucharist and receive Him in Holy Communion. We can be humble at Mass, recognizing that any gifts and talents we have, any goodness in our hearts, are flowing only from Jesus' love and power. All we have was given freely by our merciful Father (1 Cor. 4:7). United to Jesus in the Holy Eucharist, we can say with St. Paul: "It is no longer I who live, but Christ who lives in me" (Gal. 2:20).

The fullness we have of divine revelation in the Church today all started with the nomad, Abram, who had spent his life moving from place to place with his livestock and family. He used to worship the gods of his people. But one day, Yahweh, the true God, intervened and revealed Himself to Abram. He called him to go to the "land that I will show you" (Gen. 12:1). Thus God initiated a plan that continues to unfold yet today, and goes into eternity.

Abram gathered his family, his people, and went where God told him to go. God not only gave him a new land but established a covenant with him. God promised Abram He would bless him, make him a blessing to others, and even bless anyone who honored him in any way. "By you all the families of the earth shall bless themselves" (Gen. 12:3).

Abram would no longer wander aimlessly, he would now know that God had created him, loved him, and desired a personal relationship with him.

God changed Abram's name to Abraham, telling him: "I have made you the father of a multitude of nations. 6 I will make you exceedingly fruitful" (Gen. 17:5–6). We Christians are a part of the story of Abraham. We also have been called by name to follow God and receive His blessings. Our Heavenly Father has promised to lead us, bless us, and share His love with us. He has taken the initiative by loving us and sending us His Son incarnate in Jesus Christ. God has made a covenant with us and sealed it with the Precious Blood of His Son, Jesus Christ. Jesus struck that covenant with His Precious Blood on the Cross. He rose from the dead as a sign that the Father accepted the New Covenant, Jesus Christ.

Before Jesus died on the Cross, "on the first day of Unleavened Bread, when they sacrificed the passover lamb, his disciples said to him, 'Where will you have us go and prepare for you to eat the passover?'"

(Mark 14:12). They would eat the sacrificed Paschal Lamb as in the days of Moses who led the people out of Egypt, let go after the final plague, when the firstborn sons of Egypt died with the passover of the angel of death. The Jewish families were spared as they had placed, as instructed, the blood of the sacrificed lamb on the lintels of their doors that night. Each year on the anniversary of the Passover, the Chosen People would celebrate the Passover in memory. Jesus with His apostles did so as well.

> And when it was evening he came with the twelve. And as they were at table eating, Jesus said, "Truly, I say to you, one of you will betray me, one who is eating with me." They began to be sorrowful, and to say to him one after another, "Is it I?" He said to them, "It is one of the twelve, one who is dipping bread in the same dish with me. For the Son of man goes as it is written of him, but woe to that man by whom the Son of man is betrayed! It would have been better for that man if he had not been born."
>
> And as they were eating, he took bread, and blessed, and broke it, and gave it to them, and said, "Take; this is my body." And he took a cup, and when he had given thanks he gave it to them, and they all drank of it. And he said to them, "This is my blood of the covenant, which is poured out for many. Truly, I say to you, I shall not drink again of the fruit of the vine until that day when I drink it new in the kingdom of God." (Mark 14:17–25)

St. Paul makes it clear that in the Eucharist this Sacrifice of Jesus is perpetuated:

> For I received from the Lord what I also delivered to you, that the Lord Jesus on the night when he was betrayed took bread, and when he had given thanks, he broke it, and said,

> "This is my body which is for you. Do this in remembrance of me." In the same way also the cup, after supper, saying, "This cup is the new covenant in my blood. Do this, as often as you drink it, in remembrance of me." For as often as you eat this bread and drink the cup, you proclaim the Lord's death until he comes. (1 Cor.11:23–26)

Chapter 8 of Hebrews speaks of Jesus Christ in the heavenly sanctuary or the heavenly liturgy which we embrace and come into union with at every Sacrifice of the Mass. "Now the point in what we are saying is this: we have such a high priest, one who is seated at the right hand of the throne of the Majesty in heaven, a minister in the sanctuary and the true tent which is set up not by man but by the Lord. For every high priest is appointed to offer gifts and sacrifices; hence it is necessary for this priest also to have something to offer" (vv. 1–3).

Christ the High Priest in Heaven is constantly, perpetually, offering Himself to the Father in Heaven. As He perpetually does so, He has the wounds of His historical sacrifice of two thousand years ago still on His resurrected and ascended body now in Heaven.

> But as it is, Christ has obtained a ministry which is as much more excellent than the old as the covenant he mediates is better, since it is enacted on better promises. For if that first covenant [of the Old Testament] had been faultless, there would have been no occasion for a second.
>
> For he finds fault with them when he says:
>
> "The days will come, says the Lord, when I will establish a new covenant with the house of Israel and with the house of Judah; not like the covenant that I made with their fathers on the day when I took them by the hand to lead them out of the land of Egypt; for they did not continue in my covenant, and so I paid no heed to them, says the Lord. This is the

covenant that I will make with the house of Israel after those days, says the Lord: I will put my laws into their minds, and write them on their hearts, and I will be their God, and they shall be my people. And they shall not teach every one his fellow or every one his brother, saying, 'Know the Lord,' for all shall know me, from the least of them to the greatest. For I will be merciful toward their iniquities, and I will remember their sins no more."

In speaking of a new covenant he treats the first as obsolete. And what is becoming obsolete and growing old is ready to vanish away." (Heb. 8:6–13)

Chapters 9 and 10 continue with St. Paul reminding us of the inadequacies of sacrifices of the former covenant. But with the Eternal Covenant in the heavenly liturgy, we have the mediator and High Priest and Victim, Jesus Christ. He presents Himself, the New Covenant in the eternal now of Heaven. During the Eucharistic Liturgy, we enter into that eternal presentation to the Father in, with, and through Jesus Christ, who is Himself the New Covenant.

But when Christ appeared as a high priest of the good things that have come, then through the greater and more perfect tent (not made with hands, that is, not of this creation) he entered once for all into the Holy Place, taking not the blood of goats and calves but his own blood, thus securing an eternal redemption. For if the sprinkling of defiled persons with the blood of goats and bulls and with the ashes of a heifer sanctifies for the purification of the flesh, how much more shall the blood of Christ, who through the eternal Spirit offered himself without blemish to God, purify your conscience from dead works to serve the living God.

Therefore he is the mediator of a new covenant, so that those who are called may receive the promised eternal inheritance, since a death has occurred which redeems them from the transgressions under the first covenant....

... For Christ has entered, not into a sanctuary made with hands, a copy of the true one, but into heaven itself, now to appear in the presence of God on our behalf. Nor was it to offer himself repeatedly, as the high priest enters the Holy Place yearly with blood not his own [Old Covenant]; for then he would have had to suffer repeatedly since the foundation of the world. But as it is, he has appeared once for all at the end of the age to put away sin by the sacrifice of himself. And just as it is appointed for men to die once, and after that comes judgment, so Christ, having been offered once to bear the sins of many, will appear a second time, not to deal with sin but to save those who are eagerly waiting for him. (Heb. 9:11–15, 24–28)

When a soul has grasped the greatness of the reality of grace, sharing in the divine life within us, then it aspires to have a perfection of this union. On the road to perfection there is no halting or resting; one either goes ahead or slips back. There is no standing still in the authentic spiritual life. Consider the Apostle St. Paul, who teaches us in Sacred Scripture. St. Paul forgets gladly what he has accomplished. He dispels the memory of it. His only anxiety is to go forward; to constantly get nearer to the goal, which is his sublime Model, Jesus Christ. St. Paul constantly pursued to the ideal of perfection in order to attain it because he saw himself as already seized by Christ.

Not all are prepared or ready for this teaching to pursue perfection. Many will not hear it or will misunderstand it. The celebration and reception of the Eucharist is essential for the maintenance and progress of the life of the soul just as material food is necessary for the life of the body. "Unless you eat the flesh of the Son of man and drink his blood, you have no life in you.... For my flesh is food indeed, and my blood is drink indeed" (John 6:53, 55).

We begin by being born into a life of grace at Baptism without the Eucharist. We cannot remain long in grace as we grow in the natural physical life without the Eucharist. The Eucharist is necessary as an act of obedience to God's commands and as the normal requirement to perfect ourselves in the life of Christ.

Looking at Sacred Scripture we see that St. John considers the part of the Eucharist in the life of an individual soul while St. Paul regards the Eucharist in its relation to the Mystical Body. "The cup of blessing which we bless, is it not a participation in the blood of Christ? The bread which we break, is it not a participation in the body of Christ? Because there is one bread, we who are many are one body, for we all partake of the one bread" (1 Cor. 10:16–17).

St. John Chrysostom commented this way:

> Paul does not say *participation*, but *communion*, because he wishes to express a closer union. For, in receiving Holy Communion, we not only participate in Christ, we unite with him. In fact, as this body is united with Christ, so by this bread we are united with Christ.... But why do I speak of communion? Paul says that we are identically this body. For what is this bread? The body of Christ. And what do we become by receiving this bread? The body of Christ: not many bodies, but one only.

According to St. Augustine, the Eucharist is "the sacrament of piety, the sign of unity and the bond of charity." The union of the Christian with Jesus Christ and with one another is possible because of that ineffable union that Holy Communion effects. It is what the Lord Jesus meant for His Church in instituting the Eucharist. We are incorporated into Christ by Baptism and faith initially, but communion with Christ in the Eucharist is indispensable for the perfection of the Mystical Body, and for the perfection of the individual Christian.

We cannot grow in the slightest in sanctifying grace, or grow in union with Jesus Christ, by our own efforts of human nature. God has willed to make us participators in His Divine Nature and beatitude. After the germ of this divine life is given in Baptism, the growth is to be found principally in prayer and faithful and loving reception of the sacraments, especially the Eucharist.

The Eucharist is principally the sacrament of union with God. It maintains and increases divine life in us. When we receive Jesus Christ in Holy Communion, we are uniting ourselves to Life, who is Jesus who said, "I am ... the life" (John 14:6). "I came that they may have life, and have it abundantly" (John 10:10).

Jesus, Our Lord, God, and Savior gives Himself to us only when He has first been immolated in the Sacrifice of the Mass. This is why most properly Holy Communion is to be received within the context of the Sacrifice of the Mass. The Sacrifice of the Mass contains infinite power for the transformation of our souls into Jesus as it gives infinite glory to God the Father, in, with, and through Jesus Christ.

The Eucharistic Sacrifice is the great *mystery of faith*. As the priest chants after the twofold Consecration: *Mysterium fidei*. This is a mystery which cannot be explained. To understand something of it, we need Jesus Christ and the Holy Spirit. The fuller understanding of it will come only when we participate, not simply on earth in the Eucharistic Liturgy, but in the heavenly liturgy, when we ourselves are in Heaven. Then how fully, or to what intensity, we participate in the heavenly liturgy will depend on our increase and degree of grace, the Divine Nature, while still upon earth. This means the degree of grace at the moment of our death.

When Jesus announced this mystery which He was about to give us, many were scandalized and left Him. Even people among His disciples left. We look to Peter and his response to the Eucharist, as we look to Peter's successor today: "Lord, to whom shall we go? You have the words of eternal life; and we have believed, and have come to know, that you are the Holy One of God" (John 6:68–69).

Jesus' last thoughts were His love for us and of His plan to stay with us always through the Holy Eucharist:

> For I received from the Lord what I also delivered to you, that the Lord Jesus on the night when he was betrayed took bread, and when he had given thanks, he broke it, and said, "This is my body which is for you. Do this in remembrance of me." In the same way also the cup, after supper, saying, "This cup is the new covenant in my blood. Do this, as often as you drink it, in remembrance of me." For as often as you eat this bread and drink the cup, you proclaim the Lord's death until he comes.
>
> Whoever, therefore, eats the bread or drinks the cup of the Lord in an unworthy manner will be guilty of profaning the body and blood of the Lord. Let a man examine himself, and so eat of the bread and drink of the cup. For any one who eats and drinks without discerning the body eats and drinks judgment upon himself. (1 Cor. 11:23–29)

The dignity and value of the Sacrifice of the Cross that is perpetuated at every Holy Sacrifice of the Mass is derived from the dignity of the chief Priest and the Victim of the sacrifice. On Calvary the priest and victim were identical; they were Jesus Christ. They are the same today in celebrating the Eucharist. The priest acts *in persona Christi* in his words and actions at the Mass, and he offers the *immolation* of Jesus, the same He offered on Calvary.

The Council of Trent spelled it out for us in stating that the Mass is "a true and real sacrifice," which perpetuates "Christ's immolation on Calvary. The Mass is offered as a true sacrifice, properly so called"

(Sess. 22, can. 1). In "this divine sacrifice which is celebrated in the mass is contained and immolated in an unbloody manner the same Christ who once offered Himself in a bloody manner on the altar of the cross.... For the victim is one and the same, the same now offering by the ministry of priests who then offered Himself on the cross, the manner alone of offering being different" (Sess. 22, cap. 2).

The Incarnation, God become man, the Word made flesh, took place at the moment the Blessed Virgin Mother Mary replied to the archangel Gabriel: "Be it done to me according to thy word" (Luke 1:38, DRA). Thus, the cooperation of the Mediatrix of all grace, the Blessed Mother Mary, gave us the Author, the Source of all grace and the one essential Mediator.

The body of Jesus is beginning to form. The soul of Jesus Christ with intellect and will has been created. What was the first thought and act of Christ's intellect and will? What passed through the soul of Jesus at the first instance of its existence? St. Paul informs us that Christ, upon His entrance into this world as man, accepted the decree of the will of His Father. At the moment of the Incarnation, Jesus Christ embraced all He was to live and suffer as man, from the crib to the Cross, for the salvation of the world. The offering He made in His human will, united to the adorable will of His Father, will remain within His will for all eternity. St. Paul puts it this way:

> Consequently, when Christ came into the world, he said,
> "Sacrifices and offerings thou hast not desired, but a body hast thou prepared for me; in burnt offerings and sin offerings thou hast taken no pleasure. Then I said, 'Lo, I have come to do thy will, O God,' as it is written of me in the roll of the book."
> When he said above, "Thou hast neither desired nor taken pleasure in sacrifices and offerings and burnt offerings and sin offerings" (these are offered according to the law), then he

added, "Lo, I have come to do thy will." He abolishes the first in order to establish the second. And by that will we have been sanctified through the offering of the body of Jesus Christ once for all. (Heb. 10:5–10)

The first movement in the soul of Jesus Christ then was to accept the sacrifice He must make on the Cross and the entire course of the mysteries of His life leading up to and including Calvary. The least suffering of Jesus Christ, even one drop of His Precious Blood shed as a result of His free will corresponding to the Father's will, would have been sufficient to redeem a million worlds. This is on account of the infinite dignity of His Divine Person. The Eternal Father however wills that Jesus Christ should redeem us by a bloody death, shedding all His Precious Blood, upon the Cross. So much does the Father love us. So much does the Son, the God-Man love us. So much does the Holy Spirit, who is Love, love us. Jesus' last word before dying is that He has fulfilled all that the Father willed for Him to suffer. "He said, 'It is finished'; and he bowed his head and gave up his spirit" (John 19:30).

Yes, at each Sacrifice of the Mass, we are to join our hearts to Jesus, offering all we are and have, lifting up our entire life, to the Father in, with, and through Jesus Christ. "I, when I am lifted up from the earth, will draw all men to myself" (John 12:32). Thus we hear Christ's priest say each time we are at the Sacrifice of the Mass: "Lift up your hearts."

The sacrifices offered in the Old Testament were only a symbol. The reality is the blood immolation of Christ on Calvary. "Therefore be imitators of God, as beloved children. And walk in love, as Christ loved us and gave himself up for us, a fragrant offering and sacrifice to God" (Eph. 5:1–2).

There can no longer be any sacrifice perfectly pleasing to God than that of Calvary, which immolation is re-presented on the Catholic altar. It is worship of infinite value.

On July 7, 2007, the Vatican published Pope Benedict XVI's apostolic letter *Summorum Pontificum* (Of the Supreme Pontiffs) and issued his motu proprio (on the Pope's own initiative) for allowing a wider use of the Roman Missal promulgated by Pope St. John XXIII in 1962. It is sometimes called the Latin Mass, or the Tridentine Mass, after the Council of Trent. That Mass was in common use in the universal Church until the 1970 reform of the Mass for what is known as the *Novus Ordo* of the Divine Liturgy.

Pope Benedict XVI noted that "the two forms of the usage of the Roman rite can be mutually enriching" and expressed hope that the wider use of the old form, which he called the "extraordinary" form of one same Roman Rite, with its careful attention to rubrics, would encourage a more faithful and reverent approach to the ordinary form in the *Novus Ordo* Mass.

Some have interpreted that what Pope Benedict XVI was doing is what he expressed the need for as Cardinal Ratzinger (before he was elected pope and accepted the role), namely, the beginning of a reform of the reform. Some offering the *Novus Ordo* Mass misinterpreted the options as opening the door to creative ideas. Thus there were additions introduced in some places into the ordinary form that were far from what the Fathers of Vatican II intended. Some see Pope Benedict beginning the one necessary step in a long-term reform of the liturgy. He hoped that some elements of the new *Novus Ordo* liturgy would be integrated into the old Mass, while other aspects of the extraordinary form would enrich the ordinary form. It seems as though Pope Benedict envisioned a convergence of the two forms, bringing about the true organic reform of the liturgy that Vatican II envisioned.

Here is an excerpt from *Summorum Pontificum* of Benedict XVI:

The Roman Missal promulgated by Paul VI is the ordinary expression of the *"Lex orandi"* (Law of prayer).... Nonetheless, the Roman Missal promulgated by St. Pius V ... is to be considered as an extraordinary expression of that same "*Lex orandi*."... These two expressions of the Church's *Lex orandi* will in no way lead to a division in the Church's "*Lex credendi*" (Law of belief). They are, in fact two usages of the one Roman rite. (Art. 1)

As Pope Benedict wrote in his letter to the bishops that accompanied the publication of *Summorum Pontificum*: "What earlier generations held as sacred, remains sacred and great for us too, and it cannot be all of a sudden entirely forbidden or even considered harmful."

Whether a priest is offering according to the extraordinary or ordinary form, the immolation of the sacrifice of Christ on Calvary is made present on the altar, that is, the same Sacrifice of the Cross is made present. Jesus Christ, the eternal High Priest, willed that this sacrifice should be continued so long as this world lasts so that infinite worship is given by men in, with, and through Christ, to the end of time. How does Christ accomplish this will of His since He has ascended into Heaven? The answer, of course, is that He chooses certain men to be ordained as partakers of His priesthood.

This is how Bl. Columba Marmion (1858–1923) expressed the ordination of priests, who are empowered to offer the Eucharist:

> When the bishop, on the day of ordination, extends his hands to consecrate the priests, angels' voices repeat over each of them: "Thou art a priest for ever; the priestly character thou bearest shall never be taken away, but it is from the hand of Christ thou receivest it, it is His Spirit that fills thee in order to make thee Christ's minister." Christ is about to renew His sacrifice through the intermediary of men.
>
> Let us see what takes place at the altar? After some preparatory prayers and the reading of the Epistle and the Gospel,

the priests offer the bread and wine; it is the "offering" or the "offertory." These elements will soon be changed into the Body and Blood of Our Lord. The priest next invites the faithful and the heavenly spirits to surround the altar that is about to become a new Calvary, and to accompany the holy action with praise and homage. After this, he enters silently into more intimate communication with God. The moment of the Consecration comes; he extends his hands over the offering as the high priest did of old over the victim to be immolated. He recalls all the gestures and words of Christ at the Last Supper when Our Lord instituted the sacrifice: *Qui pridie quam pateretur*; then identifying himself with Christ, he pronounces the words of the Canon: "This is My Body," "This is My Blood …." By these words, the bread and wine are changed into the Body and Blood of Jesus Christ. By His express will and His formal institution, Christ renders Himself present, really and substantially, with His Divinity and Humanity, under the species which remain and hide Him from our sight….

… Since His resurrection, Christ Jesus can die no more: *Mors illi ulta non dominabitur*; it is a mystical separation of His Body and Blood that is made at the altar. "The same Christ who was immolated upon the Cross is immolated upon the altar, although in a different manner"; and this immolation, accompanied by the offering, constitutes a true sacrifice: *In hoc divino sacrificio quod in missa peragitur, idem ille Christus continetur et immolatur, qui in ara crucis seipsum cruentum obtulit* (Concil. Trid. Sess. xxii, cap. 2).

The communion terminates the sacrifice; it is the last important act of the Mass. The rite of the manducation of the victim completes the expression of the idea of substitution and above all of unity which is found in each sacrifice. In uniting himself so intimately with the victim substituted for him, man, as it were, immolates himself the more; in eating the Host, become a holy and sacred thing, he in some way appropriates to himself the Divine virtue resulting from this consecration.

In the Mass, the victim is Christ Himself, the Man-God: that is why communion is pre-eminently the act of union with the Divinity; it is the best and most intimate partaking of the fruits of alliance and Divine life gained for us by the immolation of Christ.

So, then, the Mass is not only a simple representation of the sacrifice of the cross; it has not only the value of a simple remembrance; but it is a true sacrifice, the very same as that of Calvary which it re-presents and continues and of which it applies the fruits. (*Christ, the Life of the Soul*, chap. 7)

At Vatican II, the Church called for active participation in the Divine Liturgy. What is this participation? Bl. Marmion says this of intimate participation in Christ's sacrifice:

It is the identifying of ourselves, as fully as possible, with Jesus Christ in His double office of Priest and Victim, so that we may be transformed into Him. Is this possible?

As I told you, it was at the moment of the Incarnation that Jesus was anointed Priest, and as Man was able to offer Himself to God as Victim. Now — this is a truth I have shown you at length and want you never to forget — in the Incarnation, the Word associated all humanity to His mysteries and to His Person, by a mystical union. All humanity constitutes a mystical body of which Christ is the Head and we the members. The members cannot, in principle, separate themselves from the head nor remain strangers to its action. The supreme action of Jesus, the one that sums up and crowns His life, is His sacrifice. In the same way that He took upon Himself our human nature, excepting sin, so He wills to make us partakers of the chief mystery of His life. Certainly we were not present in the body on Calvary when He was immolated for us, after having substituted Himself for us; but He has willed, says the Council of Trent, that His sacrifice should be perpetuated, with its inexhaustible virtue, by the Church and her ministers: *Seipsum ab Ecclesia, per sacerdotes, sub signis sensibilibus immolandum* (Sess. xxii, cap. 1). (*Christ, the Life of the Soul*, chap. 7)

The writings of Rev. Dom Columba Marmion, O. S. B., Abbot of Maredsous Abbey, had a most profound effect on me in my major seminary days, especially his books: *Christ, the Life of the Soul* and *Christ in His Mysteries*. My heart was thus elated when His Holiness John Paul II beatified Bl. Columba Marmion on September 3, 2000, saying: "May a widespread rediscovery of the spiritual writings of Bl. Columba Marmion help priests, religious and laity to grow in union with Christ and bear faithful witness to him through ardent love of God and generous service of their brothers and sisters."

5

The Barycenter of Catholic Life

AT EACH HOLY SACRIFICE OF THE MASS, members of Christ's Mystical Body on earth, especially those actively participating and present at Mass, come into real contact with Heaven. Heaven touches them. There is a real communion with the Church on earth and the Church in Heaven, especially activated at the offering of the Holy Sacrifice of the Cross. Jesus Christ's great act of redemption is re-presented, and the resurrected Christ is present, Body, Blood, Soul, and Divinity. The sacrificial Lamb slain but standing and living tells us that (Rev. 5:6).

I've come to appreciate ever more deeply, now that I am into my fifty-fourth year in Christ's holy priesthood, that Heaven does indeed become present each day in the Eucharistic celebration.

My mother lived in my rectory for sixteen years after I was made a pastor. When my mother was dying, she spoke of the sixteen years she had spent with me in my parish: "The years I've spent with you have been like Heaven on earth." She was always present at Mass, participated in the Stations of the Cross daily, and prayed many meditated Rosaries.

The truth is, Heaven did come to my parish each day. Heaven comes when any validly ordained priest offers the Sacrifice of the Mass. We touch Heaven each day in, with, and through Jesus Christ through His Eucharistic Sacrifice. Thus Heaven touches us. Saying this is not simply a pious expression or an exaggeration. It is a reality. Not only Jesus comes, but we come into contact with the

Communion of Saints. Thus, in those first years of grieving after my mother died, I could remember at Mass that she was with the same Jesus in Heaven who became present on the altar where I stood and who became present in my hands at the words of Consecration. As she was dying, I told her I would remember her at the altar of the Lord, and she nodded her head. I experienced my mother's presence especially at Mass.

As I write this volume on the Eucharist, I am in my senior years in Christ's holy priesthood, here at the Shrine of the Most Blessed Sacrament in Hanceville, Alabama, where I offer daily the Holy Sacrifice of the Mass. I thus appreciate ever more the glorious and holy Eucharistic Sacrifice — that we are joined to Heaven and that Heaven is joined to us in this Divine Liturgy. Here at Mother Angelica's Our Lady of the Angels Monastery of the Poor Clare Nuns of Perpetual Adoration, these contemplative nuns not only have celebrated daily the reality of the Eucharist but are in adoration of Our Eucharistic Lord day and night.

Jesus is alive in the Eucharist. We can say "the Eucharist is alive" because the Eucharist is Jesus Christ, the second Person of the Most Holy Trinity, the Eternal Word made flesh. He is present in His Body, Blood, Soul, and Divinity. The Eucharist is not so much a question of what it is but who He is.

Jesus is present and alive in the Eucharist. "I am the living bread which came down from heaven; if any one eats of this bread, he will live for ever; and the bread which I shall give for the life of the world is my flesh" (John 6:51). The Eucharist is the Living Bread, Christ Himself, come down from Heaven. He lives among us. The Eucharist is Heaven come to earth. Through the Eucharist, we touch Heaven. Pope Benedict XVI, while speaking to priests, explained that the Catholic Faith requires having "our feet on the ground and our eyes fixed toward Heaven."

The Barycenter of Catholic Life

Intimate, persevering, sacramental, and living communion with the Body and Blood of Jesus Christ brings about a profound transformation of the human person. The fruit of this involves the whole person as the Apostle Paul wrote: "For to me to live is Christ" (Phil. 1:21).

I see my life as a priest to mean all my work and efforts gravitating totally toward and around the Eucharist. As Pope Benedict XVI says of the Eucharist, it should be the barycenter of a priest's life in particular. The Eucharist should, in fact, be the center of every Catholic's life but above all the life of the priest. Everything in the priest's life should be attracted to this barycenter, for the Eucharist is the high point for which he is ordained.

The Divine Mercy image, with the red and white rays emanating from Christ's Heart, is now recognized by Catholics throughout the world. The image is based on the repeated visions of St. Faustina. The scriptural image of blood and water that flowed forth from the Savior's side when it was pierced on the Cross represents Christ's voluntary offering of His own life by which He became "the expiation for our sins [the sacrifice that atones]" (1 John 2:2).

This living presence and sacrifice of Christ becomes present in our Divine Liturgy at the Catholic altar on earth as it is constantly offered in the heavenly liturgy.

We should not be surprised that through St. Faustina Jesus has brought our attention to His living Blood present in the Holy Eucharist. Blood was essential in the sacrifices of the Old Covenant, as seen in the Letter to the Hebrews and the insistence on blood throughout Scripture. The Bible uses the expression *blood is life.* "For the life of the flesh is in the blood; and I have given it for you upon the altar to make atonement for your souls; for it is the blood that makes atonement, by reason of the life" (Lev. 17:11). The Letter to the Hebrews reminds us: "Without the shedding of blood there is no forgiveness of sins" (9:22).

Eucharist

The sacrifices in the Old Testament did not involve simply a slain animal body, for that was simply a cadaver, but the Old Testament principle was that the "warm blood," or the "live blood," in other words, the victim's life, had to be poured out. If the warm or live blood was not poured out, the sacrifice was null and void; if not the live blood, it had no effect towards reinstating a good relationship with God that had been broken by sin.

We can substitute the term *blood* with *life offered*. The sacrifice of blood embodies the meaning of "offering one's life" in obedient faith to God. At every Holy Sacrifice of the Mass, the live Blood of Jesus is offered to God the Father. In the Eucharist, His Blood is present and offered; the same Blood offered on the Cross; *the same Blood now in the Body of Jesus Christ before His Father in Heaven is offered today on our Catholic altars.*

Is it the faith of the Catholic Church that the living Blood of Jesus Christ, Our Lord, God, and Savior, together with His Sacred Body, becomes present on our Catholic altars as the very same Precious Blood that is now in Heaven? Yes.

> We believe that the Mass, celebrated by the priest representing the person of Christ by virtue of the power received through the Sacrament of Orders, and offered by him in the name of Christ and the members of His Mystical Body, is the sacrifice of Calvary rendered sacramentally present on our altars. We believe that as the bread and wine consecrated by the Lord at the Last Supper were changed into His Body and His Blood, which were to be offered for us on the cross, likewise the bread and wine consecrated by the priest are changed into the Body and Blood of Christ, *enthroned gloriously in heaven* [emphasis added], and we believe that the mysterious presence of the Lord, under what continues to appear to our senses as before,

is a true, real and substantial presence. (*Credo of the People of God*, 24)

The same resurrected Jesus who rose on Easter Sunday and forty days later ascended into Heaven is present in a unique way in the Eucharist. Heaven comes to earth; earth touches Heaven.

When we pray or chant the *Sanctus, Sanctus, Sanctus* (Holy, Holy, Holy) at each Holy Sacrifice of the Mass, countless numbers of angels gather about the altar and join us. Why? Heaven is touching earth and earth is touching Heaven. They are in union. The *Sanctus, Sanctus, Sanctus* is the prayer and song of the angels as recorded in Sacred Scripture. We borrow it from them.

> In the year that King Uzziah died I saw the Lord sitting upon a throne, high and lifted up; and his train filled the temple. Above him stood the seraphim; each had six wings: with two he covered his face, and with two he covered his feet, and with two he flew. And one called to another and said:
>
> "Holy, holy, holy is the Lord of hosts; the whole earth is full of his glory."
>
> And the foundations of the thresholds shook at the voice of him who called, and the house was filled with smoke. And I said: "Woe is me! For I am lost; for I am a man of unclean lips, and I dwell in the midst of a people of unclean lips; for my eyes have seen the King, the Lord of hosts!"
>
> Then flew one of the seraphim to me, having in his hand a burning coal which he had taken with tongs from the altar. And he touched my mouth, and said: "Behold, this has touched your lips; your guilt is taken away, and your sin forgiven." And I heard the voice of the Lord saying, "Whom shall I send, and who will go for us?" Then I said, "Here am I! Send me." (Isa. 6:1–8)

Eucharist

My first pilgrimage to Fatima was in 1974, and, starting in 1976, when I began to conduct youth pilgrimages, which I did for the next twenty years — two youth pilgrimages each summer to Fatima — I would go with the pilgrims to the Loca do Cabeço. There the angel appeared the first, and yet a third time, to the little shepherds of Fatima. The angel appeared a third time in the fall of 1916 with the Holy Eucharist. According to Sr. Lucia, the angel appeared holding a chalice with a Host, from which blood dripped down into the chalice. The angel, leaving the chalice and Host floating in midair, prostrated himself and said this prayer three times:

> Most Holy Trinity, Father, Son and Holy Spirit, I adore You profoundly. I offer You the most precious Body, Blood, Soul and Divinity of Jesus Christ, present in all the tabernacles of the world, in reparation for the outrages, sacrileges and indifference by which He is offended. By the infinite merits of the Sacred Heart, and through the Immaculate Heart of Mary, I beg the conversion of poor sinners.

Sr. Lucia wrote under obedience late in her life with the title: *How I See the Message in the Course of Time and in the Light of Events.* It was published only after her death with the imprimatur of the bishop of Leiria–Fátima, Serafim de Sousa Ferreira e Silva, on February 13, 2006. Of the above adoration and words of the angel, Sr. Lucia wrote: "This prayer was for me a great link in my union with God, a link which grasps me, takes hold of me, indissolubly engraved in my heart: Holy Trinity, one true God, in whom I believe, in Thee I hope; I adore Thee and I love Thee; accept my love and my humble adoration."

The presence of the holy angel imposed a silence on the three little shepherds of Fatima, such that they could not speak about it even to each other for days. Imagine, a holy angel from Heaven, adoring the Most Holy Trinity, prostrates himself with his countenance to the ground before Jesus Christ in the Holy Eucharist. A supernatural compulsion caused the children to do the same.

The reality of the Blessed Trinity and the presence of the Body, Blood, Soul, and Divinity of Our Lord and Savior Jesus Christ imposed its mystery on the children so that they felt a sense of nihilation and profound adoration.

Yet, with what indifference and distraction do some enter the church where the Most Blessed Sacrament is reposed, and even approach the altar and leave it in a somewhat casual manner. Having received Jesus in this August Sacrament, where is the Real Presence of the Most Holy Trinity together with the incarnate Son, some seem lukewarm. Sr. Lucia said the three shepherds witnessed an angel of God who *prostrated* himself before the Eucharist, his countenance to the ground and he adored. The same happens at every Holy Sacrifice of the Mass. Angels of Heaven are present and adore.

When years ago, through her priest nephew, Fr. Jose dos Santos Valinho, I asked Sr. Lucia to tell me the most important part of the Fatima message, Sr. Lucia (who died February 13, 2005) answered that the most important part of the Fatima message was at the beginning, at the Cabeço, where the angel appeared with the Eucharist.

When we approach the altar to receive this "living bread which came down from heaven" (John 6:51) — this Eucharist which is alive — this Christ Jesus the God-Man, Savior of the world, we should give a sign of reverence as adoration before receiving. During my years as pastor, my parishioners would genuflect when the person in front of them was receiving, or they would make a profound bow:

> When the faithful communicate kneeling, no other sign of reverence toward the Blessed Sacrament is required, since kneeling is itself a sign of adoration. When they receive Communion standing, it is strongly recommended that, coming up

in procession, they should make a sign of reverence before receiving the Blessed Sacrament. (*Eucharisticum Mysterium*, 34)

The adoration that we must render the Most Precious Blood of the God-Man will be most beneficial for our salvation, and it will render greater glory to God when we practice this devotion, especially at the time of Holy Communion.

When we receive Holy Communion, we are receiving within ourselves the very life-giving, the very redeeming, Blood of Jesus Christ, which flowed and still flows through the veins of His Sacred Body. We receive the very same Blood that was shed to its very last drop on the Cross. We receive the same Blood that redeemed the entire world — redeemed billions of men through the centuries and until the very end of the world. It is the same Precious Blood in the Sacred Body of Jesus now in Heaven at the right hand of the Father.

Jesus Christ is a member of our human race, like ourselves, but He is also God. This God-Man sends forth from His throne in Heaven, seated next to God the Father, a hymn of infinite praise. He, as man, worships in an infinite degree. Were it not for this God-Man capable of perfectly satisfying for the billions of sins that His brothers and sisters commit upon earth, God the Father would then have to cast us all into eternal fires. But God the Father, when He looks upon the many serious sins being committed upon earth, He sees at the same time His Son seated beside Him. He sees the Person of His Son joined to our own weak humanity, with a human body and soul like ours.

God the Father sees the soul of Jesus with an intellect and will, perfectly conformed with all three Persons of the Most Blessed Trinity. The Father looks at the hands, the feet, the side of Jesus; He sees there the glorified wounds of the nails and the spear, whereby His Most Precious Blood was poured out for the salvation of His brothers and sisters upon the earth. The Heavenly Father says: "At least in You, my

Son, I am well pleased. One drop of Your Precious Blood would be sufficient to have atoned for many worlds. You, my Son, are a Brother to people upon earth and the saints in Heaven. You are God, equal to myself, one in Divine Nature with me and the Holy Spirit, yet Your human nature is hypostatically fused with the Divine Nature. Down upon earth, I see Your Precious Blood offered countless times each day in the chalice of the altar at the Sacrifice of the Mass. Each day more than four hundred thousand Masses are offered throughout the world. The words of Consecration are spoken an average of five times each second, day and night. There is offered to me a perfect oblation."

Surely there is a dialogue, a hymn of praise, between the Father and His beloved Son, Jesus Christ, that goes on in Heaven. Sacred Scripture says of Jesus in Heaven that He "always lives to make intercession for [us]" (Heb. 7:25); that it is His Precious Blood that still saves us from Hell; and that the wounds from the nails are still seen in His Body in Heaven; that He sits at the right hand of the Father; that it is this human nature of the man who is also God offering perpetually His Precious Blood to the Father for us, at every second of the day and night. He is offering in Heaven in the eternal now.

In our morning offering prayer, let us unite ourselves with all the Masses being said throughout the world. Ask our merciful Lord to wash and purify the world in the torrent of His mercy, His Most Precious Blood.

It is the teaching of Sacred Scripture and the Church that the Most Blessed Trinity dwells in the soul that is in grace. By sanctifying grace one participates in the divine nature, shares in the life of God. However, many do not appreciate or realize this great gift.

It is through the priest that the grace of the sacraments is given to souls. Priests especially must strive then to make themselves more worthy receptacles to receive these graces and transmit them, in turn, to the souls under their care.

Priests should teach about the divine indwelling of the Most Blessed Trinity and its relationship to the Holy Eucharist. All Catholics need to realize, by being instructed in the fullness of the true Faith, that they come into a special union with the entire Blessed Trinity each time they receive Holy Communion in the state of grace.

Jesus complained to St. Faustina that many receive Him and treat Him as a dead object: "When I come to a human heart in Holy Communion, my hands are full of all kinds of graces which I want to give to the soul, but souls do not even pay attention to Me. They leave Me to myself and busy themselves with other things.... They treat Me as a dead object" (*Diary of Saint Maria Faustina Kowalska*, 1385).

Priests should teach, and all Catholics should realize, that the Holy Eucharist is *alive*. We receive the same Jesus Christ *alive* who is reigning gloriously alive in Heaven. As the *Catechism* teaches: "Under the consecrated species of bread and wine Christ himself, *living and glorious* [emphasis added], is present in a true, real, and substantial manner" (*CCC*, 1413). And, as Our Lord Himself taught: "I am the *living* bread ... if any one eats of this bread, he will *live* for ever.... As the *living* Father sent me, and I *live* because of the Father, so he who eats me will *live* because of me" (John 6:51, 57, emphases added).

Jesus in the Holy Eucharist does not exist alone but as the Son of God in the eternal unity with His Father and the Holy Spirit. He is present to the same degree as He is present in Heaven, that is, entirely so. The Council of Trent teaches that the Eucharist contains "the body and blood together with the soul and divinity of our Lord Jesus Christ." His Sacred Body is there, His Precious Blood is there, His immortal Soul is there, His Divine Person is there. All are present there in every particle of the consecrated Host. Since the person of God the Son united to His human nature is there, the entire Blessed Trinity is there. Note the deep meaning of the Council of Trent in teaching *"together with the soul and divinity."*

"*The Trinity is One.* We do not confess three Gods, but one God in three persons, the 'consubstantial Trinity.' The divine persons do not share the one divinity among themselves but each of them is God whole and entire" (*CCC*, 253). Where the Father and the Son are present, the Holy Spirit is also there. We receive the same Son incarnate — just as He is now gloriously present in Heaven. Thus, the Blessed Trinity dwells in the heart and soul of each person receiving Holy Communion.

When we receive Jesus Christ sacramentally, whether under the species of bread or wine or both, also God the Father and God the Holy Spirit become present with the Son incarnate. Only God the Son, made man, is received sacramentally, but, still, in a true, complete, and substantial way, the other two Persons of the Most Blessed Trinity come to us. The sacramental presence of the Body, Blood, and Soul of Jesus remain in us as long as the species remain undigested; that can vary from fifteen minutes to half an hour, depending on one's metabolism. The indwelling of the Most Blessed Trinity remains in the soul so long as one is in the state of sanctifying grace.

Catholics must become aware, with love and devotion, of the divine indwelling of the Most Blessed Trinity in the soul that is in grace and the intensity of the divine life in the soul, which increases with each worthy reception of the Eucharist.

Many of the saints experienced this indwelling of the Holy Trinity in a special way. St. Faustina wrote of it this way:

> Once after Holy Communion, I heard these words: "You are our dwelling place." At that moment I felt in my soul the presence of the Holy Trinity: the Father, the Son, and the Holy Spirit. (*Diary*, 451)

And during Eucharistic adoration:

> I knew more distinctly than ever before the Three Divine Persons, the Father, the Son, and the Holy Spirit. My soul is

in communion with these Three.... Whoever is united to One of the Three Persons is thereby united to the whole Blessed Trinity, for this Oneness is indivisible. (*Diary*, 472).

The Eucharistic Miracle of Lanciano

The greatest Eucharistic miracle recorded in Church history took place in the ancient city of Anxanum, the home of the Frentanese, in response to a Basilian monk's doubts concerning the Real Presence of Jesus in the Eucharist.

The Basilian priest was a scientist of his day. One day, after the twofold Consecration at Holy Mass, doubts flashed through his mind: "Is this really the Body and Blood of Jesus Christ?" At that moment, the Host was changed visibly into Flesh and the wine visibly into Blood, which coagulated into five globules, irregular and differing in shape and size.

The Host, as can be very distinctly observed today, has the same dimensions as the large Host commonly used today in the Latin Catholic Church. It is light brown and appears rose colored when lighted from the back. The Blood is coagulated and has an earthy color resembling the yellow of ochre.

Since 1713, the Flesh has been reserved in an artistic silver ostensorium (monstrance), delicately embossed by an artisan of the Neapolitan school. The Blood is enclosed in a rich and very old cup made of rock crystal.

The Minor Conventual Friars have been the custodians of the sanctuary since 1252; their appointment was the wish of Bishop Landulf of Chieti; their appointment was confirmed by a pontifical bull dated April 20, 1252. This church was in charge of the Basilian monks until 1176; from 1176 until 1252 the Benedictines staffed the church. In 1258 the Franciscans built the present church. In 1700 its architectural style was changed from Romanesque-Gothic to baroque.

The Barycenter of Catholic Life

The miracle was first reserved in a chapel situated at the side of the main altar. But then, from 1639 it was reserved at a side altar of the nave, which still contains the old iron chest and the commemorative inscription. In 1902 it was transferred to the present monumental marble altar, which the people of Lanciano had erected and can be seen just over the altar as the priest offers Mass.

Various ecclesiastical investigations ("recognitions") have been conducted since 1574. In 1970–1971, renewed for further study in 1981, there took place a scientific investigation by the most illustrious scientist, Prof. Edoardo Linoli, eminent professor of anatomy and pathological histology, as well as chemistry and clinical microscopy. He was assisted by Prof. Ruggero Bertelli of the University of Siena. The analyses were conducted with absolute and unquestionable scientific precision, and they were documented with a series of microscopic photographs.

These analyses sustained the following conclusions:

- The Flesh is real Flesh. The Blood is real Blood.
- The Flesh and the Blood belong to the human species.
- The Flesh consists of the muscular tissue of the heart.
- In the Flesh we see present in sections: the myocardium, the endocardium, the vagus nerve and also the left ventricle of the heart for the large thickness of the myocardium.
- The Flesh is a "HEART" complete in its essential structure.
- The Flesh and the Blood have the same blood-type: AB.
- In the Blood there were found proteins in the same normal proportions (percentage-wise) as are found in the sero-proteic make-up of the fresh normal blood.
- In the Blood there were also found these minerals: chlorides, phosphorus, magnesium, potassium, sodium and calcium.
- The preservation of the Flesh and of the Blood, which were left in their natural state for twelve centuries and exposed

to the action of atmospheric and biological agents, remains an extraordinary phenomenon.[1]

The above are the exact scientific conclusions the author of this volume obtained from Santuario Del Miracolo Eucaristico (Sanctuary of the Eucharistic Miracle). I was privileged to offer the Holy Sacrifice of the Mass in the presence of this miracle during the Jubilee Year 2000.

It would certainly seem that science, to the degree that it is able, has provided a thorough defense for the authenticity of this miracle. This is to say that the cause of the miracle cannot be naturally explained. When the five globules of blood, irregular and differing in shape and size, were weighed, each part weighed as much as the whole. This is to say whether one, two, three, four, or all five globules were weighed, the weight was always identically the same.

We are thus reminded of the teaching of the Church that Jesus Christ is whole and entire, Body, Blood, Soul, and Divinity in every particle of the consecrated Host. If the priest breaks a Host in two, three, four, five, or more parts, each part contains Our Lord entirely.

Pope Benedict XVI has reminded us that in the language of the ancient Church *Eucharist*, among other things, was called *synaxis*, meaning "meeting together." The Eucharist draws the assembly of men together to unite them and to build up the community in Christ. The assembly of the Faith thus experiences fulfillment in the Eucharist, as the center of its life.

The scope of *synaxis*, Benedict XVI reminds us, is much wider than the individual community. Jesus Christ in the Eucharist is calling us to the assembly of all the children of God. That means, the children of God on earth and also in Heaven. Jesus Christ does not assemble the

---

[1] "Eucharistic Miracle: Lanciano, Italy 8th Century A.D.," Real Presence Eucharistic Education and Adoration Association, http://www.therealpresence.org/eucharst/mir/lanciano.html.

local parish or diocesan community in order to enclose it; rather, the Eucharist calls all to assembly to open it up. We thus express willingness in Jesus Christ in celebrating the Eucharist to seek and be united with all the children of God, Heaven and earth.

Man, as described by St. Gregory of Nyssa, is the creature who wants to break out of the prison of finitude. He wants to break out of the closed confines of his ego and simplify this world. This world is too small for the human spirit of man, who sincerely seeks his potential in recognizing the existence of God, who is Love. Man yearns for that, namely God, who of his own power is beyond his reach. God, as St. Augustine observed, has made us for Himself, and we shall find no rest until we rest in Him. Thus man yearns to conquer death.

Man has long observed celebrations that have had at their heart, even when he did not clearly recognize it, a searching for eternal life that is greater than death. Man yearns to conquer death. The Christian delights joyfully that Jesus Christ has conquered death for all of us. He has destined us all for Heaven, for the resurrection of the body, for salvation, not simply of the soul, but of the whole man, body and soul. The Eucharist is the pledge of future resurrection. Because we eat the Body of the Lord and drink His Precious Blood in a worthy manner, we too shall rise, in body as well as soul, from the grave at the end of time. Jesus said: "I am the resurrection and the life" (John 11:25). We shall obtain eternal life and resurrection by faith in Jesus and walking in His footsteps.

We are able to enjoy the gift of future resurrection only through the sacrificial death of Jesus Christ, which is perpetuated at each Holy Mass. It cost the Lord His life so that we may have eternal life. The Divine Liturgy, which we call the Sacrifice of the Mass, is directed to God the Father, in, with, and through Jesus Christ, in the unity of the Holy Spirit, but it addresses us as human beings in all our depth. This depth goes far beyond the things we understand or can explain clearly with the intellect. The heart can understand when we are open to faith, love, charity, and grace. Then the mind, but gradually, grows in understanding the more our heart is open to illuminate it. Perhaps that is why this poor priest, only in his fifty-fourth year of striving to live the priesthood of Jesus Christ, after writing hundreds of articles through the years, and many books, only now can write, however poorly: *Eucharist: Heaven & Earth Unite.*

We must listen to God with the heart. We must let God in to be a part of our life; nay, the whole of our life. St. Paul said: "For to me to live is Christ, and to die is gain" (Phil. 1:21). Each one of us must become fully human, and to be fully human, each one must be touched by God. The Eucharist is where each one can be touched by God, by Heaven here on earth.

People of faith come together, responding to the Lord's call, and become one. They can be only one as the Body of Jesus Christ is but one. God's people can only be one, and that is why disunity among Christians is unfortunate and contrary to everything Jesus Christ is and why He came. Because the Orthodox have retained their valid bishops in apostolic succession and therefore have a true Eucharist, and authentic worship as instituted by Jesus Christ, we can call them a sister church. This is true, even though they lack the perfection of union with the pope, the successor of St. Peter, appointed as visible head by Jesus Christ Himself.

When the Vatican's Congregation for the Doctrine of the Faith issued, with the approval of Pope Benedict XVI, the document *Responses to Some Questions Regarding Certain Aspects of the Doctrine on the Church*, Protestant groups in various parts of the world were dismayed over the Catholic Church's description of its own identity as "Church." The Catholic Church believes she possesses the fullness of true faith and the powers of Jesus Christ in the seven sacraments. She does not consider the Protestant communities to be churches in its strictly theological sense.

The document indicated that Protestant churches are not churches in the precise sense, not in the way that the Catholic Church understands in faith the term *Church* as coming from Jesus Christ. For the true identity of "Church" there must exist the apostolic succession of bishops who are able, in the direct line of succession from the original apostles ordained by Jesus Christ, to ordain other bishops and priests. This apostolic chain is essential for a valid priesthood and a valid Eucharist and has existed for two thousand years. Protestant denominations broke away from this apostolic chain. For them the chain was broken.

Since the Catholic Church believes apostolic succession and valid sacraments, particularly the Eucharist, are essential requirements for the true Church established by Jesus Christ, it cannot recognize as "Church" those communities that lack them.

The Catholic and Orthodox aspire to full, visible unity. Protestant communities work for mutual recognition of the multiplicity and diversity of churches, even with their contradictions among each other, and especially toward the Catholic and Orthodox.

The Eucharist is for oneness in Christ. Jesus spoke of that Oneness in Him so strongly at the Last Supper when He instituted the Holy Eucharist. The Incarnation is the point in history when God breaks into our time and place and enables us to come into contact with Him in Jesus Christ. The Eucharist brings us to God incarnate and is essential for unity in Jesus Christ:

> Truly, truly, I say to you, unless you eat the flesh of the Son of man and drink his blood, you have no life in you; he who eats my flesh and drinks my blood has eternal life, and I will raise him up at the last day. For my flesh is food indeed, and my blood is drink indeed. He who eats my flesh and drinks my blood abides in me, and I in him. As the living Father sent me, and I live because of the Father, so he who eats me will

live because of me. This is the bread which came down from heaven, not such as the fathers ate and died; he who eats this bread will live for ever. (John 6:53–58)

Jesus desires for us to abide in Him and that He abides in us. The Body and Blood of Jesus Christ together with His Soul and Divinity are given to us so that we can be transformed into Jesus, that we may become one with Jesus. We eat the one Bread from Heaven and thus we ourselves become one in Christ. The dynamic of Jesus Christ enters into us and then strives to spread outwards to others; the goal is to fill the world with this dynamic.

When we adore Jesus Christ in the Eucharist there is the gesture of submission. We thereby intend to follow God; everything we will follow is based on God when we truly adore. We submit to Him who is Love. We are truly made free, liberated from within. We are being built into the holy temple of God's people where the divine presence dwells.

> You were at that time separated from Christ, alienated from the commonwealth of Israel, and strangers to the covenants of promise, having no hope and without God in the world. But now in Christ Jesus you who once were far off have been brought near in the blood of Christ. For he is our peace, who has made us both one, and has broken down the dividing wall of hostility, by abolishing in his flesh the law of commandments and ordinances, that he might create in himself one new man in place of the two, so making peace, and might reconcile us both to God in one body through the cross, thereby bringing the hostility to an end. And he came and preached peace to you who were far off and peace to those who were near; for through him we both have access in one Spirit to the Father. So then you are no longer strangers and sojourners, but you are fellow citizens with the saints and members of the

> household of God, built upon the foundation of the apostles and prophets, Christ Jesus himself being the cornerstone, in whom the whole structure is joined together and grows into a holy temple in the Lord; in whom you also are built into it for a dwelling place of God in the Spirit. (Eph. 2:12–22)

As intended by Jesus Christ, it is primarily through the Eucharist that transformation of the members of the Church takes place; that transformation is of fallen man into the likeness of Jesus Christ, that we become actually His Mystical Body and destined, like Jesus Christ, the New Adam, for future resurrection.

When we celebrate the Eucharist, we enter into the "hour" of Jesus. The presence of Jesus, His hour, comes among us, and by Holy Communion, Christ resurrected comes into us. He abides in us. When Jesus transubstantiated bread and wine into His Body and Blood at the Last Supper, He anticipated His death, He accepted, in submission, the will of the Father in His Sacred Heart, and this action was a transformation of His death into love. Then there was a transformation from His death to His Resurrection and, finally, His Ascension of His glorified body, which now exists in Heaven. That glorified Body of Heaven is in the Eucharist today. Jesus was the first of many brethren to rise from the dead, be glorified, and ascend to the Father in Heaven:

> We know that in everything God works for good with those who love him, who are called according to his purpose. For those whom he foreknew he also predestined to be conformed to the image of his Son, in order that he might be the first-born among many brethren. And those whom he predestined he also called; and those whom he called he also justified; and those whom he justified he also glorified.... Who shall bring any charge against God's elect? It is God who justifies; who is to condemn? Is it Christ Jesus, who died, yes, who was raised

from the dead, who is at the right hand of God, who indeed intercedes for us. (Rom. 8:28–30, 33–34)

Of the Eucharist and transformation Pope Benedict XVI has said: "In their hearts, people always and everywhere have somehow expected a change, a transformation of the world. Here now is the central act of transformation that alone can truly renew the world: violence is transformed into love, and death into life."

The act of faith is the assent of the mind to what God has revealed. An act of supernatural faith in the God-Man in the Holy Eucharist requires divine grace. A wrong understanding of faith can lead to a weak experience of faith. It can thus lead to a weak sense of trust and abandonment to the Lord.

What did the resurrected Jesus Christ say to the doubting Thomas who had not yet witnessed Christ risen? The Apostle Thomas, hearing from the other apostles that Christ had risen, protested that he would not believe until he could put his fingers into the place of the nails and slip his hand into His side. When Jesus later appeared and Thomas was with them, Jesus bid Thomas to come forth and do just that. Thomas did and replied, "My Lord and my God!" Our Lord Jesus Christ in turned replied: "Have you believed because you have seen me? Blessed are those who have not seen and yet have believed" (John 20:28–29).

Faith then is not believing in something we can see, nor is it simply accepting the unknown. We are speaking here of supernatural faith. It is not a mystery that we know nothing about yet accept. There are mysteries of faith that we believe with supernatural faith and about which we know a great deal even though we do not understand them. I believe that Jesus is true God, the infinite God the Son. I believe that the Son of God became true man, took on a human nature, but remained the divine second Person of the Most Blessed Trinity. I believe that the celebration of the Eucharist perpetuates both the Sacrifice of Jesus on the Cross and brings His Real Presence. I know much about what these mysteries of the Eucharist teach. I know much by faith that I do not understand. Jesus came to reveal truth about God the Father, our redemption. He returned to Heaven so He and His Father could send the Holy Spirit to bring all these things to our minds.

Hebrews 11:1 gives us a true definition of faith: "Now faith is the assurance of things hoped for, the conviction of things not seen." It means that God exists: "he rewards those who seek him" (Heb. 11:6). There is a Heaven. There is a Hell.

As Pope Benedict has written, as recorded in *Benedictus*: "'The Benedictus' [blessing] refers to the advent [coming] of the incarnate God into our midst. Christ's eucharistic coming makes a present occurrence of a promise, and brings the future into the here and now." What was promised throughout the Old Testament, what was hoped for, is accomplished and is a present occurrence of a promise each time we celebrate the Eucharist. It brings the past, Jesus' redemptive death on the Cross, and the future life we shall live in Heaven, into the here and now.

Scripture tells us that so long as we live on this earth we live by faith, not by sight. But in Heaven, we will live by sight, not by faith. We shall see God face to face, even as He is; thus, no need of faith.

What was the promise? A Redeemer who would come to save us. The Mass brings that coming to us here and now. Jesus comes to us now in His sacrifice, which He perpetuates in the Mass, and gives us Himself in Holy Communion. What is more, the Eucharist brings the future to us here and now. Heaven comes to earth. Heaven and earth unite. We come into contact with our future life in Heaven whenever we celebrate the Eucharist. That is faith lived.

Our faith does not make God real. God is the ultimate and infinite Reality. Faith is our response to the real, living God, who is present and who has made Himself known to us through His Son. The Church never bids us, "Take a leap of faith into the dark." Rather, the Church, speaking for Jesus Christ bids us to "come into the light." Jesus said, "I am the light of the world" (John 8:12).

The book of Isaiah records God telling us: "I am the Lord and there is no other.... From the rising of the sun and from the west ... there is none besides me" (Isa. 45:5, 6). By faith we are certain that God exists, that He reigns on high. We put our hope in Him, that He will reward us with strength, wisdom, and love.

Faith is the infused theological virtue by which a person is empowered to "believe that what God has revealed is true — not because its intrinsic truth is seen with the rational light of reason, but because of the authority of God who reveals it, of God who can neither deceive nor be deceived" (*Dei Filius*, 3). Faith is an exercise of the supernatural power of the Holy Spirit acting within us. We know it is true without the need to put our fingers into the place of the nails or to slip our hand into the glorified wound in the side of Jesus Christ. We look at the sacred Host elevated at Mass and in faith say: "My Lord and my God."

The Holy Miracle of Santarem

About an hour from Fatima in Portugal is the city of Santarem. In that city is "the Church of the Miracle" as it is called still today. For centuries that parish church has also been known as the Church of Santo Estevão (St. Stephen). Narrators place the date of the Eucharistic miracle some time from 1247 to 1266. I have taken many youth pilgrimage groups there, year after year, to see the miracle of the bleeding Host, which remains to the present day, and have often held its monstrance in my hands.

During these years in the village of Santarem, a poor woman whose life was made miserable by her unfaithful husband became weary of so much unhappiness. She decided to consult a Jewish sorceress for help. The sorceress promised the woman that all her difficulties would disappear if she would bring her an altar bread, that is, a Host that had been consecrated by a Catholic priest. The poor woman hesitated long over that request to commit sacrilege.

After great hesitation, the poor woman decided to commit the sacrilege, thinking then she would get help in her desperate situation. She was either greatly confused, or in great ignorance of what the Catholic Faith teaches regarding the sacraments. Why is that? On the very day that she decided to obtain a consecrated Host while receiving Communion, she first went to Confession while intending to commit sacrilege. Intending to do this while making her Confession would make her Confession sacrilegious as well as the act of desecrating the Eucharist. A mortal sin, in this case a mortal sin of sacrilege, will not be forgiven if one intended deliberately to commit a mortal sin in the future. After being heard in Confession at St. Stephen's Church, she attended Mass and proceeded to the altar at Communion time.

When the priest placed the Most Blessed Sacrament upon her tongue, she quickly disguised what she was doing. She removed it from her mouth and carefully wrapped the sacred Host in her veil. She then proceeded to leave the church. She hurried to the sorceress's cave and along the way failed to notice what was happening. Great drops of blood were saturating her veil and began to fall from it.

Others she met along the way noticed the blood from her veil. Thinking that perhaps she had been injured, they inquired why she was bleeding so profusely. Then, noting the blood, she became greatly confused and perplexed and ran quickly home. Once home, she hid the Holy Sacrament in one of her wooden chests.

Late that day, her husband returned home. She told him nothing about what she had done or what had happened. In the middle of the night, both of them were awakened and saw the house was lit up by mysterious rays of light that were penetrating through the chest. The woman then had no choice but to tell her husband about the terrible thing she had done. She and her husband spent the rest of the night upon their knees in prayer and adoration of the Most Blessed Sacrament within the chest.

At break of day, the parish priest was informed of all this. The word spread to people far and near. Many rushed to the woman's house to contemplate the holy miracle of the Eucharist that bled and had sent forth rays of light through the chest.

When the Catholic priest arrived, he removed the Most Blessed Sacrament from the chest. A procession of people was formed as the priest walked in the procession with the Most Holy Eucharist to the parish church of St. Stephen. There he placed the Host into a small case of wax and then placed it into the tabernacle.

Another Miracle of the Bleeding Host

Some time later when the tabernacle was opened for adoration of the Most Blessed Sacrament, another miracle had taken place. The priest found the wax case broken into pieces. Now the Most Blessed Sacrament he had brought from the chest of the woman's home was encased miraculously in a beautiful crystal pyx. This crystal pyx, which had been miraculously formed about the bleeding Host, was then placed in a gold-plated silver monstrance and can be seen to this very day.

In my earlier years of going to Fatima, it was seldom that pilgrims came to Santarem for few from America and other countries knew yet of this miracle that took place in the 1200s and is still to be seen to this day. Santarem is a easy driving distance from Fatima. For many years I held the monstrance in my hands as pilgrims came up to view and venerate the bleeding Host within close range.

During the first fifteen or more years that I conducted pilgrimages to Fatima for youth, twice each summer, the monstrance with the bleeding Host was in the tabernacle with other ciboria containing the Blessed Sacrament from Masses being said there for Catholic parishioners of the local parish. But then the word of the Eucharistic miracle became known among many pilgrims coming to Fatima.

Since the word spread about the bleeding Host of Santarem, often when pilgrims come to Fatima with a priest in their group, they request that their group have the Holy Sacrifice of the Mass offered at the old church of St. Stephen's. Then they want to view the miracle of the bleeding Host up close. Groups coming for this purpose have become more and more frequent.

I often worried about the safety and respect for this sacred bleeding Host as it seemed so very easy to have access to it. Once I came with a doctor from the United States who was a surgeon. He was permitted to stand immediately beside me before the tabernacle as I took the bleeding Host in the crystal pyx and examined it closely. The doctor acquainted with human blood from frequent surgeries stood there in awe and said: "Father … that is real human blood."

As the number of pilgrimages to the church with the bleeding Host continued to increase, restrictions were placed upon pilgrims. The miracle of the bleeding Host was thus placed in a less accessible place. Now, the bleeding Host is contained in a special tabernacle of its own, high up over the main altar. After Mass the sacristan pushes a button and the monstrance with the bleeding Host becomes visible; a door to a special glass tabernacle for it opens high up above the altar. Pilgrims are still permitted to view it closely at its high location but must approach it by way of stairs and from a raised sacristy room behind the sanctuary. They ascend steps up to the bleeding Host, one at a time, and see it at very close range but within its special glass tabernacle from its back. Proper lighting makes it clearly visible.

Viewing the bleeding Host has a deep effect on many pilgrims to appreciate even more deeply the Real Presence of the Body, Blood, Soul, and Divinity of Our Lord and Savior, Jesus Christ.

Eucharist

Another experience I had with pilgrims was this. One year a young man, about to enter college seminary, had an extraordinary experience associated with the bleeding Host. The rule of my youth pilgrimage groups was that no short pants were to be worn, regardless of the hot days. This young man had come from the heartland of America and flew to New York on a day with the temperatures in the nineties. His intention was to change to regular long trousers in the men's room at the airport before boarding the flight to Lisbon.

Unfortunately, the young man's flight arrived at New York behind schedule. He barely had time to catch the plane taking the many youth pilgrims across the Atlantic Ocean to Lisbon and then onto Fatima by way of Santarem. Arriving at the Lisbon airport, he kept himself always to the back of the group so that I would not spot him in the attire of short pants. It was thus we arrived at the Church of St. Stephen, which is now named the Church of the Holy Miracle.

I encouraged all the young men to fill up the front pews first. They filled the church to the back. The young man without proper attire, by his own design, to avoid my seeing him, sat in the very last pew. He never came up to view the bleeding Host at close range for fear I'd notice his attire.

He waited until we were one week into the pilgrimage before confiding to me what he had done. Here were his words: "Father, I can believe that Our Lord can perform a miracle to make a Sacred Host bleed. But why did those Portuguese turn on a recording of a loud heartbeat that carried throughout the church all the while you were up there with that monstrance with the Host in it as the young men came up one by one to view it?" "There was no recording of a heartbeat," I replied. "Perhaps you heard street noises." He answered, "Father it was a heartbeat, loud and clear. The other guys with whom I've shared this are telling me also that they heard no recording of anything."

Then the young man shared with me that a couple weeks after the pilgrimage he would be entering college seminary to study for the priesthood. I took the opportunity to share with him that what he had experienced was "a grace just for you." I said, "It was to protect your faith in the Real Presence as a future priest."

I alerted this young man that at that particular time in history in some of our seminaries there were liberal professors. "If unfortunately you end up in the seminary with a liberal professor, teaching contrary to the defined Catholic dogma of faith in the Real Presence of Jesus in the Holy Eucharist, and that the Sacrifice of the Cross is perpetuated at each Holy Mass, remember what you experienced at the Church of the Miracle, a Eucharistic miracle that now extends back over seven hundred years. Do not accept any teaching that is contrary to the Church."

The young man was in the seminary about six weeks when he phoned me that he had a professor teaching contrary to the defined dogmas of the Church regarding the Holy Eucharist. He remembered my warning, thus he phoned.

When one learns of this Eucharistic miracle in Santarem, honored by the Church for approximately 750 years, one recalls the angel at the Cabeço with the bleeding Host when He appeared to the three little shepherds at Fatima, as related earlier in this chapter and which deeply affected the future ongoing spirituality of Sr. Lucia, even into her nineties.

I recall years ago having Sr. Lucia's nephew, Fr. Jose dos Santos Valinho, ask Sr. Lucia for me, "What is the most important part of the Fatima message?" Fr. Valinho gave me her answer: "Everything that God does is important." Then Sr. Lucia added: "This is a good question. I never thought of it before. Give me a couple days to think about it." A couple days later, Sr. Lucia said, "The most important part of the Fatima message is at the beginning; at the Cabeço, where the angel appeared to us." It is easy to understand why Sr. Lucia would place the most important part of the message at the beginning. For at the Cabeço, the angel came with the Holy Eucharist for all three to receive and adore. He gave Bl. Jacinta and Bl. Francisco their first Holy Communion. The children had a compulsion of "silence" and a spirit of adoration imposed upon them. Henceforth, Francisco would spend entire days in church, before the Most Blessed Sacrament, even with his elbows on the altar, getting as close to the tabernacle as he could. Since the Blessed Mother said that she would take him and Jacinta to Heaven soon, rather than go to school, he would spend the day before the Blessed Sacrament. Lucia would find him still there when she returned from school later in the afternoon.

At the Cabeço they came to a great sense of the reality of God, three Divine Persons in one Divine Nature. There, their sense of adoration of the Blessed Trinity and the Body, Blood, Soul, and Divinity of Jesus Christ in the Most Blessed Sacrament became intense.

Jacinta, when seriously sick in her last months, would have Lucia, returning from Mass, sit near her on her bed for "she must still have Jesus within her."

There have been many Eucharistic miracles throughout the world during the centuries of Christianity. I have restricted presenting descriptive mention to a few I have personally experienced and before which I offered the Holy Sacrifice of the Mass. I've offered Mass often at Santarem, also at the Cabeço of Fatima. Finally in the Jubilee Year 2000, I examined closely and offered Mass before the Eucharistic miracle of Lanciano, described above. Yet, my faith in the Eucharist as expressed in this book flows from the gospel and the magisterial teachings of Christ's true Church kept in truth through the centuries by the power of the Holy Spirit, the Spirit of truth.

Next, we shall consider the presence of the mysteries of Jesus Christ in the Eucharist.

6

All the Mysteries of Christ Are in the Eucharist for Transformation in Christ

First, we must keep in mind that the Eucharist is a sacrifice; it perpetuates the Sacrifice of Jesus Christ offered on the Cross for the redemption of the world. *But there is more*. Participating in the Sacrifice of the Mass means offering God the Father the selfsame sacrifice of infinite value and adoration offered by Jesus on the Cross. Such is the worship we owe God. It is the only worship we can offer that is infinitely perfect and pleasing because it is offered primarily in, with, and through Jesus Christ, the High Priest. While the Eucharist re-presents, makes present primarily the immolation of Jesus Christ on Calvary, it does not exclude the remembrance of the other mysteries Jesus Christ lived, but contains them all.

To communicate to us so that we understand the mysteries that Jesus Christ once lived, and still makes present, the Church employs words. *Liturgy* is one of those words. Apart from the Church, the word *liturgy* originally meant a "public work," that is, a work done in the name of or on behalf of all the people. The Church, as it were, baptized the word *liturgy*. The Church uses it to explain the work of the Most Blessed Trinity in bringing us today the work of redemption by Jesus Christ our High Priest. *The mysteries of His life accomplished our redemption from sin, thus for our salvation, they are made present today in the Divine Liturgy of the Church.* The Paschal Mystery by which Christ accomplished our salvation is made present in the Divine Liturgy of the Church, that is, the Mass and the sacraments.

> Christian liturgy not only recalls the events that saved us *but actualizes them, makes them present.* The Paschal mystery of Christ is celebrated, not repeated. It is the celebrations that are repeated, and *in each celebration there is an outpouring of the Holy Spirit that makes the unique mystery present* (CCC, 1104, emphases added).

To the offering of Christ are united not only the members still here on earth, but also those already in the glory of Heaven. In communion with and commemorating the Blessed Virgin Mary and all the saints, the Church offers the Eucharistic Sacrifice. The Eucharistic Sacrifice is thus in union with the heavenly liturgy, with Jesus Christ in Heaven, who "always lives to make intercession for [us]" (Heb. 7:25).

The entire Blessed Trinity is involved in the celebration of the Divine Liturgy that makes present the mysteries of Jesus Christ. The priest begs God the Father to send the Holy Spirit, the Sanctifier, so that the offerings of bread and wine may become the Body and Blood of Jesus Christ and that the faithful, by receiving them in Holy Communion, may become a living offering to God.

St. Paul wrote of this as follows: "I appeal to you therefore, brethren, by the mercies of God, to present your bodies as a living sacrifice, holy and acceptable to God, which is your spiritual worship" (Rom. 12:1). While we offer Jesus Christ to God the Father in the power of the Holy Spirit at every Sacrifice of the Mass, we offer in this sacrifice of Christ made present *ourselves as well*, our bodies and minds, as living sacrifices, for we are members of Christ's Mystical Body. As the apostle continues to explain: "We, though many, are one body in Christ, and individually members one of another" (Rom. 12:5).

All the Mysteries of Christ Are in the Eucharist

God the Father is both the source and the goal of the Divine Liturgy. The Father sent Jesus Christ, and Jesus, as Head of His Body, offered Himself for all of us to the Father, and today He offers Himself yet in the Divine Liturgy as our Head, as one with us, and one with the heavenly liturgy that is eternally continuous.

From the beginning of human creation, God blessed man and woman. Man fell, but the blessing was renewed in the covenant with Noah. With Abraham the divine blessing entered into our human history of salvation. According to the *Catechism*:

> The divine blessings were made manifest in astonishing and saving events: the birth of Isaac, the escape from Egypt (Passover and Exodus), the gift of the promised land, the election of David, the presence of God in the Temple, the purifying exile, and return of a "small remnant." The Law, the Prophets, and the Psalms, interwoven in the liturgy of the Chosen People, recall these divine blessings and at the same time respond to them with blessings of praise and thanksgiving. (CCC, 1081)

We see the Eucharist prefigured already in the first book of the Old Testament and throughout the Old Testament in its various offerings of sacrifice. In Genesis 14, Abraham is returning victorious from battle and Melchizedek comes out to meet him to offer sacrifice, offering "bread and wine," as "he was a priest of God Most High" (Gen. 14:18).

St. Paul recalls this offering of bread in wine in Genesis when he writes in Hebrews:

> So also Christ did not exalt himself to be made a high priest, but was appointed by him who said to him, "Thou art my Son, today I have begotten thee"; as he says also in another place, "Thou art a priest for ever, after the order of Melchizedek." ... He became the source of eternal salvation to all who obey

him, being designated by God a high priest after the order of Melchizedek. (Heb. 5:5–6, 9–10)

Catholics who participate conscientiously and intelligently in the sacred liturgy of Holy Week are especially aware how the Paschal Lamb is Jesus' saving death and its memorial, made present, in the Eucharist. What Jesus did that first Holy Week is made present when Jesus associated the Last Supper with the Jewish Feast of Passover, or Pasch, commemorating the deliverance of the Jewish people from death by the blood of the lamb sprinkled on their doorposts in Egypt. They were saved by the blood of the lamb, just as we have been saved by the Precious Blood of the true "Lamb of God, who takes away the sin of the world," namely Jesus Christ on the Cross (John 1:29; 1 Cor. 5:7; 1 Pet. 1:19).

The angel of death saw the blood on their lintels and "passed over," sparing the firstborn son of the Jewish families but taking the others in death. Jesus is the Paschal Lamb, the symbol of Israel's redemption at the first Passover. The Eucharist today makes present the New Passover, the New Covenant, "the Lamb of God who takes away the sins of the world," in which Jesus "passes over" to His Father by His death and Resurrection. Jesus thus anticipates the final Passover of the Church into the glory of the kingdom, Heaven itself. The Jesus we come into contact with at Mass and receive in Holy Communion is the same Jesus who, in the presence of His apostles two thousand years ago on Holy Thursday night, instituted the Eucharist and the Sacrament of Holy Orders, who died on the Cross, who rose on Easter Sunday, who ascended into Heaven, and is now at the right hand of God the Father. *These mysteries become present at the Mass.*

Each one shall be able to render God a greater degree of glory for all eternity in Heaven, and participate in a greater degree of glory, in consequence of every Sacrifice of the Mass conscientiously and prayerfully participated in and every Holy Communion worthily received upon this earth. We grow in grace though each Mass and worthy reception of Holy Communion.

On must have a deep appreciation of sanctifying grace, which increases in the soul especially through the participation in the Mass and the reception of the Eucharist. Grace also increases through the other sacraments. We are speaking here not of *actual* grace by which God gives us the help to conform our lives to His will. Actual grace is fleeting, comes and goes, but sanctifying grace is habitual. We are speaking of the special fruit of the Eucharist known as sanctifying grace whereby God shares His divine life and friendship with us as a habitual gift, always present in the soul so long as we are free of mortal sin.

"Sharing in the life of God" — that is the way Jesus Christ spoke of grace. He used repeatedly the word *life* when speaking of the gift of sanctifying grace. It is the power of God, His very life in us. Jesus Christ is the efficient cause of all grace. We abide in Christ and He abides in us. "He who eats my flesh and drinks my blood abides in me, and I in him. As the living Father sent me, and I live because of the Father, so he who eats me will live because of me. This is the bread which came down from heaven, not such as the fathers ate and died; he who eats this bread will live for ever" (John 6:56–58). "I came that they may have life, and have it abundantly" (John 10:10). "It is no longer I who live, but Christ who lives in me" (Gal. 2:20).

One can get a glimpse of the plan God has for each of us in meditating on a sermon by St. Peter Chrysologus, bishop (406–450):

> A virgin conceived, bore a son, and yet remained a virgin. This is no common occurrence, but a sign; no reason here, but God's power, for he is the cause, and not nature. It is a special event, not shared by others; it is divine, not human. Christ's birth was not necessity, but an expression of omnipotence, a

sacrament of piety for the redemption of men. He who made man without generation from pure clay made man again and was born from a pure body. The hand that assumed clay to make our flesh deigned to assume a body for our salvation. That the Creator is in his creature and God is in the flesh brings dignity to man without dishonor to him who made him.

Why then, man, are you so worthless in your own eyes and yet so precious to God? Why render yourself such dishonor when you are honored by him? Why do you ask how you were created and do not seek to know why you were made? Was not this entire visible universe made for your dwelling? It was for you that the light dispelled the overshadowing gloom; for your sake was the night regulated and the day measured, and for you were the heavens embellished with the varying brilliance of the sun, the moon and the stars. The earth was adorned with flowers, groves and fruit; and the constant marvelous variety of lovely living things was created in the air, the fields, and the seas for you, lest sad solitude destroy the joy of God's new creation. And the Creator still works to devise things that can add to your glory. He has made you in his image that you might in your person make the invisible Creator present on earth; he has made you his legate, so that the vast empire of the world might have the Lord's representative. Then in his mercy God assumed what he made in you; he wanted now to be truly manifest in man, just as he had wished to be revealed in man as in an image. Now he would be in reality what he had submitted to be in symbol.

And so Christ is born that by his birth he might restore our nature. He became a child, was fed, and grew that he might inaugurate the one perfect age to remain for ever as he had created it. He supports man that man might no longer fall. And the creature he had formed of earth he now makes heavenly; and what he had endowed with a human soul he now vivifies to become a heavenly spirit. In this way he fully raised man to God, and left in him neither sin, nor death, nor travail, nor pain, nor anything earthly, with the grace of our Lord Christ Jesus, who lives and reigns with the Father in the unity of the Holy Spirit, now and for ever, for all the ages of eternity. Amen.

Each of the mysteries lived by Jesus Christ has for us a particular grace, the object of which was "to form Jesus within us." The mysteries of Jesus then are ours as much as they are His. When we come in faith and love, trusting in the promises of Jesus Christ, Jesus Himself unites such a soul intimately with each of His mysteries, the one being celebrated or contemplated. This is a divine reality.

Christ's mysteries are our mysteries, because He lived them for us. Love for His Father was the underlying motive of every act and thought in the life of the incarnate Word. "That the world may know that I love the Father" (John 14:31). But, at the Father's will and command, Jesus came forth to live these mysteries and merit for us. Jesus' love for the Father is not isolated from His love for us. Jesus loves us also in an infinite way. He came to redeem us and save us. "I came that they may have life" (John 10:10). Jesus is not speaking of our natural, physical life. Jesus is speaking of sanctifying grace when He speaks of the life for which He came. Jesus said: "I always do what is pleasing to him" (John 8:29).

It was for us that Jesus Christ, God become man, bore everything and lived through all His mysteries. He was born at Bethlehem, lived a hidden life of toil, began His public ministry preaching and working miracles, suffered, died, and rose again. For us, He ascended into Heaven, sent the Holy Spirit, and He "always lives to make intercession for [us]" (Heb. 7:25). Jesus remains in the Eucharist for us, for love of us, because it is the will of the Father.

St. Paul tells us that Jesus loved the Church and delivered Himself up for her: "Christ loved the church and gave himself up for her, that he might sanctify her, having cleansed her by the washing of water with the word, that he might present the church to himself in splendor, without spot or wrinkle or any such thing, that she might be holy and without blemish" (Eph. 5:25–27).

The reason Jesus lived all His mysteries was so that we might attain the glory of His Father where He has lived from all eternity as the second Person of the Most Blessed Trinity and where He lives now as man. Jesus "loved me and gave himself for me" (Gal. 2:20).

The mysteries of Jesus belong to us because He is our Model, our Exemplar, the Ideal of our souls to which we have been called as merited by Him. Jesus is our model of perfection and each mystery He has lived reveals His virtues and what we should strive for by His grace. We see His humility in the manger; His self-effacement in His hidden life; His zeal in His preaching and public life; His immolation in His suffering and death; and, finally, His glory in His Resurrection and Ascension. All is to give glory to the Father and attain glory for us.

"I am the way" (John 14:6), said Jesus as He went before us to give us the example. "Again Jesus spoke to them, saying, 'I am the light of the world; he who follows me will not walk in darkness, but will have the light of life'" (John 8:12).

The Eternal Father accepts each one of us in the measure that He sees His Son Jesus in us. To this resemblance, the Father predestined us from all eternity. "For those whom he foreknew he also predestined to be conformed to the image of his Son, in order that he might be the first-born among many brethren. And those whom he predestined he also called; and those whom he called he also justified; and those whom he justified he also glorified" (Rom. 8:29–30). "Even as he chose us in him before the foundation of the world, that we should be holy and blameless before him. He destined us in love to be his sons through Jesus Christ, according to the purpose of his will, to the praise of his glorious grace which he freely bestowed on us in the Beloved" (Eph. 1:4–6).

St. John the Apostle tells us that it would be a condescension on God's part simply to call us sons, even if it were only a loving expression. But what is amazing is that we are *in fact* sons and daughters of God. If we are God's sons and daughters, we must have His life and Divine Nature in us and have been begotten by God. That life we call sanctifying grace. That nature that we then possess is called divine.

> That which was from the beginning, which we have heard, which we have seen with our eyes, which we have looked upon and touched with our hands, concerning the word of life — the life was made manifest, and we saw it, and testify to it, and proclaim to you the eternal life which was with the Father and was made manifest to us — that which we have seen and heard we proclaim also to you, so that you may have fellowship with us; and our fellowship is with the Father and with his Son Jesus Christ. And we are writing this that our joy may be complete. (1 John 1:1–4)

Our Eternal Father, at this moment, sees us in our place in eternity, in Heaven, reflecting the glory of His Son. The Father predestinated us to this very resemblance of Jesus Christ from all eternity.

By Baptism, we are reborn into Jesus Christ, the character of Jesus Christ is indelibly placed into our souls. By growth in grace, Christ as the life of the soul, we become more and more like unto and one with Jesus Christ, the Son of God.

St. Paul compares our oneness in Jesus Christ to the unity of members of a human body and its head. But there is a reality in the

Church as the Mystical Body of Christ. Repeatedly, St. Paul calls the Church the Body of Christ: "For just as the body is one and has many members, and all the members of the body, though many, are one body, so it is with Christ. For by one Spirit we were all baptized into one body" (1 Cor. 12:12–13). And later, "Now you are the body of Christ and individually members of it" (1 Cor. 12:27).

At the Last Supper when Jesus instituted the Eucharist, He spoke of our union as branches are united to the vine:

> I am the true vine, and my Father is the vinedresser. Every branch of mine that bears no fruit, he takes away, and every branch that does bear fruit he prunes, that it may bear more fruit. You are already made clean by the word which I have spoken to you. Abide in me, and I in you. As the branch cannot bear fruit by itself, unless it abides in the vine, neither can you, unless you abide in me. I am the vine, you are the branches. He who abides in me, and I in him, he it is that bears much fruit, for apart from me you can do nothing. (John 15:1–5)

The Eternal Father saw us in His Son in each of the mysteries that Christ lived. Jesus Christ lived them as Head of the Body, the Church. If we consider the purpose for which the Son of God came as man to earth, the purpose why Jesus Christ came, the mysteries of Jesus Christ are more ours than His. Why? Jesus as Son of God in His very person had no need of redemption, no need of living the suffering of the Passion and so forth. Jesus took upon Himself our miseries, our infirmities:

> Surely he has borne our griefs and carried our sorrows; yet we esteemed him stricken, smitten by God, and afflicted. But he was wounded for our transgressions, he was bruised for our iniquities; upon him was the chastisement that made us whole,

and with his stripes we are healed. All we like sheep have gone astray; we have turned every one to his own way; and the Lord has laid on him the iniquity of us all. (Isa. 53:4–6)

Jesus Christ is one with us in all that He does. So closely are we united with Christ that whatever we do for another we do for or to Him: "Truly, I say to you, as you did it to one of the least of these my brethren, you did it to me" (Matt. 25:40).

Jesus Christ and His mysteries are our own, for we are His Mystical Body. When we celebrate the Eucharist, the Divine Liturgy, in bringing us the reality of Jesus Christ, brings us, thereby, His mysteries. We celebrate the Church year, as we go through the promises of the Messiah-Redeemer in the Old Testament each Advent, and then through His birth, unto Lent and Eastertide. The mysteries of Christ Jesus, which are ours, *are not only remembered, but made present in their supernatural power in the Divine Liturgy.* The Eucharist contains all the mysteries of Jesus Christ. Heaven and earth are united.

In chapter 5 of his book *Jesus of Nazareth*, Pope Benedict reflects on the Lord's Prayer, line by line. In the section, "Give Us This Day Our Daily Bread," the Holy Father commented on the meaning of the Greek word *epiousios*, typically translated as "daily" and is unique to the Gospels, specifically in the Lord's Prayer. The theologian Origen (ca. 185–254) says that it does not occur anywhere else in Greek, but that it was coined by the Gospel writers. After Origen's time, an instance of this word has been found in a papyrus dating from the fifth century after Christ. Today two principal interpretations are given for the word *epiousios*: one is "what is necessary for existence." The other interpretation states that the correct translation is "bread for the future."

In *Jesus of Nazareth*, Pope Benedict XVI tells us that the Fathers of the Church were practically unanimous in understanding the fourth petition of the Our Father, "Give us this day our daily bread," as a

Eucharistic petition. He writes: "Read in the light of Jesus' great discourse on the bread of life, the miracle of the manna naturally points beyond itself to the new world in which the Logos ... will be our bread, the food of the eternal wedding banquet."

In the Mass we participate in the great Sacrifice of Jesus Christ on Calvary. We participate in His yes to the Father that undoes the sin of the disobedience of Adam and Eve. At Mass we can truly say: "Thy Kingdom come, Thy will be done," because we are praying it in union with the re-presentation of the Sacrifice of Calvary at every Mass. We are praying it with a view to the future, our eternal life in Heaven. At Mass the yes of Jesus is sacramentally re-presented by the ordained priest. The priest thus joins his own human yes with that of Jesus on the Cross and also Jesus' yes in time and in eternity. The faithful assembled do the same by interior participation, as well as the saints in Heaven. In his book, *The Spirit of the Liturgy*, Pope Benedict XVI (then Cardinal Ratzinger) wrote:

> As St. Maximus the Confessor showed so splendidly, the obedience of Jesus' human will is inserted into the everlasting Yes of the Son to the Father. This "giving" on the part of the Lord, in the passivity of His being crucified, draws the passion of human existence into the action of love, and so it embraces all the dimensions of reality — Body, Soul, Spirit, Logos. Just as the pain of the body is drawn into the pathos of the mind and becomes the Yes of obedience, so time is drawn into what reaches beyond time. The real interior act, though it does not exist without the exterior, transcends time, but since it comes from time, time can again and again be brought into it. That is how we can become contemporary with the past event of salvation. Bernard of Clairvaux has this in mind when he says that the true *semel* ("once") bears within itself

the *semper* ("always"). What is perpetual takes in what happens only once.

At each Holy Sacrifice of the Mass, we pray the Our Father *after* the Consecration and *before* Holy Communion. This is true in all the ancient Eucharistic liturgies of the Catholic Church. This is by design because of the Eucharistic meaning of daily bread.

> In the *Eucharistic liturgy* the Lord's Prayer appears as the prayer of the whole Church and there reveals its full meaning and efficacy. Placed between the *anaphora* (the Eucharistic prayer) and the communion, the Lord's Prayer sums up on the one hand all the petitions and intercessions expressed in the movement of the *epiclesis* and, on the other, knocks at the door of the Banquet of the kingdom which sacramental communion anticipates. (CCC, 2770)

The Our Father as the perfect prayer is most properly prayed within the offering of the Holy Sacrifice of the Mass. The daily bread that we most need and ask for is the supersubstantial bread of the Holy Eucharist. Pope Benedict XVI notes that in St. Jerome's Vulgate, he translates the mysterious word *epiousios* as *supersubstantialis* (supersubstantial). The daily bread that we most need is the *supersubstantial bread* of the Holy Eucharist.

St. Ambrose also spoke of the Greek, *epiousios* of the Our Father: "He (Jesus) called it bread indeed, but He called it *epiousios*, that is, *supersubstantial*. It is not the bread that passes into the body but that bread of eternal life, which sustains the substance of our souls. Therefore, in Greek it is called *epiousios*."

As Pope Benedict teaches in *Jesus of Nazareth*, when we ask for this supersubstantial bread in the Our Father, we are really asking the Father to give us the bread of "tomorrow" today. This profound meaning of the Our Father as enunciated by Pope Benedict XVI brings us again to the celebration of the Eucharist as Heaven on earth. Bread for tomorrow we can equate with eternity, our eternal life in Heaven which exists in us even now by grace. The sharing in the life of God now is the same divine life we shall have for all eternity in Heaven. The degree of our participation in sanctifying grace is ever increasing, especially through the Mass and sacraments. The Eucharist in order of importance is primary for growth in grace.

The Eucharist is the greatest of the sacraments. That is why we call it the Most Blessed Sacrament. It contains the abiding presence of Jesus Christ, the same Christ of Heaven sitting at the right hand of God the Father.

The Mass as perpetuating the same sacrifice as the Sacrifice of the Cross is a doctrine that can be found not only in the writings of Sts. Cyril of Jerusalem, Ambrose, and Augustine, illustrious fourth-century Doctors of the Church, but the Eucharist as sacrifice is expressed in the *Didache*, an early second-century document.

The Church, in using the term *Real Presence*, safeguards the Eucharist from becoming understood as only a symbol or a sign. From the earliest centuries the Church lists saints whose Eucharistic teachings reflect the constant teaching of the Catholic Church on the Real Presence and Eucharistic Sacrifice. For example, in his letter to the Smyrnaeans, St. Ignatius of Antioch said: "The bread is the flesh of Jesus, the cup his blood."

The matter of all seven sacraments of the New Law is foreshadowed in the Old Law. In the Torah (first five books of the Old Testament), a person who was ritually unclean had to bathe. This was not to wash away dirt, but to become ritually clean. Ritual baths were everyday realities for Israelites in Jesus' day. Jerusalem is dotted with bathing pools meant for ritual bathing. The unclean person had to bathe in running water. Ritual uncleanness was symbolic of sin. The ritual bath was symbolic of cleansing of sin. John's baptism of repentance was the purest form of the ritual bath of the Old Law. Jesus Christ took this over as the matter for His sacrament of initiation into the Church. Jesus' Sacrament of Baptism actually takes away sin from the soul.

The oil used in the Sacrament of Confirmation and in the Anointing of the Sick is also prefigured in the Old Law, where it was used for ordaining priests and cleansing lepers. Our Sacrament of Penance, which requires confession and contrition, was found in the Old Law. A person who sinned had to confess his sin to the priest and bring the appropriate sacrifice. The Sacrament of Holy Orders, which confers the priesthood of Jesus Christ in three orders of deacon, priest, and bishop, requires the laying on of hands by the bishop. This gesture is seen in the Old Law, with an Old Testament priest laying his hands on the sacrificial animal, but it was also used to appoint a successor. Moses laid his hands on Joshua. Marriage today is much like the marriage of the Old Law in terms of its matter: a man and a woman promise covenant fidelity to one another and to accept the children God gives them. Jesus raised marriage to the dignity of a sacrament at the Wedding Feast of Cana.

The sacraments instituted by Jesus Christ were built on the similar sacraments of the Old Law, which then did not have the power to give grace or forgive sin. They were elevated by Jesus Christ into the seven sacraments of the New Covenant so as to extend His acts and the power of His mysteries into time and space. This brings us to the Eucharist. How was it prefigured under the Old Covenant? What rite of the Old Law did Jesus use as the matter for His Eucharist, which contains the Sacrifice of the New Covenant that we can offer to God in every age?

The death of Jesus Christ on the Cross is the sacrifice for the sins of the entire human race, and it gives infinite worship and glory to

God the Father. Scripture is clear that Jesus having died once can die no more. He has no need to die again and again for us so as to offer His Sacrifice for our redemption as the priests of the Old Law offered bulls and goats repeatedly. Since His death cannot be repeated in a physical way, His Sacrifice of the New Covenant will have to be a memorial of His one sacrificial death on the Cross. Memorial in the sense of making present now.

There is only one ritual in the entire Law of Moses that is a memorial. It is the memorial of the Passover, the memorial of the Exodus of God's people from Egypt. Of all the events in the Old Testament, the Exodus is the one that prefigures the Crucifixion of Jesus Christ. In the Exodus God claimed His people for Himself, freed them from slavery, and covenanted them to Himself.

As the Exodus from Egypt dominates the Old Testament and forms its perspective, so the Crucifixion, death, and Resurrection of Jesus dominate the New Testament. His sacrificial death and His resurrected Real Presence will be in the Eucharist, and so the Eucharist contains all the mysteries of Christ and is the source and summit of true Christian life and worship. The Eucharist is a memorial, "Do this in memory of me," but it is more. It also re-presents the Sacrifice of the Cross.

This truth must be kept clearly in mind as we worship at Mass: the Eucharist is a memorial and also a sacrifice. To appreciate its prefigurement in the Old Law, we need to study Leviticus 1–7, which gives the rules for the various types of sacrifice: burnt offering, cereal offering, peace offering, guilt offering, and sin offering. Several of these kinds of sacrifices were combined in any Old Law offering. Each of the different kinds of sacrifices expressed only a part of the total reality of sacrifice in their liturgy. All kinds of sacrifices together form the foreshadowing of Our Lord's one perfect Sacrifice of the Cross, which is of infinite value.

The sacrifices were also thought of as the "food of God." "And the priest shall burn it on the altar as food offered by fire to the Lord" (Lev. 3:11). The priests were allowed to eat from the food of the altar. It was a bond of fellowship or union between God and the priests.

There was only one kind of sacrifice that a layperson could eat: the peace offering. This expressed the layperson's priesthood because Israel was a "kingdom of priests" (Exod. 19:6). This is a prefigurement of the New Covenant in which we live: Christ established the ordained priesthood of Holy Orders and the priesthood of the faithful, that is, the priesthood of the baptized.

In the Old Covenant the layperson was not considered a priest who could enter the Temple and sprinkle the sacrificial blood. One's lay priesthood was at its climax in the peace offering, through which, like the priest, he entered into table fellowship with the Lord. Those who were ritually clean were in fellowship with God and with each other; the unclean were temporarily "excommunicated" from priestly fellowship of the people.

Only once each year did all the people come together and together offer the sacrifice, the peace offering: at Passover when they had the memorial of the Exodus. The Passover sacrifice of the lamb was a species of the peace offering. The Passover meal was the eating of the sacrifice. All the people at Passover came together and entered into table fellowship with God and each other. It was the greatest ritual expression of their communion with God and each other. This Passover sacrificial ritual was a memorial of the day when God chose and covenanted the people of Israel to Himself.

The Last Supper, when Jesus instituted the Eucharist and ordained the apostles to the fullness of the priesthood of the New Covenant, was the occasion of the Passover feast. The Passover ritual and sacrifice are now transformed into the major sacrament of the New Law, the Eucharist of the New Covenant. Participating in faith and love in the Eucharist results in union with God and with one another in the Mystical Body of Jesus Christ.

The celebration of the Eucharist is a communal meal because it is first a sacrifice, the Sacrifice of Christ's death on the Cross. The meal aspect ought not be emphasized over that of sacrifice. The Eucharist is a sacrifice before it is a meal. The Sacrifice of the Mass is not something we go through simply to have Holy Communion. The Sacrifice of the Mass we call Eucharist is first infinite worship of God in, with, and through Jesus Christ, who first offers the same sacrifice to the Father that He offered on Calvary.

Leviticus 1–7 gives all the rules for all kinds of sacrifices. Every kind of animal sacrifice followed the same six steps. The first three steps were carried out by a layperson; only the last three steps were carried out by a priest:

1. The layperson brings the sacrifice to the Temple.
2. The layperson lays his hands on the animal.
3. The layperson slaughters the animal, drains its blood, and cuts it up.
4. The priest takes the blood of the animal and sprinkles it on the altar.
5. The priest takes the flesh of the animal and burns the appropriate parts on the altar.
6. The priest cleans up the remains.

Notice that the priest does not slaughter the animal. But the priest takes the blood and the flesh of the animal into the Holy Place and there offers it. The priest sprinkles the blood on the altar and waves or burns the flesh. Yet he does not kill the animal.

In the Eucharist of the New Covenant, the priest produces the Victim of the Sacrifice of the Mass by the words of Consecration. His priesthood exercised causes the Body, the Flesh, of Jesus Christ to be present under the appearance of bread, and the Precious Blood of Jesus Christ to be present under the appearance of wine. By this He brings them into the sanctuary.

There is only one sacrifice in the New Covenant. Jesus Christ the High Priest died only once in sacrificing Himself as the Victim. This one same sacrifice is perpetuated at each celebration of the Holy Sacrifice of the Mass.

By virtue of *concomitance*, as taught by the Council of Trent, Jesus is present, whole and entire, with His Body, Blood, Soul, and Divinity under both species of the consecrated bread and consecrated wine. The ordained Catholic priest at the Sacrifice of the Mass says: "This is my Body." The power of exercising his priesthood in this manner causes *only* the Body of Jesus to become present. It causes the Body of Jesus as it exists in Heaven to be made present; this means the Body of Jesus — together with His Precious Blood and Soul, united to His Divinity — becomes present, the same as is in Heaven. This is what is meant by *concomitance*.

Again, by *concomitance*, when the priest exercises his priestly powers, *in persona Christi*, in saying over the wine, "This is my Blood," he causes *only* the Precious Blood of Jesus to become present, the Blood of Jesus as it exists in Heaven, joined to and together with His Body, Soul, and Divinity.

The priest must always consecrate both the bread and the wine into the Victim Jesus Christ for the Sacrifice of the Cross to be perpetuated. The Sacrifice and Real Presence in the Eucharist must always go together. The priest may never consecrate one without consecrating both the bread and the wine. By *concomitance* the whole Jesus is present under each species when the twofold Consecration has taken place. We can say that the priest really brings Jesus' Flesh into the sanctuary separately as the priests of the Old Covenant brought the flesh and blood to be sprinkled into the sanctuary. The ordained priest also brings Jesus' Blood into the sanctuary separately since he consecrates the bread into the Body separately and the wine into the Blood separately. These twofold and separate Consecrations make for the true Sacrifice of Jesus perpetuated in a mystical and sacramental manner. There is a real sacramental separation in the action of Consecration.

Jesus truly becomes present in the Eucharist in the manner of a sacrificial victim, His Body and Blood being consecrated separately to produce the Sacrificial Victim. The Sacrifice of the Mass is the same as the Sacrifice of the Cross, *only the manner of offering is different.* The first Sacrifice of Jesus Christ on Calvary was in a real, bloody manner. In the Mass today there is the same sacrifice. There is the same presence of both Body and Blood, but in a sacramental or unbloody, yet very real, manner. It is the great mystery of faith proclaimed after the twofold Consecration when the priest says: *Mysterium fidei.* "Let us proclaim the mystery of faith."

Mysterium fidei. What the priest is asking the people to proclaim is that the Sacrifice of Jesus on the Cross has just been perpetuated at this altar, and Christ's Real Presence, the same presence He has in Heaven, is now with us in our midst.

Bishop Arthur Serratelli, chairman of the U. S. Bishops' Committee on the Liturgy, as of November 2007, wrote a column lamenting the loss of the sense of the sacred in the Church today, and how this had diminished belief and worship among certain Catholics. He wrote:

> Living in our world, we breathe the toxic air that surrounds us. Even within the most sacred precincts of the Church, we witness a loss of the sense of the sacred. With the enthusiasm that followed the Second Vatican Council, there was a well-intentioned effort to make the liturgy modern.... And all the while, the awareness of entering into something sacred that has been given to us from above and draws us out of ourselves and into the mystery of God was gone.

In summarizing what happened, he wrote:

> Teaching about the Mass began to emphasize the community. The Mass was seen as a community meal.... Lost was the notion of sacrifice. Lost, the awesome mystery of the Eucharist as Christ's sacrifice on the Cross. The priest was no longer seen as specially consecrated.... With all of this, a profound loss of the sacred.
>
> Not one factor can account for the decline in Mass attendance, Church marriages, baptisms and funerals.... But most certainly, the loss of the sense of the sacred has had a major impact.
>
> Walk into [many churches] today before Mass and you will notice that the silence that should embrace those who stand in God's House is gone. Even the Church is no longer a sacred place. Gathering for Mass sometimes becomes as noisy as gathering for any other social event.

Acknowledging the importance that the Second Vatican Council ascribed to the liturgy, and that the use of vernacular languages was meant to facilitate the understanding of the people, Bishop Serratelli described the approach of "dynamic equivalency" and its deficiencies: "In the enthusiasm of the aggiornamento [updating], translators set to work to produce translations that expressed the Latin in modes of expression appropriated to the various vernacular languages."

Dynamic equivalency in translating Latin liturgical texts is described as translating the concepts and ideas of a text, but not necessarily the literal words or expressions. As a result, the theological richness of the original texts was too often lost and our liturgical prayer impoverished.

The Church has revisited the question of translation in light of the experience with loose translations. In 2001, the Holy See issued *Liturgiam Authenticam*, a document to guide all new translations, both of the Scriptures and of liturgical texts. This document espouses the theory of formal equivalency. Not just concepts, but words and expression are to be translated faithfully. This approach respects the wealth contained in the original text. In fact, the new instruction has as its stated purpose something wider than translation. It "envisions and seeks to prepare for a new era of liturgical renewal, which is consonant with the qualities and the traditions of the particular Church, but which safeguards also the faith and the unity of the Church of God" (*Liturgiam Authenticam*, 7).

Hopefully the change in method of translation by the official translators will have been implemented within a year after this book appears. It will greatly help to build up the Faith. *Lex orandi, lex credendi*, "The law of prayer is the law of belief," can then be recognized.

The new translation corrects our former translations of texts that did not follow the style and syntax of the Latin original. The order of the *Gloria* at the beginning of Mass is more accurate in word order and style. The beginning of the first Eucharistic Prayer, in the correct translation, begins with a direct address to God, focusing our hearts on Him and not, as before, focusing on ourselves.

The new translation is more faithful to the scriptural allusions found within the Latin. In the third Eucharistic Prayer, the words "so that from east to west a perfect offering may be made to the glory of your name," becomes "so that from the rising of the sun to its setting a pure sacrifice may be offered to your name." The new translation is more faithful to Scripture because it is more literal. The words are taken straight from Malachi 1:11. It is powerful to use God's own words in our prayer to Him! The sacred text itself is more poetic and beautiful. It evokes the beauty of sunrise and sunset that speak of the majesty of God.

Experts in theology, liturgy, and linguistics have collaborated with the bishops in producing the new translation of the Order of the Mass. They spent years to accomplish this work.

Christ's mysteries are ours, and the grace and glory Jesus Christ merited in living them are especially available to us through the Sacrifice of the Mass and the sacraments. Jesus desires to give us a share in the inexhaustible graces of salvation and sanctification that He merited for us by each of His mysteries. He desires to communicate to us the spirit of His states in living the mysteries and thereby to realize in each one of us a likeness to Himself.

There is one essential state which Jesus never leaves. He is always "the only Son, who is in the bosom of the Father" (John 1:18). When Jesus comes to us in the Sacrifice of the Mass, He still exists in Heaven as "the only-begotten Son who is in the bosom of the Father." We do indeed come into contact with Heaven when we participate with faith and love in the Sacrifice of the Mass.

Jesus Christ is the incarnate Son of God. He is the Word made flesh. He was God before He became man. He remains God in becoming man. Whether we contemplate Jesus Christ as the little infant in the manger, as an adolescent or working in the carpenter's shop of Nazareth, preaching in Judea, dying on Calvary's Cross, or manifesting to the apostles His triumphant victory over death in His Resurrection and Ascension into Heaven, Jesus is always "the only-begotten Son who is in the bosom of the Father."

As we celebrate the Church year we enter into the mysteries of Christ. This brings the graces of the mysteries of Christ to us in the Divine Liturgy. The effects will be the transformation of our souls in Christ as we give glory to God. We thus anticipate our future lives in Heaven.

The Catechism of the Catholic Church teaches us that the Eucharist unites Heaven and earth:

> To the offering of Christ are united not only the members still here on earth, but also those already *in the glory of heaven*. In

communion with and commemorating the Blessed Virgin Mary and all the saints, the Church offers the Eucharistic sacrifice. In the Eucharist the Church is as it were at the foot of the cross with Mary, united with the offering and intercession of Christ. (*CCC*, 1370)

"Christ Jesus, who died, yes, who was raised from the dead, who is at the right hand of God, who indeed intercedes for us," is present in many ways to his Church: in his word, in his Church's prayer, "where two or three are gathered in my name," in the poor, the sick, and the imprisoned, in the sacraments of which he is the author, in the sacrifice of the Mass, and in the person of the minister. But "he is present ... *most especially in the Eucharistic species.*" (*CCC*, 1373)

The mode of Christ's presence under the Eucharistic species is unique. It raises the Eucharist above all the sacraments as "the perfection of the spiritual life and the end to which all the sacraments tend." (*CCC*, 1374)

Eternity crosses all limitations of time and space, as do the sacraments. Thus the reality of the Sacrifice of the Cross, Jesus' Passion, death, and Resurrection are present to us when we participate in the Eucharist, joining us to the heavenly liturgy. The Church's *Catechism* teaches: The sacrifice of Christ and the sacrifice of the Eucharist are *one single sacrifice.... The Eucharist is also the sacrifice of the Church*" (1367–1368).

One can well appreciate why Sr. Lucia placed such great importance to the beginning of the Fatima apparitions; to the appearance and message of the angel. For it was the angel who overwhelmed the children with the presence of God, so much so that it imposed a great silence on them so that they could not speak of it even to each other.

All the Mysteries of Christ Are in the Eucharist

One sees, in what happened that spring day in 1916, why Sr. Lucia saw the Fatima message as a call to live the theological virtues of faith, hope, and love. The children fell prostrate, bowing their countenances to the ground, the same as the angel, and repeated three times with the angel: "My God, I believe, I adore, I hope, and I love You. I ask pardon for those who do not believe, do not adore, do not hope, and do not love You." That was the first vision of the angel.

The second apparition in midsummer was when they were at the well behind Lucia's house. Suddenly, the angel appeared:

"What are you doing?" He comes for a reality check. The first time, the angel had told them to pray, exercise the theological virtues, and adore God. Now he asks, "Are you doing it?" and he adds "Pray! Pray a great deal! The Hearts of Jesus and Mary have designs of mercy for you." They are to make everything they do a sacrifice in reparation for sins by which God is offended and for the conversion of sinners.

The angel appeared a third time in October, or the end of September. This apparition is so thoroughly Eucharistic that more than ever one can see why Sr. Lucia attributed what took place at the Cabeço as the most important part of the message. For here the Holy Eucharist is revealed to children, now only six, eight, and nine years of age: they see the Eucharist as both *sacrifice* and *sacrament*.

Sacrifice. That's a dogma of faith. We've heard much in recent years about many Catholics being poorly instructed, not even realizing or believing in the *Real Presence* of the Body, Blood, Soul, and Divinity of Jesus Christ in the tabernacle of our Catholic churches and which we receive in Holy Communion. Surveys have been taken on the question, "Do you believe in the Real Presence?" I had an article in the *Homiletic & Pastoral Review*, early in 2007, titled: "Do Catholics Believe in the Real Sacrifice?" We are truly Catholic only if we believe both. That is: We must believe that Jesus' Sacrifice of the Cross is perpetuated at each Sacrifice of the Mass. Secondly, we must believe that Jesus is living and substantially present with His Body, Blood, Soul, and Divinity in the Eucharist.

Explosion of the Supernatural

These fundamental Catholic truths and realities exploded in the spiritual lives of the three little shepherds with the coming of the angel at Fatima.

I am going to tell you of a true conversion account of a famous Jewish man who was very anti-Christian and anti-Catholic. Faith, hope, love, the need for adoration, overwhelmed him when something happened to him like happened to the Fatima children when the angel appeared.

First, let us see the angel appearing the third time, "holding in his hands a chalice surmounted by a Host, from which some drops of blood were falling into the chalice." We see the Body of Jesus in the Host, shedding Blood as Jesus did on the Cross in sacrifice. "Leaving the chalice and Host suspended in the air, he prostrated himself on the ground and repeated this prayer three times:

> Most Holy Trinity, Father, Son and Holy Spirit, I adore You profoundly. I offer You the most precious Body, Blood, Soul and Divinity of Jesus Christ, present in all the tabernacles of the world, in reparation for the outrages, sacrileges, and indifference by which He is offended. By the infinite merits of the Sacred Heart, and through the Immaculate Heart of Mary, I beg the conversion of poor sinners.

The children were given a Holy Communion of reparation. "Take and drink the Body and Blood of Jesus Christ, horribly outraged by ungrateful men. Repair their crimes and console your God." The children were filled with knowledge of the Eucharist as sacrifice and sacrament.

Converted in a Moment

The above experience is also what happened to the famous Jewish man who was anti-Christian and anti-Catholic, Alphonse Ratisbonne. His Jewish brother had converted to the Catholic Church and had been ordained a priest. Still Alphonse Ratisbonne remained very prejudiced against the Church and faith in Jesus Christ as Lord, God, and Savior.

The place was France — the time after the French Revolution. In 1830 the gift of the Miraculous Medal by our Blessed Mother was made to St. Catherine Labouré. Friends begged Alphonse Ratisbonne to wear the Miraculous Medal. He agreed because thus he could show his friends that he had no faith in Jesus Christ or confidence in the intercession of his Blessed Mother. Why fear what is not real? He wore the medal to show others that Jesus and Mary and the prayers of his friends would have absolutely no effect upon him.

One day, in 1841, while wearing Mary's medal, walking with a friend, Alphonse Ratisbonne entered the Church of Sant'Andrea delle Fratte in Rome. Inside is still an altar marking the very spot where the miracle took place. Alphonse's friend had walked a short distance away from where Alphonse stood, not far from the entrance door. The friend returned to Alphonse a short time later to find Alphonse a totally changed man, overwhelmed, something like the Fatima children, transformed by the angelic apparition.

Our Lady of the Miraculous Medal had appeared to Alphonse. She said nothing. But in an instant, this unbelieving intellectual Jew, without hearing so much as a word from the Holy Virgin, understood the entire Catholic Faith, including the truth about the Holy Eucharist as sacrifice and sacrament.

Mr. de Bussieres, his friend who witnessed the conversion, said: "The Catholic faith welled-up from his heart, as a rare perfume from its container, unable to be kept sealed within. *Ratisbonne now spoke of the Real Presence of Jesus in the Most Blessed Sacrament.* He spoke as a man who believed in it with all the strength of his soul, and as a man who had experienced it."

Shortly thereafter, between the Basilicas of St. Mary Major and St. Peter's, Ratisbonne was filled by an indescribable, ecstatic rapture. His friend describes it this way:

> Grasping my hands he said to me: "Oh! Now I understand the love of Catholics for their churches and the devotion which impels them to decorate and embellish them! This is no longer earth, but almost paradise."
>
> Before the altar of the Most Blessed Sacrament the Real Presence of the Divinity overwhelmed him to such a point that he visited less often, and would often leave at once, so awesome it seemed to him to remain in the presence of the Living God with the stain of Original Sin! Alphonse was not yet baptized. And he would flee to a chapel of the All-Holy Virgin.

Alphonse later became a priest himself. Together, with his priest brother, both converted Jews did remarkable evangelizing work for the Church thereafter.

Faith is a supernatural gift from God. It is infused into the soul by God. For many the realization of it comes slowly. But God can infuse faith and even the gift of the knowledge of the Faith into our souls in a moment, as He did with Ratisbonne. Think of the remarkable gift he was given. Before he was baptized and still with sin on his soul, even Original Sin, to be present before Jesus in the Most Blessed Sacrament of the altar, was too awesome and fearful for him to endure. He knew his great unworthiness before he could be baptized and have his sins forgiven.

Before Baptism, rather than remain long before the Blessed Sacrament of the tabernacle, Ratisbonne would flee to a chapel of the Mother of God for protection and help. He would fly to her who

All the Mysteries of Christ Are in the Eucharist

appeared to him and interceded as the Mediatrix of grace, to infuse in an instant both the supernatural gift of faith and knowledge of the Holy Eucharist into his heart. Immediately by faith he knew the Real Presence of the infinite God incarnate in the consecrated Host, which we receive in Holy Communion. With faith came hope and love and a deep sense of adoration of the Divinity.

The message of Fatima begins and ends with the Holy Eucharist, as sacrifice and sacrament. We who have the grace to love Our Lady of Fatima — who is also Our Lady of the Holy Eucharist — must be evangelists. We must spread knowledge, even to our fellow Catholics, that in the Holy Eucharist there is not only the Real Presence of Jesus Christ. When it is affected at Mass, there is the *Real Sacrifice*. Ask others, "Do you believe in the Real Presence?" Then ask, "Do you believe in the Real Sacrifice?" Be apostles for Jesus and Mary who have designs of mercy for you. Share your knowledge of the Eucharist as sacrament and sacrifice.

Be as guardian angels to others who may not practice their faith well through regular participation in the Sacrifice of the Mass and the reception of the sacraments, which apply to our souls the Precious Blood of Jesus Christ. Be their angels and tell them of your deep faith in the Real Presence and the Real Sacrifice of Jesus Christ perpetuated and offered at each Sacrifice of the Mass.

The Eucharist and the Church, which flows from the Eucharist, is essential in the Catholic Faith. In the Eucharist are contained all the mysteries of Jesus Christ.

7

Faith in the Eucharist as Sacrifice and Sacrament for Worship and Growth in Sanctifying Grace

The sincere practicing Catholic, whether he be a hard-laboring layman with limited education; a simple religious lay brother; or a great philosopher, theologian, and well-known, loyal churchman — in each case — each one is part of a mystery that has been accomplished: the infusion of the light of faith that is "the gift of God." Each such person has an inarticulate certitude that Jesus Christ, true God and true man is really, substantially, in the Eucharist. This knowledge does not come from reasoning nor from history or literature or science. The certitude that a poor laborer or a child may possess, more and better than a scholar, is an infused light of faith given by God. I confess to You, O Father, Lord of Heaven and earth, because You have revealed these things to little ones (see Matt. 11:25).

The late and great theologian, Fr. Reginald Garrigou-Lagrange, O. P., in his volume *Grace*, quotes the famous Fr. Lacordaire, who was speaking from experience about converts to the Faith:

> A convert will tell you: "I read, I reasoned, I desired, but I did not attain to it. Then one day — I cannot explain how — I was no longer the same: I believed; and what happened at the moment of final conviction was totally different in nature from

what preceded...." Recall the episode of the two disciples on the way to Emmaus.

Thus a sympathetic intuition sets up a bond between two men in a single moment which logic would not have produced in the course of many years. So at times does a sudden illumination enlighten the genius. There may be a scholar who studies Catholic teaching without rejecting it bitterly.... But some day this scholar gets down on his knees; conscious of man's wretchedness, he raises his hands to heaven, saying: "From the depths of my misery, O my God, I have cried unto You." At that moment something takes place within him, the scales fall from his eyes, a mystery is accomplished, and he is a changed man.

What is faith? Different people have different answers to this question. Some answers go like this: faith is believing something that you want to be true, yet you cannot prove it. Others say that it means believing only what you can see and trust. Or, faith is living in the unknown.

What did the resurrected Jesus Christ finally say to the doubting Thomas who had not yet witnessed Christ risen? The Apostle Thomas, hearing from the other apostles that Christ had risen, protested the he would not believe until he could put his fingers into the place of the nails and slip his hand into His side. When Jesus later appeared and Thomas was with them, Jesus bid Thomas to come forth and do just that. Thomas did and replied, "My Lord and my God." Our Lord Jesus Christ in turned replied: "Have you believed because you have seen me? Blessed are those who have not seen and yet believe" (John 20:28–29).

Faith then is not believing in something we can see, nor is it simply accepting the unknown. We are speaking here of *supernatural faith*. It is not a mystery about which we know nothing but still accept. There are mysteries of faith which we believe with supernatural faith and about that we know a great deal, even though we do not understand them. I believe that Jesus is true God, the infinite God, the Son of the Father, but also true man in His Divine Person. I believe that the celebration of the Eucharist perpetuates both the Sacrifice of Jesus on the Cross and brings His Real Presence. I know much about what these mysteries of the Eucharist teach. I know by faith that which I do not understand. Jesus came to reveal truth about God the Father and our redemption. He returned to Heaven so that He and His Father could send the Holy Spirit to bring all these things to our minds and so we could believe.

Hebrews 11:1 gives us a true definition of faith: "Now faith is the assurance of things hoped for, the conviction of things not seen." It means that God exists "and that he rewards those who seek him" (Heb. 11:6) There is a Heaven. There is a Hell.

In the *Summa Theologica*, St. Thomas Aquinas explains that Faith has as its material object all truths revealed by God, but chiefly the supernatural mysteries not accessible to any natural intelligence, human or angelic. But the formal object of faith, its formal motive of adherence, is God's veracity (see ST, II–II, q. 1–16), which presupposes God's infallibility. The veracity spoken of here is that of God as Author. This means God as Author not only of nature, but of grace and glory. The revealed mysteries like the Blessed Trinity and the redemptive Incarnation are supernatural. This is what St. Thomas Aquinas said:

- Faith, considered in its formal object, is nothing else than *God, the first truth* [emphasis added]. For faith assents to no truth except in so far as that truth is revealed. Hence the medium by which faith believes is divine truth itself (ST, II–II, q. 1, art. 1).

- ✣ The formal object of faith is the first truth, adherence to which is man's reason for assenting to any particular truth (ST, II–II, q. 2, art. 2).
- ✣ In faith we must distinguish the formal element, i.e., the first truth, far surpassing all the natural knowledge of any creature; and second, the material element, i.e., the particular truth, to which we adhere only because we adhere to the first truth (ST, II–II, q. 5, art. 1).
- ✣ The first truth, as not seen but believed, is the object of faith, by which object we assent to truths only as proposed by that first truth" (ST, II–II, q. 4, art. 1).
- ✣ Since the act by which man assents to the truths of faith is an act beyond man's nature, he must have within, from God, the supernatural mover, a principle by which he elicits that act" (ST, II–II, q. 6, art. 1).
- ✣ The believer holds the articles of faith by his adherence to the first truth, for which act he is made capable by virtue of faith" (ST, II–II, q. 5, art. 3, ad. 1).

What was promised throughout the Old Testament, what was hoped for, is accomplished and is a present occurrence of a promise each time we celebrate the Eucharist. It brings the past — Jesus' redemptive death on the Cross — and the future — the life we shall live in Heaven — into the here and now. Such is the Eucharist.

Sacrifice of the Mass

The principal Priest who offers the Sacrifice of the Mass is Jesus Christ. The priest celebrant we see at the altar is the instrumental minister. While he possesses certain powers of Jesus Christ, those powers are the very powers of Jesus Christ. At the time of Consecration, the priest celebrant does not speak in his own name, not even precisely in the name of the Church. He speaks the words of Consecration in the name of Jesus Christ the Savior, who is always interceding for us (see Heb. 7:25).

Christ Jesus offers each Mass *actually*, as He instituted the Sacrifice, gave His power as High Priest to consecrate to the apostles, and commanded that it be done by the apostles and successors (bishops and priests) until the end of the world. This is the doctrine as explained by St. Thomas Aquinas.

If the priest as the instrumental minister should be distracted and, at the moment of saying the Consecration words, "This is my Body.... This is my Blood," had only a virtual intention of consecrating, still, Christ, the one High Priest, who is the principal cause, still wills actually, here and now, this transubstantiating Consecration. Christ's humanity, joined to His divinity, is the physically instrumental cause of the twofold transubstantiation.

An Immolation Takes Place

In the Sacrifice of the Mass there is an unbloody sacramental immolation, which re-presents the bloody immolation of the Cross. The fruits of the Cross are given to us at Mass. John of St. Thomas explained it this way:

> The essence of the Eucharistic sacrifice consists in the consecration, taken, not absolutely [that is, not physical] but as sacramentally and mystically, separative of the blood from the body.... On the cross the sacrifice consisted in the real and physical separation of Christ's blood from his body. The action, therefore, which mystical and sacramentally separates that blood is the same sacrifice as that on the cross, differing therefrom only in its mode [of offering] which there [on Calvary] was real and physical and here [today is real but] sacramental.

The immolation that is present in the Sacrifice of the Mass is the sacramental immolation, the sacramental separation, by the double Consecration, of His Blood from His Body, whereby His Blood is shed sacramentally.

The Sacrifice of the Mass, which contains the shedding of Christ's Blood sacramentally, is not less worthy in value than the sacrifice as offered on the Cross of Calvary. Why is this? Because it is *one and the same sacrifice*, only the manner of offering differs. The Eucharist is simultaneously sacrifice and sacrament. There is a re-presentation of the bloody immolation of Calvary. St. Augustine said that the visible sacrifice of the Mass is the sacrament, the sacred sign, of the invisible sacrifice.

The Council of Trent expressed the doctrine this way: "In the two sacrifices there is one and the same Victim, one and the same priest, who then on the cross offered himself, and who now, by the instrumentality of his priests, offers himself anew, the two sacrifices differing only in their mode."

They differ in the manner of offering, not in the reality of Christ's sacrifice, for the sacrifice of the Eucharist is the same Sacrifice of the Cross. In reality there is one sacrifice, not two sacrifices, but the Council was expressing the physical or bloody offering on Calvary, and the offering in a sacramental manner today. The bloody sacrifice and the unbloody sacrifice are one and the same sacrifice. The sacrifice Jesus offered at the Last Supper, the sacrifice He offered on Calvary on the first Good Friday, and the Sacrifice of the Mass today, are not three sacrifices, but one and the same sacrifice.

Sanctifying Grace

Sanctifying grace, which increases within us principally through the Sacrifice of the Mass and the sacraments, is the seed of glory. We need sanctifying grace to live in the glory of Heaven, seeing God face to face even as He is. Sanctifying grace is the supernatural life of the soul. This grace is received into the essence of the soul. Charity is received into the soul faculty which we call the will. Charity is an infused virtue residing in the will. The infused virtue of charity can come only into a soul that is living a supernatural life, so empowered by sanctifying grace. That grace can grow and grow, and does grow, especially by active interior participation in the Sacrifice of the Mass. It grows by the loving reception in faith also of the Lord's Body, Blood, Soul, and Divinity in Holy Communion.

When we receive Holy Communion, we are receiving within ourselves the very life-giving, the very redeeming, Blood of Jesus Christ, which flowed and still flows through the veins of His Sacred Body. We receive the very same Blood that was shed to its very last drop on the Cross. We receive the same Blood that redeemed the entire world — redeemed billions of men through the centuries and until the very end of the world.

Jesus Christ is a member of our human race, like ourselves, but He is also God in His Person and therefore eternal in His divinity. This God-Man sends forth from His throne in Heaven, seated next to God the Father, a hymn of infinite praise. He as man worships in an infinite degree. Were it not for this God-Man capable of perfectly satisfying for the billions of sins that His brothers and sisters commit upon earth, God the Father, would then have to cast us all into eternal fires. But God the Father, when He looks upon the many serious sins being committed upon earth, sees at the same time His Son seated beside Him. He sees His Son joined to our own weak humanity, with a human body and soul like ours. He sees that His Son in His humanity is head of all humanity.

God the Father sees the soul of Jesus with an intellect and will, perfectly conformed with all three Persons of the Most Blessed Trinity.

The Father looks at the hands, the feet, the side of Jesus; He sees there the glorified wounds of the nails and the sword — whereby His Most Precious Blood was poured out for the salvation of His brothers and sisters upon the earth. He redeemed us and made infinite satisfaction for us. The Heavenly Father says: "At least in You my Son I am well pleased. One drop of Your Precious Blood would be sufficient to have atoned for many worlds. You my Son are a Brother to people upon earth and the saints in Heaven. You are God, equal to Myself, one in Divine Nature with Me. Yet your human nature is hypostatically fused with the Divine Nature. Down upon earth, I see Your Precious Blood offered countless times each day in the Chalice of the Altar at the Sacrifice of the Mass."

Surely there is a dialogue, a hymn of praise between the Father and His Beloved Son, Jesus Christ, that goes on in Heaven. Sacred Scripture says of Jesus in Heaven that He is always living "to make intercession for [us]" (Heb. 7:25).

In our Morning Offering prayer, let us unite ourselves with all the Masses being said throughout the world. Ask our merciful Lord to wash and purify the world in the torrent of His mercy, His Most Precious Blood.

Sanctifying grace makes us children and heirs of God. It is *habitual* in the soul, that is, it remains so long as one is free of mortal sin. This grace is a constant supernatural quality of the soul that sanctifies and makes a person just and pleasing to God. This grace is the result of the condescension and benevolence shown by God toward us. It is an unmerited gift that flows from the benevolent disposition of God. Grace is entirely gratuitous. Man has absolutely no claim or right to grace.

Yet, as children of God, we should be at home in our Father's house. "For you did not receive the spirit of slavery to fall back into fear, but you have received the spirit of sonship. When we cry, 'Abba! Father!' it is the Spirit himself bearing witness with our spirit that we are children of God, and if children, then heirs, heirs of God and fellow heirs with Christ" (Rom. 8:15–17).

Grace is the supernatural gift that God, of His free benevolence, bestows on rational creatures for their eternal salvation. The gifts of grace are supernatural, that is, they surpass the being, powers, and claims of our created nature. The infused virtues and the gifts and fruits of the Holy Spirit accompany sanctifying grace. These gifts are indispensable for us to reach the Beatific Vision.

The Beatific Vision we shall have in Heaven is called *beatific* because it produces happiness in the will and the whole being. Such is the human life in Heaven. The blessed share in the divine happiness, where the beatitude of the Most Blessed Trinity is, the consequence of God's perfect knowledge of His own infinite goodness. There we shall share in the living of the life of God without the veil of faith. The good holy angels enjoy the Beatific Vision. It was possessed by Jesus Christ in His human nature even while He was in this mortal life on earth.

As defined by the Church, the souls of the just in Heaven "see the divine essence by an intuitive vision and face to face, so that the divine essence is known immediately, showing itself plain, clearly and openly" (Denzinger, 1000–1002). The souls of the saints "clearly behold God, one and triune, as He is" (Denzinger, 1304–1306).

Sanctifying grace is real and intrinsic in our soul. God's great and precious promises have made us "partakers of the divine nature" (2 Pet. 1:4). God is the principal cause of grace, as sanctifying grace is a participation in the Divine Nature. This sanctifying grace begins in the soul at Baptism. We grow especially through the Eucharist but therein is God too, the God-Man Jesus Christ, the essential Mediator. The entire Blessed Trinity is present in the Holy Eucharist, for where the Son is present, as Person of the God-Man, all three Persons of the Blessed Trinity are present. The priest is the instrumental cause of effecting the Eucharist, but the chief priest of the Mass and all the sacraments is Jesus Christ Himself. Only fire ignites, so Deity (true God) alone can deify, that is, sanctify us into the likeness of Christ, giving us a share in His divine life. This happens in our Eucharistic union with Jesus Christ.

The human soul, which is immortal, has an aptitude, a potential as a spirit in God's likeness, to receive all that God can will to give it. God can give the soul anything that is not self-contradictory. The soul has the potency to receive grace, glory, and even the hypostatic union (which was done in one case, the created human soul of Jesus Christ). Thus the soul can increase to an ever-higher degree of grace and glory. The potency of the immortal soul can never be so completely actualized as not to be still more actualizable. We can always keep growing in the likeness of God by an increase in our share in the Divine Nature.

This is what the Holy Eucharist is about. It perpetuates the Sacrifice of Jesus on the Cross. It gives us, if we are well-disposed in the dispositions of our heart, an increase in our sharing in the life of God, which Jesus Christ has in its plentitude.

The increase of sanctifying grace in one's soul requires some movement of the will as a disposition of the heart. "Direct your heart to the Lord," says Samuel (1 Sam. 7:3). The disposition cannot of itself engender grace. Yet to the man who under actual grace does what he can in his own power to prepare himself for justification, habitual or sanctifying grace is given infallibly. This is not because the preparation proceeds from our own free will. It is because it comes from God who moves efficaciously and infallibly. St. Thomas Aquinas put it this way: "If God who moves intends that man attain grace, he attains it infallibly" (ST, I–II, q. 112, art. 3).

Man receives a higher or lower degree of grace in proportion to the dispositions of his heart. God is Love and does not force Himself or His grace upon anyone. God, who is the first cause of each degree of disposition, distributes His free gifts more or less abundantly. Thus the Church, Christ's Mystical Body, is adorned with different levels of grace, charity, and ultimately glory.

Can we be certain that we are in the state of grace? It would require a special revelation to have absolute certitude. We can have a relative certitude, a moral and conjectural certitude. Whenever we receive Jesus in the Holy Eucharist, our conscience, with a moral conjectural certitude, must inform us we are already in the state of sanctifying grace. St. Paul the Apostle realized he could not have absolute certitude on the state of his soul, and so he wrote: "I do not even judge myself. I am not aware of anything against myself, but I am not thereby acquitted. It is the Lord who judges me" (1 Cor. 4:3–4).

Without a special revelation, we cannot know with genuine certitude whether God dwells by grace in our souls or not. Yet, if we have a clear conscience, are conscious of no mortal sin since our last good confession, find our joy in the Lord Jesus, and are desirous of union with Him, then we should feel free and anxious to receive Our Divine Lord in Holy Communion so as to grow more in Christ's likeness.

We are the adoptive sons and daughters of God. Scripture teaches this clearly that we are the children of God. Jesus Christ is God's Son by nature, Divine Nature that is. At Baptism we become God's sons and daughters by baptismal grace, by adoption. We are baptized into the Lord Jesus Christ. We can then grow in grace throughout our lives on earth by cooperating with God's love for us. God's love, since it is not merely affective, but is effective, produces something real in the soul, namely, grace, a participation in the Divine Nature, which justifies and sanctifies. Thus God's act of adoption is not a mere human adoption. Having adopted us as His children, God wills to feed us, chiefly through the Eucharist.

Essentially, sanctifying grace is justice, rectitude. It means *sanctity* for the human person. Sin is essentially iniquity, defilement, disorder.

For justification of an adult there are acts enumerated by the Council of Trent: faith, fear, hope, love, contrition, and firm proposal. St. Thomas Aquinas required chiefly faith and contrition, but he also noted filial fear, humility, hope, and love of God. Contrition is included in firm proposal.

Do we have to have all these acts explicitly present in our consciousness? Explicitly, two of them are required, namely, faith, which is in the intellect, and love, which is in the will. The others can be contained virtually in the above two. Contrition for sin must ordinarily be present, but it can be contained virtually in the act of love, even if a man is not explicitly thinking of his sins but of his love for God. Hope can also be virtually contained in charity.

St. Margaret Mary Alacoque (1647–1690), the Apostle for the Sacred Heart of Jesus, wrote as follows in a letter:

> It seems to me that our Lord's earnest desire to have his Sacred Heart honored in a special way is directed toward renewing the effects of redemption in our souls. For the Sacred Heart is an inexhaustible fountain and its sole desire is to pour itself out into the hearts of the humble so as to free them and prepare them to lead lives according to his good pleasure.
>
> From this Divine Heart three streams flow endlessly. The first is the stream of mercy for sinners; it pours into their hearts sentiments of contrition and repentance. The second is the stream of charity which helps all in need and especially aids those seeking perfection to find the means of surmounting their difficulties. From the third stream flow love and light for the benefit of his friends who have attained perfection; these he wishes to unite to himself so that they may share his knowledge and commandments and, in their individual ways, devote themselves wholly to advancing his glory.

This Divine Heart is an abyss of all blessings, and into it the poor should submerge all their needs. It is an abyss of joy in which all of us can immerse our sorrows. It is an abyss of lowliness to counteract our foolishness, an abyss of mercy for the wretched, an abyss of love to meet our every need.

Therefore, you must unite yourselves to the Heart of Our Lord Jesus Christ, both at the beginning of your conversion in order to obtain proper dispositions, and at its end in order to make reparation. Are you making no progress in prayer? *Then you need only offer God the prayers which the Savior has poured out for us in the Sacrament of the Altar.* Offer God his fervent love in reparation for your sluggishness. In the course of every activity pray as follows: "My God, I do this or I endure that in the Heart of your Son and according to his holy counsels. I offer it to you in reparation for anything blameworthy or imperfect in my actions." Continue to do this in every circumstance of life. And every time that some punishment, affliction or injustice comes your way, say to yourself: "Accept this as sent to you by the Sacred Heart of Jesus Christ in order to unite yourself to Him."

But above all preserve peace of heart. This is more valuable than any treasure. In order to preserve it there is nothing more useful than renouncing your own will and substituting for it the will of the Divine Heart. In this way his will can carry out for us whatever contributes to his glory, and we will be happy to be his subjects and to trust entirely in him.

Jesus said, "Apart from me you can do nothing" (John 15:5) St. Paul said: "I can do all things in him who strengthens me" (Phil. 4:13). Thus there is the absolute necessity of grace for our salvation, sanctifying grace. "What have you that you did not receive?" (1 Cor.

4:7). This means the absolute gratuity of grace. Only God who is the Author of grace, can move a man to a supernatural end. The ultimate end is Heaven. The sanctifying grace in our souls at this moment is the same eternal life we shall live in Heaven, but then, without the veil of faith.

8

Priesthood and Eucharist Go Together

Permit me in this chapter to talk in a personal manner, from my heart, as one priest among thousands, about the priesthood of Jesus Christ among men. Once ordained a Catholic priest in the Sacrament of Holy Orders, a man is a priest forever, for all eternity. As we advance in this chapter more and more the profundity, the depth, of the priesthood of Christ in men will develop with a scriptural basis.

Upon entering college seminary in 1947, following high school, one of the first books I read was on the life of the Curé d'Ars, St. John Vianney, patron of parish priests. My ideals of the priesthood were already quite sublime, thanks to parish priests, the good Franciscan sisters who gave me formal education, and especially my family.

Then, beginning my first year of college seminary, I learned about this holy priest, St. John Vianney. He was born in a small town near Lyons, France, in 1786. His struggles to be educated and ordained impressed me greatly. Even more so was the way he lived Christ's Priesthood. Let me share with you then what this patron of parish priests wrote of the Catholic priesthood.:

> Oh, how great is a priest! The priest will not understand the greatness of his office until he is in heaven.... Go to confession to the Blessed Virgin, or to an angel. Will they absolve you? No. Will they give you the Body and Blood of Our Lord? No.
>
> The priest has the key of the heavenly treasures; it is he who opens the door; he is the steward of the good God, the

distributor of His wealth.... The priest is not a priest for himself, he does not give himself absolution, he does not administer the sacraments to himself.... He is for you.

After God, the priest is everything. Leave a parish 20 years without priests; they will worship beasts. When people wish to destroy religion, they begin by attacking the priest, because when there is no longer any priest there is not sacrifice, and where there is no longer any sacrifice, there is no religion....

The priest continues the work of redemption on earth.... If we really understood the priest on earth, we would die not of fright but of love.... The Priesthood is the love of the Heart of Jesus. (*Catechism on the Priesthood*)

The humble Curé d'Ars would spend up to sixteen hours daily in the confessional. From many countries of the world, people, even cardinals and bishops, flocked to him for Confession. It is said he spent three-fourths of his priestly life in the confessional. And lines waiting to go to Confession, or hear him preach, ran into eight days. The world came to Ars to witness the priesthood in action — in this humble priest who at first was not accepted for ordination, until his pastor went to battle for him.

Years ago, when I was in Ars, France, I was able to see the bed and curtains that the devil had set ablaze in John Vianney's simple bedroom. The evil spirits attempted to keep this holy priest from rest, since he was touching multiple thousands of souls with the love of the Hearts of Jesus and His mother. I saw the Curé's simple study as the saintly priest had left it, his breviary, eyeglasses on a small table, even some blood stains on the wall from his penitential scourging. There was the single cooking pot over the fireplace where the Curé prepared his potato or two, which was about all he ate in a day. His rectory was extremely poor. Yet his parish church of Ars was different. Nothing was too good for the house of God. He had the best vestments for Mass that he could obtain. I prayed before his incorrupt body enclosed in glass — for intercessory protection in living Christ's holy priesthood today. I saw his hands which had been raised in absolution hundreds of thousands of times.

St. Padre Pio was another holy priest, closer to our times, a priest of Jesus Christ for fifty-eight years. He attracted millions of souls throughout the world. This saintly priest was an apostle of love of God and neighbor. For millions, St. Padre Pio was above all a priest. He was a priest in the confessional, where he spent many hours each day; in church; in his small cell; in the realization of charitable social works. Grown and mature men became as little children, spiritual children, in his presence.

St. Padre Pio reflected Jesus Christ the Priest so visibly, that, for fifty years, he bore in his body the stigmata, the wounds of Christ's Crucifixion in his hands, feet, and side.

Padre Pio, often considered to be a "living crucifix," was never more in evidence than at the Sacrifice of the Mass. Perfume would fill the Church as he offered the Eucharistic Sacrifice. All who assisted at Padre Pio's Mass could detect the expression of his participation in the sufferings and death of Jesus Christ. At the same time, they sensed his ecstatic rapture.

During the Jubilee Year 2000, when I went to Rome, a high point of the pilgrimage for me was to be able to offer the Sacrifice of the Mass at the tomb of this beloved priest-saint, then newly canonized. It was a spiritually uplifting experience to realize that before me was the tomb of this stigmatic priest who read souls, bilocated, and loved God and fellow men intensely.

Yes, I am still learning more and more how a man who is ordained a priest must also be a victim, as Jesus Christ was both Priest and Victim. A priest must bear Christ's wounds and walk the road of Calvary.

Men like St. John Vianney and St. Padre Pio helped me understand how victimhood and priesthood are not separated.

Jesus Is the Chief Priest of Every Mass

While it was so much in evidence in the life of the holy priest St. Padre Pio of Pietrelcina, the reality of what the Sacrifice of the Mass is, in which anyone of us can participate, is the same. It is the same *Sacrifice of the Cross*, whether the priest consecrating and offering be St. Padre Pio, St. John Vianney, Pope St. John Paul II, Pope Benedict XVI, St. Philip Neri, or any ordained country priest in a remote corner of the world.

For a priest to act *in the Person of Christ*, he must follow the approved Divine Liturgy of the Church, without additions or omissions to what the Church has prescribed, to effect what Jesus has accomplished on the Cross of Calvary.

Celibacy Is for Marriage to the Church

The understanding of the priesthood of Jesus Christ and celibacy have always gone hand in hand. Holy Ordination is a marriage to the Church. The Church, the Mystical Body of Christ, is the family of the priest. The priest dedicated to his calling experiences fatherhood, spiritual fatherhood, in making the sacraments possible and available. This is true especially by feeding the faithful with the Body and Blood of Jesus Christ, having just offered the infinite act of Eucharistic Sacrifice that perpetuates Jesus' Sacrifice of the Cross, and forgiving the sins of his spiritual children.

The priest also experiences fatherhood at Baptisms when souls are born to new life, and in a special way in the confessional, where souls are restored to grace, made to live again, or made more perfect and pure from imperfections.

The priesthood of Jesus Christ is the greatest vocation on earth. The priesthood is eternal. It is of Jesus Christ, true God and true man. The priesthood is not simply for the individual ordained man, but to glorify God and work for the salvation of souls. A Judas here and there does not diminish what Jesus Christ bestowed on the apostles.

Priesthood Gives Eternal Indelible Character

An ordained priest has the indelible character of Jesus Christ the High Priest on his soul in virtue of ordination by the bishop, who is directly part of the apostolic chain going back to Jesus Christ. That indelible seal of Jesus empowers the ordained man with the power to perpetuate Christ's Sacrifice of the Cross as he pronounces the words of Consecration over the bread: "This is my Body." And over the wine *in persona Christi*, "This is my Blood." This effects, then, the Real Presence of the God-Man, Jesus Christ on the altar. The very seal of Jesus Christ, the Priest, imprinted on the ordained man, now characterizes his soul for all eternity. There is an ontological change in the soul of the ordained man. It is the same soul, but, as Baptism makes one a new creation in Christ Jesus, Holy Orders makes the baptized and confirmed soul additionally identified in power and entity with Jesus Christ the High Priest.

Mary, Mother of Vocations

The priest has the sacred power not possessed by angels. Not even Mary, the Mother of God, Mother of the eternal High Priest, can consecrate bread and wine into Jesus Christ or forgive sins. He has the privilege and the power of transubstantiation and reconciliation. He possesses the powers of Jesus Christ to change the substance of bread and wine into the living substance of the Body, Blood, Soul, and Divinity of Our Lord and Savior, Jesus Christ. He forgives sins in Jesus' name. Devout Catholics can well understand why Mary beholds every validly ordained priest as a special beloved son.

When I celebrated my twenty-fifth anniversary as a priest of Jesus Christ, it became clear in my mind why I had a deep devotion to Mary from a very young age. I realized then, more clearly, that every man called to the holy priesthood of Jesus Christ received his priestly vocation as the fruit, not only of the calling by Jesus Christ, but also, through the intercession of Mary, the Mother of God. I believe Mary is involved in every authentic priestly vocation, whether the man ordained realizes it or not. She is the Mediatrix of Grace. She is the Mother of the Church, Mother of Priests. She is Mother of Vocations. It seems to me that a priest who does not have a deep devotion to Mary has not heard his calling from Jesus Christ clearly enough.

How did the world get the first Priest, Jesus Christ? The archangel Gabriel was sent to Mary. It required Mary's cooperation, her yes, her "Let it be to me according to your word" (Luke 1:38). And the "Word became flesh and dwelt among us" (John 1:14). Mary is the Mother of Grace. She is the Mediatrix of all grace. She is the Mother of us all, but especially of priests, and in a special way. Through Mary as Advocate and Mother, through her intercession, grace is bestowed upon souls. The Holy Spirit is the uncreated divine Advocate. Mary, the Holy Spirit's spouse, is the created human advocate. All her privileges and greatness flow from her vocation as the Mother of God. She prays always: "My soul magnifies the Lord" (Luke 1:46).

We grow in grace especially through the sacraments. For the Holy Eucharist, we need the priesthood. Without the Eucharist, there is no Church. Mary, Mother of the Church, will intercede so that we have priests, so that we have Jesus Christ in the Holy Eucharist. The Catholic Church is the Church of the Eucharist.

Priesthood and Eucharist Go Together

When I conducted youth pilgrimages to Fatima for many years, with about two hundred of the young men eventually being ordained to the holy priesthood, I would be asked, "How did you get your vocation to the priesthood?" I would answer: "A priest is called 'father' as he is a father to souls. Having six, eight, ten, thirteen, or more children would never have satisfied me. I needed hundreds, in fact thousands of children in Christ. From the first year of ordination until forty-eight and a half years later, I would teach our holy Catholic Faith to children and teenagers, grades one to twelve, each week of the school year. A father must teach and form his children. When the bishop decided I was to retire, I obeyed in retiring from the pastorate of a parish. I would be without an assignment. Shortly before the date of retirement, July 1, 2003, came, I was happy to have the Mother Vicar (Sr. Catherine) of Our Lady of the Angels Monastery and Shrine of the Most Blessed Sacrament, founded by Mother Angelica near Hanceville, Alabama, invite me to come here to offer Mass daily in the lower church. Since I was convinced that there was no such thing as a "retired priest," I accepted the invitation to come to Hanceville, where, at the time of writing this, I am in my fifty-fourth year as a priest.

My first twenty-five years of striving to live the priesthood of Jesus Christ convinced me ever more deeply that a priestly vocation is the fruit of the intercession of Mary, Mother of Priestly Vocations. That conviction grew in me during the second twenty-five years in the priesthood and continues to grow. I pray for more young men to listen so as to hear the call. It is most important for the priest to have a personal relationship with the Heart of Jesus Christ, with Christ the High Priest. But it is also important for the priest to have a knowledge of, love of, and personal relationship with Mary, Mother of Jesus Christ, Mother of the Church. She was the medium, through the power of the Holy Spirit, through which the Church got Her invisible Head. His physical body was formed in her body.

Pope Pius XII in his encyclical *Mediator Dei* wrote:

> It is the same priest, Christ Jesus, whose sacred person his minister truly represents. Now the minister, by reason of the sacerdotal consecration which he has received, is truly made like to the high priest and possesses the authority to act in the power and place of the person of Christ himself [*virtute ac persona ipsius Christi*].
>
> Christ is the source of all priesthood; the priest of the old law was a figure of Christ, and the priest of the new law acts in the person of Christ.

For a priest to grant absolution to a penitent in serious sin, and thus restore one to the state of sanctifying grace, restoring the Divine Nature and life in the soul, is a greater act than to raise a dead man back to natural life.

A Priest Is a Priest Forever

As in the case of Baptism and Confirmation this share in Christ's office is granted once for all. The sacrament of Holy Orders, like the other two, confers an *indelible spiritual character* and cannot be repeated or conferred temporarily. (*CCC*, 1582)

The grace of the Holy Spirit proper to this sacrament is configuration to Christ as Priest, Teacher, and Pastor, of whom the ordained is made a minister. (*CCC*, 1585)

With these brief reflections, I can only express my great gratitude to Jesus Christ for having chosen this unworthy individual to be His priest among thousands of others more worthy. My heart goes out in great love to any young man I see seriously considering the priesthood of Jesus Christ.

Priesthood and Eucharist Go Together

Since boyhood I've loved the Sacred Heart of Jesus, even just the mention of the Sacred Heart of Jesus. I still love to speak the words, for they speak words of love. In time my devotion to the Immaculate Heart of Mary has grown, and I've appreciated ever more the alliance between the Hearts of Jesus and Mary. Yes, Mary leads to Jesus. But Jesus also leads us to love His mother. The heart of each priest is called to be bonded into the alliance of Jesus and Mary with the Father in the union of the Holy Spirit.

Were it possible, and were it the will of Jesus Christ, I would love to exercise the priesthood of Jesus Christ upon earth until the end of time. Since that hardly seems the will of God, and this mortal body already experiences the weaknesses of time, I pray that my last day on earth may be a day when, as every day before, I will be able to celebrate the Eucharistic Sacrifice, which perpetuates the Sacrifice of the Cross.

And when, God willing, I enter Heaven, I pray that it be in the company of Mary and St. Michael with my guardian angel, and that I immediately recognize Jesus, my Brother Priest, the Source of the Priesthood. For it is Jesus and Mary primarily who call men to the ordained priesthood. The good guardian angel, appointed by Mary, knows our vocation before we do, and he works for us to become enlightened to God's calling. Mary as Mediatrix, dependent on Jesus Christ, surely calls too, for she wills whatever her Son wills, she does whatever He tells her and bids us do the same. The grace He merited, she bestows.

God willing, as I behold the Blessed Trinity face to face, I hope to meet face to face also my guardian angel who has been ever at my side these long years upon earth that went all too quickly. The guardian angel, appointed also by Mary, Queen of the Angels, is the one, as said, who discovers our vocation in life, long before we do. Throughout life the good angel works for us to live true to our calling.

I thank the Lord Jesus for sustaining me for fifty-four years in His holy priesthood. I thank him for holding me close to His Heart when

Eucharist

the Cross became heavy and I felt alone. I thank Mother Mary, Mother of Mercy and Consolation, for interceding for me, day by day, that as one of her beloved sons, I might in some small way reflect the image of her Son, Christ Jesus, the High Priest. I write these lines here in the prayer they may touch some young man's heart aspiring to the holy priesthood of Jesus Christ, or lift up the heart of some priest suffering loneliness so that he realizes he is never alone.

When I was required to retire from being a pastor of a parish, I wrote the following poem:

> When I was young, Jesus touched my soul
> He invited me to walk the less traveled road
> I answered Jesus' Call, "Come follow Me."
> He gave me souls, to point to Heaven's Key.
>
> The life of a priest, has been glorious indeed
> Beset with trials, amidst good and bad seed
> To leave all things and follow in His steps
> To bring souls to Jesus until in Heaven we've met.
>
> If we give up all things and follow Him today
> He rewards a hundredfold, the Life, Truth, the Way
> He promises persecution to those who with Him stay
> He gives us His Mother, His Words are ours to say.
>
> Life in the priesthood, passes quickly with the years
> Preaching the full gospel, the Word of God one hears
> Souls reborn in Baptism; Souls restored to grace,
> Souls fed with Christ's Body, regardless of race.
>
> A glorious life for man, Christ's holy priesthood
> Years passed quickly, still at the altar he stood
> An old priest now, with a heart in spirit young
> Full of joy and gratitude, for a life not done.

"There's no such thing as a retired priest," he said
"There are souls to be nourished, until I'm dead."
I pray Jesus, before Paradise, that my last day on earth,
I may offer His Eucharistic Sacrifice, of infinite worth.

With Jesus, Mary, angels and saints, from Heaven I'll be
Doing good upon earth, interceding for all, including thee
In Heaven there's no time, only NOW, so I will not grieve
From there an harmonious song of love, I'll forever weave.

The reason I am happy as a priest is because I feel fulfilled in Jesus Christ. I still look for more opportunities each day to reach out to others for the good of their souls and for the glory of God.

I remind young priests that we priests are promised by God's Word that we will never be tempted beyond our strength. The extraordinary graces of Jesus in the sacraments are there, and they are there for each one of us daily.

Recently I found in my notes, yellowed with age and written down either as a seminarian or as a young priest, the following thought: "Celibacy in the priesthood: while at times one may find oneself feeling lonely, that loneliness is designed to cause a vacuum which for the priest can only be filled with love for Jesus Christ and the people of His holy Church."

I can honestly say that in my fifty-plus years as a priest of Jesus Christ, I have never been lonely for very long. Yes, there have been lonely moments. And those lonely moments were times to renew my commitment and vows and come aside with Jesus.

Rather than loneliness, there have been more times, many days, when I longed to be alone for a while. I wanted to be alone so as to be alone with God so that my life might be centered on God alone. I wanted to be alone at times so as to be more fruitfully in a spirit of prayer, in order to prepare articles, books, sermons, classes, lectures, to love Jesus. I can say I've never been seriously tempted to break any priestly vows. I've been too occupied with the practice of the priesthood, reaching out to others to bring them to Jesus and present them to His Mother, to give time to temptation. My greatest joy has been and continues to be preaching the Word of God, offering the Divine Liturgy, administering the sacraments, and teaching youth the Way, the Truth, the Life.

A Priest Is Not a Priest for Himself

I realize that a priest's life centered on God, even God alone, must still involve God's people. For the very nature of priestly powers and duties is to act in the Person of the Head of the Body of Christ, the Mystical Body of Christ, of which people become members through Baptism. After Baptism he must feed them in the name and Person of Jesus Christ. The Catholic priest not only represents Christ but acts *in persona Christi* in offering the Holy Sacrifice of the Mass and administering the sacraments. Jesus Christ also acts through the priest when he reads the Scriptures in Church and teaches the Word of God, as pointed out by the Second Vatican Council.

Jesus Christ is Truth. He is the "way, and the truth, and the life" (John 14:6). The priest commissioned to teach the Word of God must always preach and teach the truth. Never should he compromise the truth of faith and morals. If he attempts to do so, he is compromising Jesus Christ.

The priest should preach the truth in season and out of season. He should preach the full gospel, the fullness of truth, whether at a particular time and place it is popular or unpopular to do so. If in preaching the truth, a priest, even when prudent, becomes controversial, he should be grateful, for Jesus Christ was a man of contradiction to the world, to the world's way of thinking and acting. Preaching is not to entertain, but to give knowledge of Jesus Christ so that souls can be formed in Christ's love.

A Priest Should Be a Sign of Contradiction

When the Christ Child was presented in the Temple, Simeon, inspired by the Holy Spirit, took the Child in his arms, blessed God, and said to Mary, His Mother, "Behold, this child is set .... for a sign that is spoken against (and a sword will pierce through your own soul also)" (Luke 2:34–35). It is interesting that, whereas Luke tells us that His father and His Mother marveled at what was said about Him, the above quoted words were directed not to both St. Joseph and the Blessed Virgin Mother, but only "to Mary, his Mother."

Those called to the priesthood of Jesus Christ are called not only to be good, but to be holy, to be a sign of contradiction to the world. If a priest carries out his mission, as not simply a good man but as a true priest, he will be spoken against, he will be contradicted, even persecuted. If he seeks to be a popular priest, one who entertains, one who speaks what people in general want to hear, he will not be a holy priest. He then will not be fulfilling the mission for which he was ordained.

"Blessed are those who are persecuted for righteousness' sake, for theirs is the kingdom of heaven" (Matt. 5:10). Yes, Jesus promised a hundredfold to those who leave all things, even family members, and follow and serve Him in His holy Church, even in the face of persecution.

"If any man would come after me, let him deny himself and take up his cross and follow me. For whoever would save his life will lose it; and whoever loses his life for my sake and the gospel's will save it" (Mark 8:34–35). If such words of Jesus Christ apply to all, how much more to the priest who has the indelible character of Christ the High Priest forever sealed on his soul.

Seminarians and young priests should get ready for this. To them I say in Jesus' name: not only will you be criticized, even persecuted, by those who do not want to hear the truth, you will receive such treatment at times even from some priests and fellow religious. If you give your whole heart to Jesus in full-time work and concern for souls, you will be a threat to many who should be working with you, encouraging you.

Pope St. John XXIII called for the ecumenical council known as the Second Vatican Council during the early years of my priesthood. I was enthusiastic, then, for what the Council stood for. I remain enthusiastic for it now. One who has actually read prayerfully and studied the sixteen documents of the Second Vatican Council will find nothing disharmonious with the first two thousand years of the teachings of Jesus Christ and His Church. There is nothing disharmonious in the Second Vatican Council with the other twenty ecumenical councils. The pre-conciliar and post-conciliar Church are one and the same Church.

Pope Benedict XVI has emphasized that there is a continuity in the Church. It is not correct to speak of the old Church before the Second Vatican Council and the renewed Church, or the one following the Council. There is one Church established by Jesus Christ, which will exist until the end of the world and then in Heaven. Each Holy Sacrifice of the Mass embraces the heavenly liturgy, or one might say, the heavenly liturgy embraces us on earth as we participate in perpetuating the Sacrifice of the Cross in the Eucharistic Sacrifice first offered by Jesus Christ at the Last Supper, forever offered in Heaven.

The development of Catholic doctrine builds. It does not contradict what went before. Fr. John A. Hardon, S. J., who was the theological advisor to an apostolate for the family I founded, once said to me that given the conditions of the modern world, the problems of the Church today would be much greater if there had been no Second Vatican Council.

Most of the years I've worked to practice Christ's holy priesthood have been years beset with struggles and contradictions. The true teachings of Christ's Church have always been a contradiction to the world. But what happened during and after the Second Vatican Council was that some, even within the Church, became the source of unnecessary contradictions that disturbed many of the faithful so that they were no longer faithful.

If some theologians and priests and religious are not faithful, how can they guide and inspire the faithful to remain faithful or grow in the Faith? They are then rather the cause, in too many cases, for others to weaken in the Faith, or even to lose faith all together.

The only way a priest will be happy in the priesthood is if he consistently lives and teaches the fullness of the true Faith and is consistent in a priestly spiritual program that he lives daily. Watering down the content of the Faith and morals of Catholicism will bring much tension and unhappiness to the priest himself and to others. If a priest thinks he will be more popular or liked by making the demands of the gospel and of the Church easier for people, by hiding or weakening the demands of Christ to carry one's cross daily, the truth is that priest will be miserable in this life. He will endanger his place in eternity, for he is not living out the mission Jesus Christ gave him when he was ordained nor cooperating with the graces promised in virtue of Holy Orders.

Yes, there are those who slap such priests on the back if the priest attempts to offer cheap bargains on an easy way to salvation. In reality, behind the scenes, usually not visible to the priest in his blindness, he is criticized much. Not only is he criticized when he does not teach the truth, if he is observant, he will notice, the numbers practicing the true Faith will dwindle. He will recognize no fruit from his labors, only decay, because then he would not be laboring in Jesus' name or Person.

Eucharist

Might as Well Be Criticized for Teaching Truth

Why is it that conservative fundamentalist communities are growing rapidly while communities among the mainline churches that have become very liberal in their doctrines see their membership falling rapidly in numbers? Why? The answer should be obvious. They are not being fed solid meat. Their people are starving for substance while their ministers or priests are attempting to entertain them and make them feel good about themselves. They are preaching the world, not Christ Crucified. They are attempting to adapt to the world that is not spiritual.

At the time of the death (April 2, 2005) and funeral (April 8) of Pope St. John Paul II, the public, including world leaders, spoke of his greatness. Millions went to Rome for his funeral. Major television networks occupied most of their time for a week reporting on this pope who was so admired by the world. The center of Rome had to be closed to traffic. People were asked through the media to refrain from coming to Rome. There was no more space. Hundreds of millions followed the funeral worldwide via television and radio.

Three days before the official funeral, Archbishop Angelo Comastri, vicar for Vatican City State, said it well as he concelebrated a Mass with other bishops for the repose of the pope's soul at the altar of the Chair of St. Peter's: "Today we see a river of people filing before the Pope because he, with his testimony, has awakened our faith and, therefore, our community. This is John Paul II's last silent homily."

People waited in line two or more miles long. Some were in line more than ten hours so as to file past the body of the pontiff known and loved throughout the world. Fifteen to eighteen thousand people per hour filed past the pope's body. It was estimated that more than four million people filed past his remains in St. Peter's.

Dignitaries came from 138 nations. Leading representatives of Christian bodies were present as well as heads of state. The Holy Synod of Greece approved the request of Orthodox Archbishop Christodoulos of Athens to accompany the president of Greece to the funeral. Leaders of the world Jewish community were present, too.

After the Mass ended, bells tolled and twelve pallbearers presented the coffin to the crowd one last time before carrying it on their shoulders back inside the basilica for burial. Crowds in the square chanted *santo subito*, a Latin phrase meaning "sainthood at once."

Cardinal Ratzinger (later Pope Benedict XVI) in the homily at the funeral Mass said: "Thanks to his being profoundly rooted in Christ, he was able to bear a burden which transcends merely human abilities: that of being the shepherd of Christ's flock, his universal Church." Yet, he radiated happiness.

For a priest to be happy his life must be "rooted in Christ." The priest who engages in worldly activities and entertainments, and who compromises true teachings on Catholic faith and morals, is not one whose life is rooted in Christ. He will be unhappy as a priest because he then is not living a priestly and Christlike life.

When Pope John Paul II became an old man with stooped shoulders, not able to walk unaided, and with trembling hands from Parkinson's, still young people by the hundreds of thousands came to greet him. They listened to his messages packed with proclamations of true faith and morals. These large crowds of teenagers and young adults would applaud whenever Pope John Paul II spoke tough love. They applauded when he encouraged them to use the Sacrament of Confession frequently. They applauded him when he stood up for purity and holy marriages. They applauded whenever he spoke for human life and dignity. They applauded him when he spoke against the drug culture. They applauded when he publicly condemned evils in the world.

Even if all these youth who applauded did not always live what he taught, they nonetheless recognized the truth when they heard it;

they recognized Jesus Christ in the truth and demonstrated that truth is attractive, even if it's difficult sometimes to live; yet each of us must strive to live Truth. Failures, yes. They recognized that in applauding at the encouragement to frequent the Sacrament of Reconciliation.

Is there a message in all this for seminarians and priests today? "Be not afraid" to proclaim Christ Jesus, His true faith and morals, and do so openly and without reservations. Preach the full gospel.

"Be not afraid" were among the first words of Pope John Paul II when he stepped onto the balcony of St. Peter's Basilica on October 16, 1978, immediately after being elected the 264th pope of the Roman Catholic Church. He immediately proclaimed Christ Jesus in a fearless manner. He challenged all to do the same without fear. He was a true shepherd, chosen for these times, and he suffered for all of humanity.

When I personally met Pope John Paul II on July 25, 1979, I asked him to give me one sentence to live by in my priesthood, for the apostolate for youth, which grew to an apostolate for the total family which I direct. He placed both hands on my shoulders, saying: "You must make your work in the spirit of the Sermon on the Mount."

When he was in Gemelli Hospital, recuperating from gunshot wounds, I took about 150 youth to sing for him beneath his hospital window. He threw signs of affection and Signs of the Cross for blessing.

On Wednesday, three days before his death, he appeared at his window, weak, face distorted with pain, and tried to speak and bless the people. His pain and effort spoke volumes of his commitment. He was teaching in this way of his loyalty to Christ and His Church, to all humanity to the very end.

There is much unhappiness among people today. Why? In short, the reason is because they are not living their God-given vocations in the manner God intends. The priest will be happy only if he lives the priesthood to the full as a divine vocation, not as another job.

Priesthood and Eucharist Go Together

Religious, laity, whatever be their vocation in life, will not find happiness apart from Jesus Christ.

Many youth today are confused and not happy. They lack direction. They lack guidance. They often lack an understanding of the very basics of Catholicism. And what they lack is often for two reasons. True faith has not been taught consistently. True faith has not been lived consistently by their parents. That, together with the parents' training them in living the Faith, is essential. Too often their parents also have not been taught and formed correctly and do not know how to teach and form their children. Sometimes youth, even when well taught, allow themselves to be captivated and formed by the world and the passions of fallen man. That is why the formation must consist in resisting the world, the flesh, and the devil.

If faith formation and love for Jesus in the Eucharist is lived and is the focus of the family's spiritual life, young people will be highly motivated to live moral lives. There will then be many youth answering the call to Christ's holy priesthood. There is a deep mystery to the reality of the Eucharist and the priesthood. They cannot be fully understood in the life of this world. Eucharist and priesthood involve mysteries of our Catholic Faith.

If all that God wanted to communicate to us could be easily understood by the human mind, if the truths of the Faith — including Christ's priesthood and Christ's Real Presence in the Eucharist, with His Sacrifice made present in the Mass — were easy to understand, we would not need the Holy Spirit to explain the "mysteries" to us. But we do need the Holy Spirit, and we need to be open to the Holy Spirit.

As Jesus was about to leave this world in His physical and visible presence, He assured the apostles: "But the Counselor [or Advocate], the Holy Spirit, whom the Father will send in my name, he will teach you all things, and bring to your remembrance all that I have said to you" (John 14:26). This was so important for the apostles to understand that Jesus repeated it: "When the Spirit of truth comes, he will guide you into all the truth; for he will not speak on his own authority, but whatever he hears he will speak, and he will declare to you the things that are to come. He will glorify me, for he will take what is mine and declare it to you" (John 16:13–14).

Jesus is speaking all these words as His earthly mission is ending, as He is instituting the Holy Eucharist on the eve of His sacrificial death, which the Eucharist perpetuates; that Eucharist brings us all the mysteries of Christ as well through the Church year.

The apostles did not understand everything Jesus was teaching them. When He explained parables and gave them specific direction, they did not get it all; they even got it wrong sometimes. In washing His disciples' feet, when He came to Simon Peter, who said to Him, "Lord, do you wash my feet?" Jesus answered, "What I am doing you do not know now, but afterward you will understand" (John 13:6–7). "'And you know the way where I am going.' Thomas said to him, 'Lord, we do not know where you are going; how can we know the way?'" (John 14:4–5).

The apostles often did not understand, but they did not assume it was impossible. They would come again and again to Jesus to ask Him questions. They listened to His teachings and pondered His answers. They tried to understand them. They wanted to know Jesus and understand Him the best they could. His presence among them stirred their hearts to know and love more.

The fuller understanding of the apostles awaited Pentecost, the descent of the Holy Spirit who becomes the Soul of the Church. If we are open to the Holy Spirit today and listen to Him in His Church, we have the great advantage of understanding even more deeply the mysteries of Jesus Christ. The Church, aided by the Holy Spirit, has had two thousand years to meditate, inheriting the insights of great spiritual teachers and saints, the popes, and bishops united with the popes, for over twenty centuries. The pope and bishops form the Magisterium and present to us the final teachings and interpretations of all that Jesus taught.

The mysteries of Christ as part of the deposit of faith left to the Church by Jesus Christ, especially concerning the Eucharist, are so profound that from the beginning of the Old Testament through the New Testament, revelation is gradually given to mankind. This prepared mankind slowly to appreciate and understand these mysteries in greater depth. If we are attune to what God is doing and revealing to us, beginning already in the book of Genesis, leading up to the founding of the Church which grows out of the Old Covenant into the New Covenant, we see the finger of God always at work to reveal Himself and help us understand.

Picture in your mind the awesome ceremony with which Moses had to seal God's covenant with the Israelites. He declares "all the words" of the Lord to the multitude at the foot of Mount Sinai. "Moses came and told the people all the words of the Lord and all the ordinances; and all the people answered with one voice, and said, 'All the words which the Lord has spoken we will do'" (Exod. 24:3).

Then Moses poured half of the blood of the sacrificial young bulls onto the altar as an offering to the Lord and sprinkled the rest on the people. Finally, Moses and the elders ate a holy meal before God.

What happened next?

> The Lord said to Moses, "Come up to me on the mountain, and wait there; and I will give you the tables of stone, with the law and the commandment, which I have written for their instruction." ... Then Moses went up on the mountain, and the cloud covered the mountain. The glory of the Lord settled on Mount Sinai, and the cloud covered it six days; and on the seventh day he called to Moses out of the midst of the

cloud. Now the appearance of the glory of the Lord was like a devouring fire on the top of the mountain in the sight of the people of Israel. And Moses entered the cloud, and went up on the mountain. And Moses was on the mountain forty days and forty nights. (Exod. 24:12, 15–18)

Notice how closely this sequence of events parallels the central actions of our worship of the Sacrifice of the Mass in the New Covenant under which we now live. Something similar to Moses' ceremonies takes place at Mass today: the reading of the Word of God, the profession of faith, the offertory and Consecration, and, finally, Holy Communion. When this worship is offered with basic understanding from the heart, one desires to obey the commandments of God.

The covenant that God made with His people on Mount Sinai was sealed with the blood of animals. That blood symbolized the life of the people who offered it and sealed their determination to carry out all that they had heard and professed. The declaration of Moses: "Behold the blood of the covenant which the Lord has made with you" (Exod. 24:8), foreshadowed Jesus' words at the Last Supper: "This is my blood of the covenant, which is poured out for many for the forgiveness of sins" (Matt. 26:28).

The New and Eternal Covenant of our redemption in Jesus Christ has been sealed by Jesus' own blood poured out for us. This blood is pure, living, of infinite and eternal value. It is now offered in Heaven. It is offered on earth on our Catholic altars. The blood of sacrificial bulls sealed the Israelites in their decision to obey the Law of the Old Covenant and keep the Ten Commandments God would give them. That blood of animals of the Old Covenant was symbolic. The blood offered in the New Covenant today is not merely symbolic but is Christ's own blood really present, and once offered is always in an eternal act of offering to the Father in Heaven. Jesus' blood was poured out to bestow divine power and seal us for all eternity. Whereas the sacrifices of the Old Covenant made the people ritually clean, the blood of Christ in the New Covenant makes our interior, our souls, pure and holy and empowers us to grow in sanctifying grace while infinite glory is given to God in the Sacrifice of the Mass.

Such then being the arrangements, the priests always used to enter into the first tabernacle to perform the sacred rites; but into the second tabernacle the high priest alone entered once a year, not without blood, which he offered for his own and the people's sins of ignorance. The Holy Spirit signified by this that the way into the Holies was not yet thrown open while the first tabernacle was still standing. This first tabernacle was a figure of the time, inasmuch as gifts and sacrifices are offered that cannot perfect the worshipper in conscience, since they refer only to food and drink and various oblations and bodily regulations imposed until a time of reformation.

> But when Christ appeared as a high priest of the good things that have come, then through the greater and more perfect tent (not made with hands, that is, not of this creation) he entered once for all into the Holy Place, taking not the blood of goats and calves but his own blood, thus securing an eternal redemption. For if the sprinkling of defiled persons with the blood of goats and bulls and with the ashes of a heifer sanctifies for the purification of the flesh, how much more shall the blood of Christ, who through the eternal Spirit offered himself without blemish to God, purify your conscience from dead works to serve the living God....
>
> But when Christ had offered for all time a single sacrifice for sins, he sat down at the right hand of God, then to wait until his enemies should be made a stool for his feet. For by a single offering he has perfected for all time those who are

sanctified. And the Holy Spirit also bears witness to us. (Heb. 9:11–14; 10:12–15)

Jesus died once, made the offering of Himself, shedding all His blood once. Scripture tells us that this sacrifice does not have to be repeated time after time for this sacrifice is eternal, infinite. The sacrifice of Himself — in sacramental form at the Last Supper, physically on Good Friday, and re-presented at each Sacrifice of the Mass today — these are not three different sacrifices but one and the same Sacrifice of Jesus Christ. That one sacrifice is present on earth today and is present eternally in Heaven. Scripture tells us that Christ Crucified but now risen, still bearing the wound marks but now glorified, always makes intercession for us at the right hand of God the Father. His glorified wound marks remind the Father of man's redemption, and Jesus' Heart is eternal in His offering of His sacrifice.

> But you have come to Mount Zion and to the city of the living God, the heavenly Jerusalem, and to innumerable angels in festal gathering, and to the assembly of the first-born who are enrolled in heaven, and to a judge who is God of all, and to the spirits of just men made perfect, and to Jesus, the mediator of a new covenant, and to the sprinkled blood that speaks more graciously than the blood of Abel. See that you do not refuse him who is speaking. For if they did not escape when they refused him who warned them on earth, much less shall we escape if we reject him who warns from heaven. (Heb. 12:22–25)

The church building is meant to be "a sacred building designated for divine worship" (CIC, 1214). It is more than just a place where we gather. Physical church buildings "signify and make visible the Church living in this place, the dwelling of God with men reconciled and united in Christ" (CCC, 1180).

The altar on which the Eucharistic Sacrifice is celebrated is central to every Catholic church. The Eucharist is the summit and source of the Church's life. The Eucharist makes the Church and the Church makes the Eucharist.

Jesus gave us the Eucharist on the evening before He died. He celebrated God's deliverance of Israel and the redemption that He Himself was accomplishing for all in the context of the Passover meal. This was in remembrance of the Paschal Lamb. The Pasch was the Jewish feast celebrated annually at God's command to commemorate the deliverance of the Jews from the bondage of Egypt. The deliverance of God's people was conditioned by the sacrifice of an unblemished lamb, whose bones could not be broken, and whose blood was sprinkled on the doorposts of every Hebrew house on the night that the angel of death passed over Egypt. The firstborn son of every home without the blood of the lamb was thus met with death.

The deliverance of the Jews from Egypt was a foreshadowing of the Christian Pasch, when, through the Sacrifice of the true Lamb of God and the application of the merits of Christ's Precious Blood, mankind would be freed from the bondage of the devil and of sin. In the early Church, Good Friday was called the Pasch of the Crucifixion. Easter Day was called the Pasch of the Resurrection. The following Sundays were referred to as "after the Pasch."

The main feature of the Jewish Pasch was the sacrificial meal, which ended with the eating of the Paschal Lamb, followed by the seven-day Feast of Unleavened Bread. At the time of Jesus Christ, the Passover meal united the Jewish family from sunset to midnight on the fifteenth of Nisan (Nisan in the Jewish calendar was the seventh month of the civil and first of the religious year, usually coinciding with parts of March and April). Its celebration by the Savior, a memorial of the Old Passover feast of the Old Covenant, was the occasion for His instituting the Eucharistic worship and the priesthood of the New Covenant. This Eucharist will assure our Passover into Heaven.

The mystery of the Eucharist is so great that it cannot be explained in a single concept. The very context of the giving of the Eucharist reminds us of the structure of a meal. " 'Take, eat.' ... And he took a cup... gave it to them, saying: 'Drink of it, all of you' " (Matt. 26:26–27). The Eucharist is the sacrificial meal bringing us to union with God and union with our fellow men; we enter into a profound communion with the Lord Jesus. He abides in us and we in Him (see John 15:4).

Israel under the Old Covenant had communion sacrifices in which part of the victim was offered to God and another part given to the people to eat. In this way Israel expressed its desire to be one with God. When Moses ratified the covenant with Israel, Moses, Aaron, and his two sons Nadab and Abihu, along with the seventy elders, went up the mountain. Then in a very rare statement in the entire Old Testament, we are told, "they beheld God, and ate and drank" (Exod. 24:11). At the birth of God's Chosen People, the meal on the mountain prefigured the fellowship that God desired to establish with all His children. This is accomplished today at the Lord's altar where we eat and drink in His sight, and enter into fellowship, sharing the very life of God Himself.

The narratives of the Last Supper help us understand that the Eucharist is not just a meal but a sacrifice: (Matt. 26:26–28; Mark 14:22–23; Luke 22:19–20; 1 Cor. 11:23–25). Jesus is the Suffering Servant who offers Himself in sacrifice, pouring out His blood for the New Covenant.

The Sacrifice of the Cross begins at the Supper (1 Cor. 11:26). In the Upper Room, Jesus makes present in an unbloody manner His self-offering, which takes place physically on the Cross on Good Friday. In every celebration of the Eucharist, Jesus Christ makes present to us that same sacrifice offered once for all on Golgotha. *The*

Eucharist is not a sacrifice repeated again and again; rather, it is the one same Sacrifice of the Cross made present to us in every age as it is always present in Heaven.

St. John Chrysostom wrote:

> For when you see the Lord sacrificed, laid upon the altar, and the priest standing and praying over the victim, and all the worshippers empurpled with that precious blood, can you then think that you are still among men, and standing upon the earth? Are you not on the contrary, straightway translated to heaven, and casting out every carnal thought from the soul, do you not, with disembodied spirit and pure reason, contemplate the things which are in heaven? (*De Sacerdotio*, III, 4)

Jesus Christ, who will come at the end of time, comes to us in every Holy Eucharist. The Eucharist draws us up into Heaven. We enter the Holy of Holies in every Eucharist, the Body of Christ, and we are sanctified (see Heb. 9:11–14).

How awesome that the very Body and Blood Jesus offered at the Last Supper and physically on the Cross Good Friday is the very same Body and Blood of Jesus now in Heaven and which is offered to us at every Sacrifice of the Mass. It perpetuates all this and what was offered once by Christ the High Priest is eternally offered and accepted in Heaven in the eternal now. Into this we enter at Mass. This is the Mystery of Faith. This is the reality of the Eucharist. *Heaven and earth are united at every celebration of the Eucharist.*

A true sacrifice presupposes a priesthood. Before there is a true sacrifice there must be a priest commissioned to offer it in the name of all. In the Old Testament, under the Jewish Law, the priest was chosen by God from the tribe of Aaron. He was consecrated to service in the Temple with a special anointing. The priesthood of Jesus Christ is transcendent and totally unique. At the moment of the Incarnation, the second Person of the Most Blessed Trinity, who is the person of the Word, was hypostatically united to humanity, to a human nature.

The High Priest Jesus Christ is the incarnate Word; He is "the Christ," which means "the Anointed" one. He did not have an outward anointing such as that which designated the consecrating of kings, prophets, and priests of the Old Testament. Rather it was the Divinity outpoured on the humanity of Jesus Christ, making His human nature one with the Son of God. He became the God-Man, and at the very moment of His conception in the Virgin Mary by the Holy Spirit, Jesus is "anointed," at that moment, consecrated and constituted priest and pontiff. He thus becomes mediator between God and man. He is one with the Father. His Father thus ordains Him supreme High Priest.

"So also Christ did not exalt himself to be made a high priest, but was appointed by him who said to him, 'Thou art my Son, today I have begotten thee'; as he says also in another place, 'Thou art a priest for ever, after the order of Melchizedek'" (Heb. 5:5–6).

Being the Son of God the Father, Jesus Christ the High Priest is able to offer sacrifice worthy of the infinite God. He is the eternal High Priest because the union of His Divinity and humanity in the Incarnation, is the union anointing Him pontiff, which is indissoluble. St. Paul says: "But he [Jesus] holds his priesthood permanently, because he continues for ever" (Heb. 7:24).

St. Paul recalled the mysterious person of Melchizedek, who appears in the Old Testament and then disappears from Scripture, at least in action. He offered bread and wine, and his name means "King of justice," and Scripture says he was "King of Salem," which means "King of peace." He prefigures Jesus Christ, who offers yet today as He did at the Last Supper His sacrifice through the use of bread and wine.

"Every high priest ... is appointed ... to offer gifts and sacrifices for sins" (Heb. 5:1).

Priesthood and Eucharist Go Together

The first men, conscious of God, offered fruits and immolated the best of their flocks so as to testify that God was their Supreme Master in all things. As divine revelation was given, God gave the forms and norms for sacrifice in the Mosaic Law. First there were holocausts, sacrifices of adoration. The victim was entirely consumed. There were then peace offerings of thanksgiving or petition: a part of the victim was burned, another part reserved for the priests, and a third part attributed to those for whom the sacrifice was being offered. Finally there were expiatory sacrifices for sin.

St. Paul informs us that all these forms of sacrifice were only symbolic. They represented the sacrifice of infinite value to give glory to God and wash mankind of sin, that is, the sacrifice to come of Jesus Christ on the Cross. Of all these Old Covenant figures the high point was the sacrifice of expiation, which was offered only once a year by the high priest. He acted in the name of all the people of Israel. The victim was substituted for the people.

In this yearly sacrifice of expiation, a victim was presented to God by the high priest. He was robed in priestly vestments; he placed his hands upon the victim while the people remained prostrate in adoration. This represented that the victim was substituted for the faithful. It represented them before God, laden with the sins of the people. The victim was then immolated, laid upon the pile and burnt. The sacrifice was seen as ascending to the throne of God and was a symbol of offering themselves. The high priest, having sprinkled the horns of the altar with the blood of the victim, would then enter into the Holy of Holies to sprinkle the blood likewise before the Ark of the Covenant, considered the special presence of God. As a consequence of this sacrifice, God would renew His covenant of friendship He had made with His Chosen People.

All these forms of striking or renewing God's covenant with His people passed away with Christ's self-sacrifice.

Jesus has obtained a more excellent ministry now, just as he is mediator of a better covenant, founded on better promises. If that First Covenant had been faultless, there would have been no place for a second one. But God, finding fault with them, says: "Days are coming, says the Lord, when I will make a New Covenant with the House of Israel and with the House of Judah. It will not be like the Covenant I made with their fathers the day I took them by the hand to lead them forth from the land of Egypt."...

But when Christ came as High Priest of the good things which have come to be, he entered once for all into the sanctuary, passing through the greater and more perfect tabernacle not made by hands, that is, not belonging to this creation. He entered, not with the blood of goats and calves, but with his own Blood, and achieved eternal redemption....

This is why he is mediator of a New Covenant; since his death has taken place for deliverance from transgressions committed under the First Covenant, those who are called may receive the promised eternal inheritance (see Heb. 8:6–9; 9:11–12, 15).

Indeed, priesthood and Eucharist go together.

9

Eucharistic Adoration

Adoration of Our Divine Lord and Savior was spoken of in chapter 4 of this volume. However, adoration is so important we here extend its consideration further.

The Church desires that we devoutly look at the Most Blessed Sacrament and adore Jesus Christ, present in all His Godhead. We there adore the entire Blessed Trinity present in the Eucharist. Where one Person of the Trinity is present the other two Persons must also be present, for the three Persons of God are non-divisible. God is never partly present. God is present in all three Divine Persons in virtue of the humanity of Jesus Christ, whose Person is God the Son.

At the elevation of the Sacred Host, we should look up at the Host and whisper, "My Lord and my God." Pope St. Pius X granted an indulgence to all the faithful who would look at the Sacred Host with faith, devotion, and love, either at the elevation of the Mass or when solemnly exposed in the monstrance, whispering, "My Lord and my God."

Would that all parents would teach their children, even before they begin grade one, the practice of adoring the God-Man, Jesus Christ with the words, "My Lord and my God," every time they witness the elevation at Mass. The author of this book was taught the practice from his earliest years and attributes his faith and love for Jesus in the Most Blessed Sacrament to this simple devotion.

Eucharist

We have the Apostle Thomas to thank for the words of adoration, "My Lord and my God." Thomas was slow to believe when he heard that Jesus had risen from the dead. He said that he would not believe until he could put his fingers in the place of the nails and his hand into His side: "Now Thomas, one of the twelve, called the Twin, was not with them when Jesus came. So the other disciples told him, 'We have seen the Lord.' But he said to them, 'Unless I see in his hands the print of the nails, and place my finger in the mark of the nails, and place my hand in his side, I will not believe'" (John 20:24–25).

Obviously the other apostles who had been present behind locked doors for fear of the Jews on the evening of the first Easter Sunday had told Thomas that Jesus had risen from the dead and had retained the marks of crucifixion. Jesus had appeared to them, coming right through the doors and standing before them, showed them His hands and His side that bore, now glorified, the wounds from the nails and the spear rammed through His sacred side. They knew that Jesus thus gave evidence that He was the same Jesus taken captive and nailed to the Cross and there died. They rejoiced that He had risen and that it was He who appeared to them saying, "Peace be with you."

It was on this evening of the very day He rose from the dead that Jesus breathed on them and said: "Receive the Holy Spirit. If you forgive the sins of any, they are forgiven; if you retain the sins of any, they are retained" (John 20:22–23). Those words of the resurrected Jesus initiated the Catholic practice of the Sacrament of Reconciliation, commonly known as *Confession*. Jesus would act through His apostles and their successors to forgive sin just as He gave them the power to consecrate bread and wine into His Body and Blood when He said: "Do this in remembrance of me" (Luke 22:19).

Now that He had redeemed mankind by His suffering, the shedding of His blood, and His death on the Cross, Jesus gives His Church the power to forgive sin also in His name. He had merited the forgiveness of sin on Calvary. Now He bestows the power of His redemption to forgive sins to His apostles, the first bishops and priests: "Receive the Holy Spirit. If you forgive men's sins, they are forgiven them" The Catholic Church teaches that if one of Her members is conscious of having committed a mortal sin since their last good confession, they must repent and go to Confession before receiving the Lord's Body, Blood, Soul, and Divinity in Holy Communion.

Growth in grace comes especially by participating in the Sacrifice of the Mass and the sacraments. After the Mass and the reception of Holy Communion, adoration of Jesus Christ in the Most Blessed Sacrament where He is united to the entire Blessed Trinity is a major way to grow in grace while giving glory to God.

Fr. Lukas Etlin, O.S.B., born in Sarnen, Switzerland, on February 28, 1864, and most devoted to faith and love for Jesus Christ in the Most Blessed Sacrament, gives the account he received from the Most Reverend Mermillod. Fr. Etlin, so devoted to love and adoration of the Most Blessed Sacrament, was killed in a car accident the very month and year the author of this book was born. And so his account touches me deeply as I hope it will readers.

The saintly Archbishop Mermillod told Fr. Etlin that while he was still vicar at Geneva, he was instrumental in converting a Protestant without knowing it. This was by merely making the genuflection reverently before the Most Blessed Sacrament, as every Catholic should do upon entering the Church or before leaving it. The genuflection should be made whenever passing before the tabernacle. In his book *The Holy Eucharist*, Fr. Etlin said:

> He [Mermillod] had the pious custom of paying a last visit to the Most Blessed Sacrament every evening in order to attend to the perpetual light and to see if the doors were locked and

to assure himself that no one was hidden in the church, for he feared that a sacrilegious robbery might be committed. When he had carefully looked after everything, he knelt on the altar steps for a short time, after which he made a reverent genuflection, kissed the floor as a sign of profound reverence before the Most Holy Sacrament and then returned home.

One evening … he finished his devotions as usual. Upon rising from his knees, he was startled by a noise. Suddenly the door of a confessional opened and a very distinguished lady came forth. "What are you doing here at this hour, Lady?" asked Mermillod.

"I am a Protestant, as you know," she answered. "I have been present at the sermons you have given during Lent on the Real Presence of Jesus Christ in the Sacrament of the Altar. Your arguments have convinced me of the truth of this doctrine. Only one doubt remained, and that was … does he himself believe what he says? I wished to see if, when alone or in secret, you would conduct yourself before the Holy Eucharist as one who believed in It, and I had firmly resolved to be converted if your conduct corresponded with your words. I came, I have seen, I believe."

This lady became one of the most zealous Catholics of Geneva.

It is the author's practice, not only to genuflect when entering the Chapel where is the Most Blessed Sacrament, but in doing so to pray: "Blood and Water which gushed forth from the side of Jesus as a fountain of mercy for us, I place my trust in You." Other times I adore with the words: "Most Holy Trinity, Father, Son, and Holy Spirit, I adore You profoundly, and I offer You the Most Precious Body, Blood, Soul, and Divinity of Jesus Christ, present in all the tabernacles of the world, in reparation for the outrages, sacrileges and indifferences by which He is offended. By the infinite merits of the Most Sacred Heart of Jesus and through the Immaculate Heart of Mary, I beg the conversion of poor sinners."

Another prayer I love to say often before the Most Blessed Sacrament is: "My God, I believe, I adore, I hope, and I love You! I ask pardon for those who do not believe, do not adore, do not hope, and do not love You."

Also, "O Most Holy Trinity, I adore You! My God, My God, I love You in the Most Blessed Sacrament."

St. Ignatius had the practice of saying: "Jesus in the Tabernacle is my God and my All! He is my Heaven on earth."

St. Crescentia of Kaufbeuren often said: "Two things constitute my Heaven on earth: The holy Will of God and the Most Blessed Sacrament!" St. Francis Xavier, after a long day's work for the salvation of souls, would frequently spend the entire night in prayer before the Most Blessed Sacrament.

The same is true of one closer to our own day. The Capuchin priest, Blessed Fr. Solanus Casey (1870–1957), who grew up in a family of ten boys and six girls on a Wisconsin farm along the banks of the Mississippi. At times he would spend the entire night before the Most Blessed Sacrament. Fr. Benedict Groeschel, C F.R., tells how years ago at St. Bonaventure Friary, Detroit, Michigan, late during the night, when he himself could not sleep, something like two in the morning, he had entered the chapel and turned on the lights over the tabernacle to see Fr. Solanus Casey in ecstasy before the Most Blessed Sacrament, totally unaware of his surroundings other than the Divine Presence. Yet, Fr. Solanus, a simple man, was a simple priest, not a man of letters, although he sometimes wrote like a poet. He was ordained a priest "simplex" — not permitted to hear confessions or preach. Yet, because of his saintly virtues, thousands flocked to this simple priest who was assigned the role of porter. Many miraculous healings took place through his intercession.

According to Fr. Groeschel, people spoke of him as "the brother who says Mass." The Fr. Solanus Casey's love and devotion for the Real Divine Presence was unto spending the whole night sometimes before the Most Blessed Sacrament, even unto ecstasy at times.

St. Francis Borgia would go to the church seven times each day to adore the Real Presence; St. Mary Magdalene de' Pazzi, thirty-three times; St. Ignatius and St. Stanislaus Kostka would spend all their free time before the tabernacle adoring their God. When St. Vincent de Paul would go on visits to the poor and suffering, he entered every church along the way to adore Jesus and the Most Blessed Trinity in the Holy Eucharist. St. Leonard of Port Maurice and St. Benedict Labre, whenever they arrived at a city, would direct their first steps to a church where was the Most Blessed Sacrament.

St. John Bosco, who lived in the nineteenth century, known as a patron saint of youth, when he was ordained made the resolution to visit his Lord frequently in the Most Blessed Sacrament. He became an apostle to youth under his care and influenced them with no compulsion to follow his example in frequent visits of adoration to their Eucharistic God.

St. Dominic, founder of the Dominicans, went to the church for adoration a number of times each day. Tradition recounts that on St. Mary Magdalen's day, in the year 1206, St. Dominic was walking at nightfall on the way from Fanjeaux, in the south of France, to Prouilhe, pausing on the hill to contemplate the magnificent panorama stretching out before his eyes. Here he retired, like his Divine Master, to pray and make supplication for sinners. With all the ardor of his soul, he implored guidance from on high for a project he had in mind: how to provide a secure refuge for the young maidens who, by his preaching, were being converted from heresy to the true Faith.

Eucharistic Adoration

The Lord answered his anguished prayer in a marvelous manner. Suddenly, the clouds opened and a globe of fire emerged, circled, and swooped down and remained poised over the ancient chapel of Our Lady of Prouilhe. It was the sign of God for which St. Dominic prayed, the Seignadou, as the place is still known today. As if to reassure him, the same extraordinary phenomenon was repeated on the following two nights, designating the cradle of the feminine branch of the great Order of Preachers that he was soon to bring into existence.

St. Dominic hesitated no longer. He set about building a modest habitation in Prouilhe where, on November 22, 1206, he installed the first community of nine members, whom he associated with himself, the "holy preacher." On December 27 he enclosed the sisters and gave them a simple habit, a white tunic, and black cappa and veil, and later the white scapular of the Dominican Order.

Thus St. Dominic, beginning with the contemplative nuns, was assured of an apostolate of prayer and penance to draw divine blessings on the labors of the Preachers of men he would found ten years later. The Queen of Heaven inspired him to undertake another crusade, preaching the mysteries of salvation to his hearers, who prayed the Lord's Prayer and the angelic salutation of the Ave Maria, which blossomed into the devotion of the Holy Rosary.

To combat the errors of the Albigensian heresy, which was propagated in the region of Albi — hence its name — St. Dominic gave himself, day and night, to preaching, prayer, and penance. After Prouilhe, he chose Toulouse for the center of action, gathering his first sixteen male disciples and forming with them the first Community of Preachers. Thus the Order of St. Dominic was born, approved by the Holy See in 1216, ten years after the first seedling had been planted in Prouilhe.

Yet today, there continues the Dominican Nuns of Perpetual Rosary. At Fatima, daily they have exposition of Jesus in the Most Blessed Sacrament for adoration in the monstrance in the Monastery of Pius

XII, and as in other areas of the world, at least some of them are praying the Rosary constantly around the clock.

Shrine of the Most Blessed Sacrament, Hanceville, Alabama

St. Clare was born at the end of the twelfth century in Assisi, Italy and was advised by St. Francis of Assisi. She expressed to him her desire of becoming the spouse of Christ. He first sent her to the Benedictine nuns. But then Clare's sister Agnes wanted to join her. St. Francis placed them in a small house adjacent to the Church of St. Damian, and soon their mother and many other persons joined them. Their rule entailed austerities unknown until then in monasteries for women. They walked barefoot, slept on the ground, observed perpetual abstinence from meat, and made poverty and adoring Jesus in the Most Blessed Sacrament the basis of their lives.

The extraordinary devotion of St. Clare to the Most Blessed Sacrament was rewarded by a miracle. On the day when the Saracens, who were besieging Assisi, tried to enter the Convent of St. Damian, she met them at the door holding the monstrance with the Most Blessed Sacrament and put them to flight.

On August 11, 1253, St. Clare was visited by a choir of virgins in white robes, among whom was one who surpassed in beauty all the others, and she went to meet her spouse. Two years later she was canonized by Pope Alexander IV.

The Poor Clare Nuns of Perpetual Adoration today are a continuation of the Eucharistic love, devotion, and adoration of St. Clare and her sisters in religious life, in their love and spirit of Eucharistic adoration.

Mother Angelica, who founded Eternal Word Television Network (EWTN), which reaches millions throughout the world, together with the Monastery of Our Lady of the Angels, established and had built the adjoining Shrine of the Most Blessed Sacrament. Her Poor Clare Nuns of Perpetual Adoration are in adoration around the clock, twenty-four hours a day. The main church has a monstrance seven and a half feet tall. Pilgrims come from all over America, sometimes from other countries. Their faith is revitalized. Many return again and again.

I wrote this book near that Monastery of Our Lady of the Angels, where there are approximately forty-five nuns (professed or in formation) of the Poor Clare Sisters of Perpetual Adoration. They have sent nuns to other states to start or revitalize Poor Clare communities. Recently, one of their sisters went to France.

It is my privilege as a priest to offer the Holy Sacrifice of the Mass daily in the lower church of this Shrine of the Most Blessed Sacrament, also to spend some time daily in Eucharistic adoration in the upper church. Often Catholics, after the Mass, desire to speak to me, or seek where confessions are heard. Their faith becomes alive again or is strengthened.

Pilgrims come to the shrine here to adore Jesus and the Most Blessed Trinity in their special presence through the Most Blessed Sacrament. As a senior priest, offering Mass at the Shrine of the Most Blessed Sacrament seven days a week, I can attest that many conversions take place at this Shrine.

St. Vincent de Paul became successively a parish priest and chaplain to the galley slaves. St. Francis de Sales entrusted to him later the spiritual direction of the nuns of the Visitation. Preaching especially to country people, he founded members of a congregation under the title of Priests of the Mission, or Lazarists. They made a special vow to undertake this apostolic work: he sent them to preach missions and to establish seminaries. While especially known for his concern for the poor, St. Vincent de Paul entered every church along his way to visit and adore the Most Blessed Sacrament. If the church happened to be locked, he would perform his devotions outside at the door.

In order to help poor foundlings, young girls whose virtue was exposed to danger, and others insane, invalid, or sick, he founded, in conjunction with St. Louise de Marillac, the Congregation of the Sisters of Charity. After a life reminiscent of the apostolate of St. Paul the Apostle, and which caused Pope Leo XII to proclaim him the special patron of all charitable associations, St. Vincent died in 1660 at St. Lazarus's house in Paris.

For centuries we see that the great saints recognized by the Catholic Church had a profound love and sense of adoration of Our Lord in the Most Blessed Sacrament. In our own times there are still many who find their Heaven on earth before the Most Blessed Sacrament.

St. Mother Teresa of Calcutta, founder of the Missionary Sisters of Charity, was described in *Time* magazine, while she was still living, in an article with the headline, "Saints Among Us." I share here some quotes from Mother Teresa, which I collected while she was still living on this earth:

> Where do our Sisters get this joy, this happiness, to be able to continue to do this kind of work [with the poor] day after day? It is true, it is labor; it is not only work — it is hard labor. But we wouldn't be able to do it unless we had Mass and Holy Communion in the morning. I remember last year or so when the Prime Minister of Yemen asked for our Sisters to come there, I made only one condition: I can only give you the Sisters if you allow a priest to come. For without Jesus I cannot send them. He accepted. So now after many years, there is Mass and Holy Communion in Yemen, there is a tabernacle, surrounded with Moslems who previously had not had a sign of Christianity. Now there is a living God amongst them. I know I would not be able to work one week if it were not for that continual force coming from Jesus in the Blessed Sacrament. He is so lovable and so easily approached.

Eucharistic Adoration

A few days ago one of our Brothers came to me in great distress. He said, "My vocation is to serve the lepers and the dying." (We are taking care of about 46,000 lepers.) After listening to him I said, "Your vocation is to belong to Jesus, and because you belong to Jesus He wants you to put your love for Him in action in serving the lepers." Our love for Christ in action is the service of our poor.

The other day a Hindu gentleman came to our home for the dying. He said, "The presence of the work, the actions of the Sisters radiating the joy and compassion of Christ, make me feel that God is — that God loves the world — that Christ has come once more into this world and He is going about doing good." This comment from a Hindu who found Christ in the simple work of the Sisters is a tremendous grace. *That is why we try to pray our work by doing it with Jesus, by doing it for Jesus and by doing it to Jesus.*

One time when Mother Teresa came to the United States she said: "I wouldn't be able to work one week if it were not for that continual force coming from Jesus in the Blessed Sacrament." Each day she and her Sisters begin and end their day before Jesus in the Most Blessed Sacrament. Besides Holy Mass, they spend a Holy Hour in silent adoration each day before their Eucharistic Lord.

The soul has to be heated with the fire of grace, the presence of the Holy Spirit, of Jesus abiding within it. This growing intensity comes through fervent and frequent Holy Communion. Otherwise there will be lukewarmness and eventually loss of faith and love for God. If fervent and frequent Holy Communion is neglected for a length of time, the heat of the soul goes out of the soul.

Even if a soul is frequent in the reception of the Holy Eucharist, but often cold water comes in by way of entertaining sinful thoughts and the reception is routine, with hardly a thought to what one is doing, whom one is receiving, the soul will gain little. One who is receiving with no fervor and is not open to the interior participation required for fruitful participation in the Mass and sacraments, will prevent what Jesus intends to accomplish in us.

The fact that hundreds of Communions do not produce sanctity for those of indifferent spirituality does not distract from the truth that here is a plenitude of love and grace to be obtained, and already contained, in the Holy Eucharist. One Holy Communion received by a soul with great faith and love could be sufficient to make a great saint. Jesus has willed that the life of a Christian should be a Eucharistic life.

Our life *does* depend upon the Holy Eucharist. For the Christian there is no religion as God wills it apart from Eucharistic religion. Our spiritual life must be fed by the Bread of Life. God's gift to us in the Holy Eucharist is love as He gives Himself. This is true because the nature of God is Love. When God communicates Himself to man, He is actualizing to the fullest degree His love for His creatures made in His own image and likeness.

Sr. Lucia of Fatima wrote, under obedience to her bishop, of the angelic and Marian apparitions. The angel brought them the Eucharist in the fall of 1916, and when Mary, the Mother of God, appeared on May 13, 1917, the *feast of Our Lady of the Eucharist*, at that first apparition of Our Lady, while pronouncing the words, "the grace of God," Our Lady opened her hands for the first time. Sr. Lucia described the experience of Our Lady opening her hands, as "shedding on us a light so intense that it seemed as a reflex glancing from her hands and penetrating to the inmost recesses of our hearts, making us see ourselves in God." As a result, the children fell to their knees, repeating, "Oh, most Holy Trinity, I adore Thee! My God, my God, I love Thee in the most Blessed Sacrament!"

The ultimate purpose of receiving Jesus Christ in Holy Communion is eternal life in Heaven. Jesus made that very clear in telling us we could not have the eternal and divine life needed for Heaven unless we ate His Body and drank His Blood: "Truly, truly, I say to you, unless you eat the flesh of the Son of man and drink his blood, you have no life in you; he who eats my flesh and drinks my blood has eternal life, and I will raise him up at the last day" (John 6:53–54). Jesus kept repeating Himself on the points He was making that He really is the Living Bread come down from Heaven. "I am the bread of life.... I am the living bread which came down from heaven; if any one eats of this bread, he will live for ever" (John 6:48, 51).

Jesus' first public miracle at Cana in Galilee is rich in doctrine. We can only hint at the deep implications here. "On the third day there was a marriage at Cana in Galilee, and the mother of Jesus was there; Jesus also was invited to the marriage, with his disciples. When the wine failed, the mother of Jesus said to him, 'They have no wine.' And Jesus said to her, 'O woman, what have you to do with me? My hour has not yet come.' His mother said to the servants, 'Do whatever he tells you'" (John 2:1–5).

Sometimes the Wedding Feast of Cana is spoken of as the beginning of Jesus' public ministry. His public ministry, however, really begins at His baptism. This is not the same as the Sacrament of Baptism. Jesus is taking the sins of the world upon Himself and will do penance and make reparation for all of humanity as the Second Adam, the new Head of the human race. Thus He permits Himself to have the baptism of John. At His baptism by John in the River Jordan: "And when he came up out of the water, immediately he saw the heavens opened and the Spirit descending upon him like a dove; and a voice came from heaven, 'Thou art my beloved Son; with thee I am well pleased'" (Mark 1:9–11).

This was the beginning of His public ministry when God the Father gives public testimony by the sign of the dove and the sound of the Father's voice that Jesus is the Son of God; that Jesus is the Christ, the Anointed One. Jesus then goes into the desert to make special reparation for mankind, and His supreme act of reparation, repairing the bridge between man and God, will be His sacrificial death on the Cross. God the Father will give testimony, the sign that He accepts this redemptive act of His Son, by raising Him from the dead, the Resurrection. Both the sacrificial death and the resurrected Christ are contained in the Eucharist. The infinite act of adoration given on Calvary, confirmed as accepted by the Father on the first Easter Sunday, are contained, perpetuated in the Eucharist.

The miracle of changing water into wine is done at the request of the Blessed Mother. Calling His Mother "woman" is entirely courteous as this form of address was normally given by Jesus to women He encountered during His ministry (See Matt. 15:28; Luke 13:12). Mary is called "woman" by Jesus as He hung dying on the Cross. The mother of the Messiah in Revelation 12:1–5 is described as the "woman clothed with the sun." We are thus reminded of the symbolic reference to Eve, "the woman" of Genesis. At the Fall of our first parents, God in consequent punishment, yet in promising a redeemer, said: "I will put enmity between you and the woman, and between your seed and her seed" (Gen. 3:15).

We can appreciate in looking at Sacred Scripture as a whole that Mary and the Eucharist are closely associated as this "woman" conceived the human nature of the Son of God, who is present in the Eucharist and whom we receive in Holy Communion. It was our Blessed Mother's intercession that influenced Jesus to work His first public miracle, which foreshadowed the Eucharist. Water is changed into wine at a wedding feast; at the banquet of the Last Supper, Jesus will change wine into His Precious Blood. It all foreshadowed the heavenly banquet for which we need the Eucharist to enter. "My hour has not yet come." The hour is the hour of Jesus' Passion, death,

Resurrection, and Ascension (John 13:1), all mysteries contained in the Eucharist.

The richness of doctrine in the Cana miracle also involves the sanctification of marriage, Jesus raising marriage to the dignity of a sacrament at Cana. Worthy participation and reception of the Eucharist is required for marriage partners to grow in holiness.

God first loves us. His love comes to us not because we first love Him. God loves us first and elicits our absolute dependence and surrender. His mercy calls us to never hesitate to ask pardon for ourselves and for others. The Incarnation did not begin or end at a certain hour in time. Its work is continued in the Eucharist. While this is true in the Most Blessed Sacrament in the tabernacle or in the monstrance where the God-Man is publicly adored and loved, it is more true and efficacious when the Most Blessed Sacrament is received into our bodies and souls. The benefits of the Incarnation reach their deepest and fullest expression in Holy Communion received in the context of participating in the Sacrifice of the Mass. The fruits of adoring Jesus in the Most Blessed Sacrament are great. Still, the primary purposes for the institution of the Holy Eucharist were to perpetuate Jesus' sacrifice and to feed His people with His Body, Blood, Soul, and Divinity.

God is the Alpha and the Omega. Jesus is the First and the Last, the Beginning and the End. We try to become holy by pleasing God with worship that He has given us in instituting the Holy Eucharist. But even the desire to pray, to worship, comes from God. The desire to offer the Eucharist to the Father at the Sacrifice of the Mass is an actual grace from God as is the desire to receive Jesus in Holy Communion. The same is true to desire to adore Jesus in the Most Blessed Sacrament. We must respond of our own free will. When we respond in faith and love to such callings, we not only please God but grow in sanctifying grace.

The Holy Eucharist is Christ's means to enable us to embody the words of St. Paul: "It is no longer I who live, but Christ who lives in me" (Gal. 2:20).

St. John Vianney spoke frequently about the Most Blessed Sacrament:

> In heaven, where we shall be glorious and triumphant, we shall see Him in all His glory. If He presented Himself before us in that glory now, we should not dare to approach Him, but He hides Himself like a person in a prison and seems to say, "You do not see Me, but that does not matter; ask of Me all you wish and I will grant it." He is there in the Sacrament of His love, sighing and interceding incessantly with His Father for sinners.
>
> To what outrages does He not expose Himself, that He may remain in our midst! He is there to console us, and therefore we ought to visit Him. How pleasing to Him is the short quarter of an hour that we steal from our occupations, from something of no consequence, to come and pray to Him, to visit Him, to console Him for all the outrages He receives! When He sees pure souls coming eagerly to Him, He smiles upon them.... They come with that simplicity which pleases Him so much, to ask pardon for all sinners, for the outrages of so many ungrateful souls.
>
> What happiness do we not feel in the presence of God, when we find ourselves alone at His feet before the holy Tabernacle! Come, my soul, redouble thy fervor; thou art alone adoring thy God; His eyes rest upon thee alone. This good Savior is so full of love for us, that He seeks us everywhere.
>
> As, if we had the eyes of Angels with which to see our Lord Jesus Christ who is here present on this altar and who is looking

at us, how we should love Him! We should never more wish to part from Him; we should wish to remain always at His feet. It would be a foretaste of heaven. All else would become insipid to us. But see, it is faith we lack. We are poor blind people; we have a mist before our eyes. Faith alone can dispel this mist.

Presently, my children, when I shall hold Our Lord in my hands, when the good God blesses you, ask Him to open the eyes of your heart; say to Him with the blind man of Jericho, "O Lord, make me to see!" If you say to Him sincerely, "Make me to see!" you will certainly obtain what you desire, because He wishes nothing but your happiness. He has His hands full of graces seeking someone to whom to distribute them, but alas, no one will have them! Oh, indifference! Oh, ingratitude! My children, we are most unhappy not to understand these things! We shall understand them well one day, but it will then be too late.

In the last encyclical of the twenty-seven-year reign of Pope John Paul II, *The Church of the Eucharist* (*Ecclesia de Eucharistia*), this great pope states in its introduction:

> The Church draws her life from the Eucharist. This truth does not simply express a daily experience of faith, but recapitulates *the heart of the mystery of the Church*.... The Church was born of the Paschal Mystery. For this very reason the Eucharist, which is in an outstanding way the sacrament of the Paschal Mystery, *stands at the center of the Church's life*.... In the Paschal Event and the Eucharist which makes it present throughout the centuries, there is a truly enormous "capacity" which embraces all of history as the recipient of the grace of the redemption. This amazement should always fill the Church assembled for the celebration of the Eucharist.

Eucharist

Again we review what many readers may have heard St. Mother Teresa say repeatedly while still on earth about the Eucharist: "Where do our Sisters get this joy, this happiness, to be able to continue to do this kind of work [with the poor] day after day? It is true, it is labor; it is not only work, it is hard labor. But we wouldn't be able to do it unless we had Mass and Holy Communion in the morning." And yet, in the summer of 2007, when the tenth anniversary of her death came, the secular news media was filled with reports about the lack of faith Mother Teresa experienced, even at Mass and before the Holy Eucharist. Before we attempt to explain, here is a brief review of her life.

"A Calling within a Calling"

Mother Teresa of Calcutta (1910–1997) was beatified on October 19, 2003.

Agnes Bojaxhiu was born in Skopje, Yugoslavia on August 27, 1910. Five children were born to Nikola and Dronda Bojaxhiu but only three survived. Agnes was the youngest, with an older sister, Aga, and brother, Lazar. Nikola was a contractor, working with a partner in a successful construction business. He was heavily involved in the politics of the day. Lazar tells of his father's sudden and shocking death, which may have been due to poisoning because of his political involvements. With his death, life changed overnight as the mother assumed total responsibility for the family, Aga, only fourteen, Lazar, nine, and Agnes, seven.

While much of her young life was centered in the Church, Mother Teresa revealed that it was not until she was eighteen that she ever thought of being a nun. In her early years, however, she was fascinated with stories of missionary life and service.

At eighteen, Agnes chose the Loreto Sisters of Dublin, missionaries and educators founded in the seventeenth century to educate young girls. In 1928, the future Mother Teresa began her religious life in Ireland, far from her family and the life she had known. She never saw her mother again in this life and now spoke a language few understood. A sister novice of this period remembered her as "very small, quiet and shy." Another member of the congregation described her as "ordinary." Mother Teresa always valued her beginnings with the Loreto Sisters and maintained close ties. Unwavering commitment and self-discipline were always a part of her life and stayed with her always.

In 1929, Agnes was sent to Darjeeling, India, to the novitiate of the Sisters of Loreto. In 1931, she made her first vows there, choosing the name Teresa, honoring both saints of the same name, Teresa of Avila and Therese of Lisieux. Finally she was sent to St. Mary's High School for girls in a district of Calcutta to teach history and geography. This she enjoyed for the next fifteen years. It was in the protected environment of this school for the daughters of the wealthy that Teresa's new "vocation" developed and grew. Then Teresa received her "second calling" on that fateful day in 1946 when she traveled by train to Darjeeling for a retreat. Jesus appeared to her as a poor man and gave her the call to give her life over to the service of the poor. She called this a "calling within a calling."

Teresa pursued every avenue during the next two years to follow what she "never doubted" was the direction God gave her. She was "to give up even Loreto where I was very happy and to go out in the streets. I heard the call to give up all and follow Christ into the slums to serve Him among the poorest of the poor."

Sr. Teresa had to be released formally, not from her perpetual vows, but from living within the convents of the Sisters of Loreto. She confronted the Church's resistance to forming new religious communities and sought permission from the Archbishop of Calcutta to serve the poor openly on the streets. She had to figure out how to live and work on the streets, without the safety and comfort of the convent. Teresa decided she would set aside the habit she had worn during her years as a Loreto Sister and wear the ordinary dress of an Indian woman: a plane white sari, edged with blue, and sandals.

First Teresa went to Patna for a few months to prepare for her future work by taking a nursing course. In 1948 she received permission from Pius XII to leave her community and live as an independent nun. So back to Calcutta she went and found a small hovel to rent to begin her new undertaking.

Sr. Teresa began by teaching the children of the slums, something she knew well. Without equipment, she made use of what was available — writing in the dirt. She strove to make the children of the poor literate, to teach them basic hygiene. As they grew to know her, she gradually began visiting the poor and ill in their families, and others all crowded together in the surrounding squalid shacks, inquiring about their needs.

Teresa was frequently exhausted as she found a never-ending stream of human needs in the poor. Despite the weariness of her days, she never omitted her prayer, finding it the source of support, strength, and blessing for all her ministry.

Missionaries of Charity Soon Begin

Within a year Sr. Teresa found more help than she anticipated. It seems many were waiting for her example to open their own lives to charity and compassion. Young women came to volunteer their services and later became the core of her Missionaries of Charity. Others offered food, clothing, the use of buildings, medical supplies, and money. As such support and assistance grew, more and more services became possible to huge numbers of suffering people.

Thus, the Missionaries of Charity were born in Calcutta, nourished by the faith, compassion, and commitment of Mother Teresa. They have grown like the mustard seed of the Scriptures to almost five thousand sisters today. Vocations come from all parts of the world, serving those in great need wherever they are found. There are homes for the dying; refuges for the care and teaching of orphans and abandoned children; treatment centers and hospitals for those suffering from leprosy; and centers and refuges for alcoholics, the aged, and street people — an endless list. While much smaller in number, there are also brother and priest divisions of the Missionaries of Charity.

Mother Teresa continued her work among the poorest of the poor until her death in 1997. Always she depended on God for all of her needs. The world was astounded by her care for those usually deemed of little value. In her own eyes she was "God's pencil — a tiny bit of pencil with which He writes what He likes." While countless honors came to her, to honors she was not in the least attracted.

Though frail and bent, with numerous ailments, Mother Teresa always returned to her work, to those who received her compassionate care for more than fifty years. Months before her death, when she became too weak to manage the administrative work, she relinquished the position of head of her Missionaries of Charity. When asked what she thought would happen to her work and religious congregation after she was gone, she replied, "It is His concern."

There are now three known saints with the name Teresa who suffered the dark night of the soul. We can look for intercessors for our faith struggles to St. Teresa of Avila, St. Therese of Lisieux, and St. Mother Teresa of Calcutta who, it seems, suffered that pain of thirst the longest.

Mother Teresa's Long Dark Night Was Strong Faith

Time magazine headlined the long dark night of the soul experienced by St. Mother Teresa this way: "Mother Teresa's Crisis of Faith." The *London Telegraph* and numerous news outlets reported that Mother

Teresa "was tormented by a crisis of belief for 50 years." The mentality of the media was seen in their questions such as, "Can she still be made a saint?" It demonstrated a lack of knowledge regarding the Church's understanding of faith.

In October 2003 Pope St. John Paul II referenced St. Teresa's spiritual struggles at her beatification. It was not in reality lack of faith, but strong faith and love:

> Mother Teresa shared the passion of the Crucified One, particularly during her long years of "interior darkness." In the darkest hours, she clung with even greater tenacity to prayer before the Blessed Sacrament. This harsh spiritual struggle allowed her to identify even more with those she served every day, experiencing the pain and even rejection they felt.

Special interest in this extraordinary founder of the Missionaries of Charity came from the published book, *Mother Teresa: Come Be My Light*. Fr. Brian Kolodiejchuk, postulator for the cause of canonization of the saintly nun, who died in 1997, compiled her letters and writings, including a number that revealed St. Teresa's trials of great spiritual dryness in what theologians call "the dark night of the soul."

While Mother Teresa experienced the silence of God in her soul, even at special prayer times, she demonstrated joyous love through her every action, gesture, and expression. God writes straight with crooked lines. Paradoxically, the divisive aspect of the stories has done what many Church synods could not accomplish in the minds of people. Liberal and traditional Catholics joined forces to correct the record and to recognize Mother Teresa as an example for all people who suffer spiritual loneliness. Millions more can now identify with her in sufferings, physical and spiritual.

While people today try to dispel feelings of loneliness with analysts, medications, or pop spirituality, St. Teresa embraced her loneliness and clung to her faith in Jesus, which, though often devoid of feelings, was solid and profound. What many have failed to notice, in fact, is that a good number of her expressions of solitude are addressed to Jesus Himself. Blessed Teresa converted "her feeling of abandonment by God into an act of abandonment to God." How many times have we gone to Mass, not "feeling it," as some would say. Our lips moving, our gestures mechanical, but we remain distant from the reality of God and His love for us. That is when we prove our inner faith by not giving into temptations to abandon God.

"Without suffering, our work would just be social work, not the work of Jesus Christ, not part of the redemption," said Mother Teresa. Fr. Kolodiejchuk said: "Mother surrendered and accepted the darkness. Fr. Neuner [one of her spiritual directors] helped her to understand it by linking the darkness with her charism, of satiating Jesus' thirst."

She used to say that the greatest poverty was to feel unloved, unwanted, uncared for, and that's exactly what she was experiencing in her relationship with Jesus. Her reparatory suffering, or suffering for others, was part of her living her charism for the poorest of the poor. So for her, the suffering was not only to identify with the physical and material poverty, but even on the interior level, she identified with the unloved, the lonely, the rejected. She gave up her own interior light for those living in darkness, saying, "I know this is only feelings."

In one letter to Jesus, she wrote: "Jesus, hear my prayer — if this pleases you. If my pain and suffering, my darkness and separation gives you a drop of consolation, my own Jesus, do with me as you wish, as long as you wish without a single glance at my feelings and pain." Scholars of mysticism, following St. John of the Cross, easily recognized in the experience of Mother Teresa what is called "the dark night of the soul." Tauler described that stage of the spiritual life this way:

Now, we are abandoned in such a way that we no longer have any knowledge of God and we fall into such anguish so as not to know any more if we were ever on the right path, nor do we know if God does or does not exist, or if we are alive or dead. So that a very strange sorrow comes over us that makes us think that the whole world in its expanse oppresses us. We no longer have any experience or knowledge of God, and even all the rest seems repugnant to us, so that it seems that we are prisoners between two walls.

In an article titled "The 'Atheism' of Mother Teresa," Fr. Raniero Cantalamessa, O.F.M. Cap. (preacher to the papal household), wrote:

> The interminable night of some modern saints is the means of protection invented by God for today's saints who live and work constantly under the spotlight of the media. It is the asbestos suit for the one who must walk amid the flames; it is the insulating material that impedes the escape of the electric current, causing short circuits....
>
> Mother Teresa was able to see her trial ever more clearly as an answer to her desire to share the *sitio* (thirst) of Jesus on the cross: "If my pain and suffering, my darkness and separation give you a drop of consolation, my own Jesus, do with me as you wish.... Please do not take the trouble to return soon. I am ready to wait for you for all eternity."
>
> It would be a serious error to think that the life of these persons was all gloom and suffering.
>
> Deep down in their souls, these persons enjoy a peace and joy unknown by the rest of men, deriving from the certainty, stronger than doubt, of being in the will of God.... The joy and serenity that emanated from Mother Teresa's face was

not a mask, but the reflection of profound union with God in which her soul lived.

Mother's Joy before Her Death

Fr. Benedict J. Groeschel, C.F.R., told of how he saw Mother's joy before her death.

> A few weeks before her death, Mother Teresa was in New York. The sisters very kindly invited me to offer Mass for her the day before she left for Calcutta. It was obvious that she was dying....
>
> After Mass, I met a person I had never known. She was bubbly, exuberant, joyous, and telling Fr. Andrew Apostoli and me of the wonderful growth of the Missionaries of Charity. She was not bragging, but triumphantly rejoicing in the Lord....
>
> As we were leaving, I commented to Fr. Andrew that we would never see her again, that she was obviously beginning to go through the gates of eternity. This is not an unknown phenomenon in the lives of certain mystic saints. They begin to enter eternal life while they are still in this world.
>
> I want many people to know of this triumphant exultation of Mother Teresa in the last days of her life.

Mother Teresa made a private vow in 1942 never to refuse Jesus anything under pain of mortal sin. Then four years later, September 10, Jesus gave her the inspiration to begin the Missionaries of Charity. Jesus spoke clearly by interior locution. In 1946 and 1947, Mother Teresa experienced real intimate union, real contemplative union with God. Her confessor, Fr. van Exem, spoke of her being very close to the state of ecstasy.

Years later, she wrote in letters to Fr. Neuner about this inspiration of Jesus speaking to her. She was moved from Calcutta to a place called Asansol in January 1947, and she says: "There it was, as if Our Lord gave Himself to me in the full. The sweetness and consolation of those past six months passed but too soon."

After That Came the Darkness

Fr. Brian Kolodiejchuk, postulator for her cause, has stated the following:

> When the work started... there was this terrible sense of loss, this untold darkness, this loneliness, this continual longing for God....
>
> In another letter she says she can't be distracted because "my mind and heart are continually with Him." So that's why it's not a crisis of God not existing; it seems to her, "Where did He go?"...
>
> She's feeling rejected and unwanted by the One she loves. So you have to see everything in the context of a love relationship.... She often describes herself as the spouse of Jesus.... So the trial as she's perceiving it is: What happened? Do I have any faith?
>
> It's not that she really doubts, but it seems to her where did the faith go? The love I had and love I was feeling is all gone....
>
> I put a quote from her in the front of the book: "If I ever become a saint, I will surely be one of darkness. I will continue to be absent from heaven to light the light of those in darkness on earth."...
>
> And then, in the midst of this darkness, she'll say ... her mission from heaven is to those in darkness.... In another

letter she says, "If my darkness is a light to others…" It's a kind of paradox: that through darkness she is the light.

Jesus' words to her in 1947 were, "Come, be my light."

Mother Teresa never doubted the Real Presence or the Sacrifice of the Cross perpetuated at Mass. She knew her faith was not founded on feeling or Eucharistic miracles but in belief in the proclamation of Our Lord Jesus which she received with faith through the action of the Holy Spirit. Her ready, simple, and direct answers and statements to everyone, whether the heads of countries, or simple, humble people, the clarity of the truth that echoed from her lips were obviously guided by the Holy Spirit. Her faith did not depend on feelings but on Jesus Christ, true God and true man. In the depths of her soul, she knew and believed: "I wouldn't be able to work one week if it were not for that continual force coming from Jesus in the Blessed Sacrament."

Consider the stories from people who had to do without the Eucharist for months, even years, in concentration camps, Russian prison camps, and the like. It has happened in history in various parts of the world where people were without priests for many years. These people did not attempt arbitrary celebrations of the Eucharist themselves. They waited, they prayed, they longed for the day when they would have again Christ's priest to give them Jesus Christ in the Eucharist. Marvelous stories have come out of concentration camps when a priest prisoner found a piece of bread and a little wine, even fermented from grapes in secret, and consecrated them into the Body and Blood of the Lord and perpetuated His Sacrifice in the midst of their own sacrificial living. These people knew what the Eucharist is and what it means.

Loving God means adoring Him. Adoration or worship at its height is "sacrifice," surrendering of all things to God. When we kneel in adoration before Jesus made present in the Eucharistic Sacrifice, we are in the presence of the resurrected Christ, the heavenly Christ at the right hand of the Father. The Eucharist bears within it the mystery of the Cross and the presence of the resurrected Christ. The Transfiguration of Jesus Christ speaks of who is present in the Eucharist.

It is not all-important that one experiences feelings of exhilaration when in the presence of Jesus Christ in the Eucharist. We should seek and adore the God of consolations, not simply the consolations of God. It may happen to us, as it happened for years to great saints, that like Abraham going to offer sacrifice, we offer not anything prepared by ourselves but what God has provided. Abraham told Isaac that God will provide for the sacrifice. He did not know that God would provide the ram. He trusted God in his heart to take care of him and Isaac. In the dark night of his incomprehension, he knew that God is a loving, providing God. He put his trust in God when he understood nothing. He trusted in the One who seemed to oppress him and called for the sacrifice of what was dearest to him, but he loved God more than what was dearest to him so that he was willing to sacrifice his own son. We must trust God in the dark night of the incomprehensible, God whom we love in the Eucharist.

In the depths of our soul we believe and know that Jesus is present in the Eucharist, and so we adore Jesus and the entire Blessed Trinity there. If He gives us consolations at times, fine, accept them, appreciate them. But believe and adore even when you don't feel it. Then you are most pleasing to God. God rewards not so much His own consolations He gives you, but your own faith, trials, sacrifices, love, when you don't feel His presence.

The God who seems at times to allow torments in our lives is the very One who truly loves us so that He laid down His life for us on the Cross. God allows us to prove our love and faith when trials of darkness beset us. The essence of the Eucharistic Sacrifice is the Sacrifice of Jesus Christ Himself, to whom we must add our own living sacrifice of our bodies and souls.

Eucharistic Adoration

When Jesus Christ was calling me to His holy priesthood and I was a young teenager, I would go to the Church, genuflect, sit there, and experience the power, the presence, the force of Jesus Christ coming from the Most Blessed Sacrament in the tabernacle. How often as a priest have I desired that same experience to be with me often when it was not. But Jesus in the Most Blessed Sacrament is the hidden Jesus. He even keeps Himself hidden within our minds and souls, sometimes for years. But He is then just as real, just as present, and always incomprehensible. He cherishes our love especially when we don't feel His embrace.

10

The Holy Eucharist and the Holy Angels

THE CELESTIAL BEINGS, persons called angels, are always present in adoration wherever the Eucharistic Lord is present. Angels gather about the tabernacle. Before discussing the angels further, we list in brief sentences from defined dogmas of our Catholic Faith regarding Jesus Christ. Scriptural bases for the Church's teachings on Jesus Christ were given in an earlier chapter with many references. Each sentence below was carefully worked out by the authority of Christ's own teaching Church under the protection of the Holy Spirit working through the pope and bishops:

Jesus Christ is true God and true Son of God. Christ took to Himself a real body, not a phantom body. Christ assumed not only a real human body but also a human rational soul. Christ was truly generated and born of the Virgin Mary. The Divine and human natures of Jesus Christ are "hypostatically" united, i.e. joined to each other in one Divine Person, the second Person of the Eternal and Most Blessed Trinity. In the hypostatic union, each of the two natures of Christ continues unimpaired, untransformed, and unmixed with the other. Each of the two natures of Christ has its own natural will and its own natural manner of operation. The hypostatic union of Christ's human nature with the Divine Logos, or Word, took place at the moment of conception in the Blessed Virgin Mary. The hypostatic union can never cease. The hypostatic union was effected by the three Divine Persons acting in common. Only the second Divine Person assumed to Himself a human nature. Not only as God, but also as man, Jesus Christ is God's natural Son. The God-Man, Jesus Christ, is to be worshipped with one single kind of worship, the absolute worship of latria, which is due to God alone. Christ's divine and human characteristics and actions are to be predicated on the one Word Incarnate. Christ being God-Man was free from all sin, original as well as personal. The eternal Son of God became man in order to effect the redemption of men. Fallen man is incapable of redeeming Himself. The God-Man Jesus Christ is the eternal High Priest. Christ offered Himself on the Cross for mankind as a true and proper sacrifice. Christ, by His Sacrifice on the Cross, has redeemed mankind and reconciled us with God. Christ did not die only for the predestined. Christ, by His Passion and death, merited reward from God.

The good holy angels are in fact creatures of love. If one were to see the lowliest among them as he really is, whose nature is higher than our human nature, that one holy angel would be so bright and beautiful and holy that one would think he was seeing God, and the vision might well outdistance our dreams of what the all-holy God is like. "What no eye has seen, nor ear heard, nor the heart of man conceived, what God has prepared for those who love him" (1 Cor. 2:9).

The number of angels is great: "innumerable" (Heb. 12:22), "thousands of thousands" (Rev. 5:11), "legions" (Matt. 26:53). Each good angel is loving and powerful and different in nature from one another. Each angel is always active, not only in the moments when we may become aware of angelic activity.

The angels possess a higher perfection of intellect, will, and power than man (2 Pet. 2:11). The angel wills with all his power. When the angel acts there is no struggle or conflict. He destroys all opposition with irresistible might. Pope St. John Paul II spoke often, as did Pope Benedict XVI, of the need for a new evangelization and civilization of love. The role of the angels will be involved in inflaming the Church with a new fire, new activity, increased knowledge, discernment, and reverence and adoration for the Eucharist.

The angels praise God in Heaven, and they reflect His glory on earth. The angels are created even more in the image of God than are men. The angels are a part of that spiritual communion of God's intellectual Persons, and they act and interact in their relationships, not only with God, but with each other and with us. We are destined for that same place which will be home forever with all the holy angels and saints.

In biblical history, as God begins to form His people from whom the Messiah will come, we discover early on the role that God gives to angels in communicating with mankind.

In the eighteenth chapter of Genesis, we are told how three angels were entertained by Abraham. In them Abraham recognized the Lord coming to his home. From among these angels in visible form as men, one of them said, "I will surely return to you in the spring, and Sarah your wife shall have a son" (Gen. 18:10). Both Sarah and Abraham were advanced in age, normally beyond childbearing years. Abraham, however, now realizes for the first time that he will have a son of Sarah as a miraculous birth is predicted.

Abraham and Sarah, when the time became right, were soon to have their son Isaac, marking the beginning of Abraham becoming the father of a populous nation, and "all the nations of the earth bless themselves, because you [Abraham] have obeyed my voice" (Gen. 22:18). As Abraham accompanies the three angels from his place and looked down toward Sodom, it was revealed to Abraham that Sodom and Gomorrah were about to be destroyed due to wickedness, and the reason for their destruction was the sin of homosexuality (Gen. 19:1–11).

The three angels, representative of the Lord, are a hint of the Blessed Trinity, which was not fully revealed until the coming of the

New Covenant when the archangel Gabriel appears to the Virgin Mary of Nazareth with the good news about the coming miraculous conception and birth of Jesus Christ. We even see a hint and foreshadowing of God's presence in the Eucharist in Abraham's experience. The Byzantine icon of these three holy angels depicts a chalice on the table and the vine and branches behind the central figure. While on this earth we shall never come to appreciate the great beauty, power, and role of even the lower choirs of angels, much less those mighty seraphim and cherubim who are in the ring of adoration closest to the Blessed Trinity. We can never comprehend any of the angels in their proper magnitude.

God in His creation has surrounded Himself threefold. First there are His creatures, who are entirely spiritual, the choirs of angels, who are above the nature of man. Below man is the created material universe — the mineral, plant, and animal world.

God, in becoming man in Jesus Christ, has become one with all of His creation. Man stands in the middle between the entirely spiritual world of the angels and the material world below. The Son of God descended to the center of God's creation in becoming man Himself. Sacred Scripture tells us that God never said to an angel, "Thou art my Son" (Heb. 1:5). Only to the God-Man Jesus Christ has God the Father been able to say that in thus becoming one with all levels of His creation. God the Son became one with the spiritual and material world — for is not the body of man composed of all lower forms of creation while his soul is spiritual like the angels?

God in becoming man, hypostatically united to all elements of His creation, material and spiritual, also willed that His Son should give us Himself in the Eucharist, transubstantiating bread and wine of the earth into Himself substantially.

The realm of the heavenly spirits, while for us incomprehensible, is full of wonders and is intellectually inconceivable in this life. Yet, as seen by God, it is a world well ordered, full of measure and law, full of harmony and beauty. If we were given sight of the work of the angelic world around us in our daily lives, we would be amazed beyond words in our inability to express it. Yet, if we keep conscious of the good holy angels, especially one's guardian angel, we can gradually grow to perceive their invisible world about us, these good holy spirits admonishing, warning, and helping us in everyday affairs. They are continuously working to lead us to the Triune God; to Jesus Christ in His Incarnation; to the Church, which is Christ's Mystical Body; and to Mary, who is their Queen as she is our Queen and Mother.

One of the most well-known books I've ever written is *The World and Work of the Holy Angels*. The book is based on sound Catholic theology and spirituality and remains popular. It contains the scriptural basis for devotion to, and knowledge of, the angels. Having been consecrated for years, both to the Immaculate Heart of Mary and to the holy angels, it is a joy to share a few words here about angels and the Eucharist.

Quiet and unnoticed, the angels are ever at our side, working with the force and power of love, desiring to lead us to God's merciful love, which awes them so, that we may glorify God with them and win salvation. The Sacred Heart of Jesus and the Immaculate Heart of Mary, and what these two inseparable Hearts mean, have been especially manifested for these modern times. The guardian angel of each one of us, well aware of the power of these two inseparable Hearts and the acceptance of God's will that they be venerated by us alongside each other, works constantly in their regard for God's glory and our salvation.

Leading Us to the Eucharist

St. Bonaventure wrote, "All the angels in heaven are begging our Blessed Lady, in her graciousness, to honor them with some of her commands." St. Augustine wrote, "Even St. Michael is always anxiously awaiting the honor of going at her bidding to render service to her." The good guardian angels doubtlessly have a role in influencing the minds and hearts of the people on earth who are especially dedicated in love to the service of Mary.

We see the angel at Fatima leading the children to offer to God the Father, Son, and Holy Spirit the Most Precious Body and Blood of Jesus Christ present in tabernacles throughout the world. There are the special angels assigned to the tabernacles, to adore the Real Presence, while man often forgets to do so.

If there is anything that can put deep awe in the angel it is the mystery of the Incarnation of his Lord and God, who is present in the Sacred Host and in the chalice after the twofold Consecration by the ordained priest. What pain to witness indifference and even desecration by humans who treat the infinitely merciful Savior of mankind in that way. At times there is sacrilegious Communion. What further spiritual pain this causes the angels!

Mary selects angels with strong intercessory power to bring us to her Son by the exaltation of His Cross, and this is done especially through the Sacrifice of the Mass, which perpetuates Calvary's Sacrifice. She brings us also to the tabernacle, which contains the glorified Victim where tabernacle angels always adore.

Our guardian angels, perfectly open to Our Lady and the higher angels, work on our behalf to lead us to Our Eucharistic Lord. Every angel carries out the will of God in some task or mission, and the guardian angel of each one of us has you or me as his particular vocation or mission. Every angel longs to become a guardian angel once, and he longs with his entire spirit to be allowed

- to belong to the sheltering mantle of Mary;
- to be assigned by Mary, Mother of the Church, to a soul being baptized into Christ's Mystical Body upon earth;

- to look upon God so clearly through his protégé in holy Baptism; and
- to build God a throne in the heart of his protégé so as to be united with God.

The above-named joys of the angel exceed the joys of man, except that of the joy of a man of faith and love, who is able to receive Jesus Christ in Holy Communion. You see, the angel may never receive Holy Communion, that great sacrament of love and growth in grace. It belongs to the important duties of every guardian angel above all to alert a correct and clear conscience in his protégé. And what spiritual pain guardian angels have when they behold souls who receive the sacramental Body, Blood, Soul, and Divinity of the God-Man in Holy Communion while in the state of mortal sin! If the words "the Word became flesh" are enough to cause a trembling of awe in the angel, what, then, of the human who receives the Word made flesh into a blackened soul? Angels always adore the Holy Eucharist, but what pain for them to see the Sacred Species trampled upon, received into a soul in mortal sin!

But in the case of the soul in grace receiving Our Lord — the Body, Blood, Soul, and Divinity of Jesus Christ — the angel adores God within the body and soul of the recipient, who for some minutes becomes another tabernacle. Those fifteen and more minutes that the Sacred Species remain within one is a time of profound adoration of God Incarnate within us by the guardian angel.

The good holy angel longs to have us come to adore before the Most Blessed Sacrament. He adores with us. He learns more about the love and mercy of God through us, his charge. No angel has ever directly experienced the mercy of God for no angel has ever had a sin forgiven. The angel cannot change his mind. He could never change, convert, say, "I'm sorry." The trial of the angels was once and final. When the good angel becomes a guardian to any one of us, he learns more about the mercy of God.

Eucharist

The angelic world is a world much vaster and more incomprehensible than our own, and yet it is a world where these spiritual beings are our fellow companions. We catch glimpses of this spiritual world, often at unexpected moments. Through his supernatural light, the very sight of the angel always calls forth the opening of the soul for a message, and this light is accompanied by an inner consciousness of beatitude at being in the presence of such a good heavenly being, and all this together is only the glorification of the one God.

When we face humiliations, rather than react in pride, the angels whisper into our hearts, "Say thank you! Say thank you!" In every darkness he shows us Mary, our Mother, the Morning Star of eternal happiness. In every feeling of being abandoned by God, the angels remind us, "GOD IS."

The angel at Fatima gave the children a lesson in adoration and prayer. The angel eventually led them to Mary, the Temple of God. The children were told that the Hearts of Jesus and Mary had a plan or design of mercy for them. God has a plan or design for each one of us. God, through the angel, wants to bring us to a disposition of mind and heart where we can fulfill our mission. Our guardian angel, who is always conscious of us, works to carry out this plan of God. Our guardian angel knows our mission: *reparation*. Only in receiving Holy Communion, a Communion of reparation, are the children able to fulfill their mission. Eucharistic reparation becomes primary in their lives. They long to receive Jesus in the Holy Eucharist and spend hours adoring His Real Presence in the tabernacle.

Only by the Cross can the members of the Church become more like Jesus Christ. This requires the experience in a faith consciousness that the Divine Liturgy of the Holy Eucharist truly perpetuates Christ's Sacrifice of the Cross. The Church has to be an adoring Church, in communion with the angels and saints to the glory of the Most Holy Trinity.

Our Lady's deepest silence was under the Cross. Angels love silence. Only in Mary can the angels reveal themselves to us. Mary is always the Mediatrix, and angels always work with her.

The angels are communicative with Mary and therein discover more of her humanity. The angels crave to know more about the Incarnation in the body and soul of man. Christ emptied Himself, restricted His glory to become man (Phil. 2:5–11), and so do the angels when they become guardians. The power of the angel is then restricted. A seraphim comes down to the last choir when assigned as a guardian. He remains what he was created, but, by nature of his mission, he steps down to his protégé on earth. The angel can speak to us through our conscience. The angel may use another person to turn our attention to what he desires.

We meet the angel in Mary, the Cross, and in order. If Mary did not help us, we would never find our angel. Mary instills obedience, humility, and silence in us to find our angel. All angels are in the service of Mary but some more than others. Mary under the Cross leads us to our angel. In the heart of the Cross, we meet the angel.

If one stays before the tabernacle for an hour a day, it is also a new experience for one's angel. The angel finds out more about the mystery of his Lord become man, that is, the Incarnation, whenever we go before the Real Presence. The angel then learns more about Jesus dying on the Cross, where is the infinite outpouring of mercy. Contemplating the mystery of the Incarnation and the Cross before the Most Blessed Sacrament, with each of us before the Most Blessed Sacrament, or during the Sacrifice of the Mass, brings deeper enlightenment to the angel.

We can know God only in purity. "Blessed are the pure in heart, for they shall see God" (Matt. 5:8). We must purify our hearts to know Our Lady and to know more our angel. Meeting us at the Cross, the angel comes to know more about the Incarnation, and we come to know more about glory, which the angel already knows in view of the Beatific Vision he always has. If we don't grow in a spirituality centered in the Holy Eucharist and the Cross, we hinder our angel from growing in knowledge of the Incarnation.

Several Masses during the liturgical year are dedicated to the angels. There is the feast of the Guardian Angels on October 2 and the Archangels Michael, Gabriel, and Raphael on September 29. Catholic countries like Portugal, Spain, and Brazil have long celebrated a feast day in honor of the guardian angel of their nation. There is a special angel assigned to the United States, and it would be well to promote such a devotion.

Bishop Robert J. Baker, bishop of Birmingham in Alabama, requested October 2, 2007, the feast of the Guardian Angels, as the time for his Mass of installation. When he was previously installed as bishop of Charlotte, it was the feast of the Archangels.

In Scripture, angels precede the coming of the Lord. This was true in the well-known and approved Fatima messages. In the third apparition of the angel, the central Eucharistic mysteries of our Faith are reaffirmed. The Holy Eucharist, whose testimony is found in the sixth chapter of St. John's Gospel, is seen as the spiritual sun of our lives, which finally transforms us into light, light of the Light of God.

The first apparition of the angel leads to prayerful adoration, the second to contemplation and atonement; but in the third apparition, it is seen that only through an intimate union and loving action with Jesus Christ in the Most Blessed Sacrament of the Holy Eucharist can we reach great holiness.

We can be sanctified only through Jesus, who abides in us through the Holy Eucharist. Our Lord Himself told us:

> Abide in me, and I in you. As the branch cannot bear fruit by itself, unless it abides in the vine, neither can you, unless

you abide in me. I am the vine, you are the branches. He who abides in me, and I in him, he it is that bears much fruit, for apart from me you can do nothing. (John 15:4–5)

In chapter 7, there was already related events concerning the Angel of the Eucharist at Fatima. It is worth considering again in this chapter on the the Holy Eucharist and the holy angels.

Holding in his hands a chalice surmounted by a Host, from which some drops of blood were falling into the chalice, the angel left the chalice and the Host suspended in the air and prostrated himself on the ground and repeated this prayer three times:

> Most Holy Trinity, Father, Son and Holy Spirit, I adore You profoundly. I offer You the most precious Body, Blood, Soul and Divinity of Jesus Christ, present in all the tabernacles of the world, in reparation for the outrages, sacrileges and indifference by which He is offended. By the infinite merits of the Sacred Heart, and through the Immaculate Heart of Mary, I beg the conversion of poor sinners.

The children, impelled by the supernatural force all around them, imitated the angel of the Holy Eucharist. In a century that was to witness, even among many Catholic people, a weakening of faith in the Real Presence of the God-Man in the Holy Eucharist, the children experienced this Eucharistic presence of the Lord and felt so intensely the presence of God that they were completely overwhelmed and absorbed by it. For a considerable time, they were unconscious of their bodily senses and, even for some days after, their physical actions were impelled, as it were, by that supernatural Being. Their total persons became absorbed in the supernatural, as is the constant work of the angels.

It was in this angelic and Eucharistic apparition that the central mystery of the holy Faith unfolded for the children. It was revealed that the angels join men in adoring the presence of God in the Holy Eucharist and that angels adore God where Jesus Christ is sacramentally present in tabernacles of Catholic churches the world over. The guardian angel of each one of us then surely joins us when we kneel in adoration before the tabernacle and at the Consecration of the Mass. In fact, the guardian angel leads us, inspires us, to such adoration.

It was later revealed at Fatima that in the end the Immaculate Heart of Mary will triumph. That triumph will be a Eucharistic one as souls are made holy, being led not simply to the Immaculate Heart; by following the inspiration of the angels and the prayers of Mary, her Immaculate Heart will direct men to the supreme sacrifice perpetuated in the Holy Eucharist where her Son always abides.

The good holy angels, who never directly experienced the mercy of God, are in awe of the Cross. Infinite condescension, God become man. But there is more. The God-Man dies on the Cross for sinful mankind. God becoming man and then dying on the Cross, such an infinite ocean of mercy is a loving mystery to angels and men. The Cross is at the middle for angel and man. The angel works to lead us closer to the Cross as our great love and source of mercy. When we have love for Christ Crucified, the angel has greater influence over us so that we can be formed into the image and likeness of Christ.

The multitude of good holy angels were gathered about Christ Crucified on Calvary. Lucifer and his followers had outwitted themselves. They had influenced many of God's people under the Old Covenant to seek a worldly Messiah, not a spiritual Messiah whose kingdom is not of this world. Satan had entered into Judas and influenced the very people who should have recognized in Jesus Christ, their Lord, God, and Savior, as the long-expected Messiah, instead of working for His Crucifixion. But it would be that very suffering and death of Jesus on the Cross that would defeat the devil. When Jesus died on the Cross, Satan was hurled a defeating blow and crushed, as predicted would be the case in Genesis 3:15.

The devil hates the Cross. Evil spirits work to keep us from the Cross, for the Cross is what crushes the head of the serpent and brings our salvation. This is why the devil hates the Eucharist, both as sacrifice and sacrament. He hates it as sacrifice, for Christ's own offering of Himself on the Cross is made present at Holy Mass. He hates the Eucharist as sacrament because we are sanctified in receiving it worthily and grow close to the entire Blessed Trinity through the humanity of Christ when we adore it.

While the angel has tremendous love and respect for every Christian in grace, he looks with special awe at the priest who has the power of Jesus Christ Himself to perpetuate the Sacrifice of the Cross while changing bread and wine into the God-Man. St. Gregory Nazianzen said that the angels themselves venerate the priesthood.

St. Francis of Assisi, the Seraphic Doctor, who toward the end of his life bore the marks of Christ Crucified in his body, so profoundly venerated the priesthood, which can perpetuate the Cross, which brings the Real Presence of Christ's Body, Blood, Soul, and Divinity, that he did not consider himself worthy to advance beyond the diaconate.

At the Sacrifice of the Mass when the moment of the *Sanctus* arrives, countless angels gather about the altar to join in this hymn of praise and glory. From Sacred Scripture we know that this is the prayer of the angels, which we borrow from them.

What grace and mercy the holy angels see outpoured in every Sacrifice of the Mass! Jesus having died physically in a bloody manner on that first Good Friday will die in such a manner no more. But God is not bound by space or time. Sacramentally, Jesus Christ can perpetuate the same Sacrifice of Calvary at each Holy Mass. It is a dogma of the Catholic Faith that He does. And the angels who adored and were in profound awe at His mercy on Calvary experience the same and renew their adoration and awe at every Holy Sacrifice of the Mass. Would that we saw and loved the Cross as do the angels.

Sr. Faustina, in her diary (470–472), mentions her experiences with angels. From her, whose mission it was to make popularly known the rich mercy of God, it is not surprising to learn of her encounters with angels who contemplate God's mercy through their associations with men.

The saintly soul of St. Padre Pio (d. 1968) bore for fifty years the wound marks of Christ Crucified and was especially devoted to the angels from his childhood. The angel of Padre Pio surely led him to the Cross. The familiarity of Padre Pio with angels has had a widespread effect of renewing devotion to the angels.

United to the good angel, one gathers strength at the altar. The angel leads one to love the Cross as the greatest support. One is led to bless oneself reverently, not hurriedly and unconsciously, with the Sign of the Cross. Each day, as the alarm goes off in the morning or we awaken to start a new day, we begin with the Sign of the Cross. It is taught to children, students, the sick. The Cross is kept in the classroom, the living room of the home, bedrooms, and so forth. The Cross stirs up love for God in us and inspires us to offer our daily crosses in union with Christ Crucified.

The good guardian angel is most pleased each time we participate in the Sacrifice of the Mass or stop by the church to visit Jesus in the Most Blessed Sacrament in the tabernacle. There one's good guardian angel is present at the Sacrifice of the Cross perpetuated, and he adores the Eucharistic Lord together with us. Whenever we participate in the Sacrifice of the Mass or adore our Eucharistic Lord in the tabernacle, the holy angel ever at our side discovers even more of the mercy of God as he witnesses its effect in us and sees more clearly what we behold by faith.

The good holy angel witnesses the infinite mercy of God outpoured in the Sacrifice of the Cross perpetuated. Before the Real Presence of his and our Eucharistic King, as we approach the altar or submit our souls to the tribunal of mercy in the confessional, he adores God before the tabernacle and is in awe of our sins being forgiven. No angel has ever had a sin forgiven, yet here in the confessional he witnesses it happen. "Just so, I tell you, there is joy before the angels of God over one sinner who repents" (Luke 15:10).

The angels respect us because of our real adventure of liberty, which is increased with the dignity of being coheirs with Christ. All this is within the sacramental life of the Church. The angels want to share in our sacramental life, to adore with us the Precious Blood of Jesus Christ, which is renewed each day on the altars of the world. They want to rejoice for each sinner who is converted.

In the Eucharistic Communion, they want to unite themselves with us to Christ. It is the ideal of the angels to share with us our life here on earth until the culmination of our supernatural life. It is an honor for them, and a joy, because in that way they will actively share in the tremendous adventure of the eternal destinies of man!

Our joy and friendship in Heaven will be shared with the angels. If our happiness must depend on the adventure of our liberty used well here on earth, the angels have the right to a share in such joy. The good holy angels even now, as associated with us, are in the joy of the heavenly Beatific Vision, which they always behold. They work to have us share it too.

St. Francis, the Cross, Angels, and Eucharist

As the good holy angels love the Cross, we can well understand St. Francis of Assisi's love. He bequeathed to his order a special devotion to the Passion of Jesus as a precious heritage. This devotion soon spread and became general throughout the Church. The love of Christ Crucified filled his soul. St. Francis had a compassion for the suffering Jesus. St. Francis was not long converted from his carefree life before he felt himself pierced with the love of the divine Crucified One.

The voice of Christ came to him in the church of St. Damian, which was then in ruin: "Go, Francis, and repair my house; you see clearly that it is fallen in ruins." With more purification and enlightenment, Francis realized Jesus wanted to use him to upbuild His Church, the Mystical Body of Christ throughout the world.

The companions of St. Francis relate: "One day he was walking alone near the Church of Saint Mary of the Portiuncula weeping and lamenting aloud. A holy man heard him and thought he was suffering. Seized with pity he asked him why he wept. Francis answered: 'I bewail the passion of my Lord Jesus Christ, and I ought not to feel ashamed to go throughout the world thus weeping.'" The man then began to weep with him. It was often noticed that when he had just been praying his eyes were filled with blood because he had wept so much and so bitterly. "Not content with shedding tears, he used to deprive himself of food at the memory of the passion of the Lord."

St. Francis taught this prayer to his followers so as to make them give unceasing honor to the Passion of the Savior: "We adore thee, O Christ, in all the churches of the whole world, and we bless thee because by thy holy Cross thou hast redeemed the world."

Shortly before the apparition of the stigmata, Francis composed this prayer:

> O my Lord Jesus Christ, two graces do I beseech Thee to grant me before I die: the first that, during my lifetime, I may feel in my soul and in my body, so far as may be possible, that pain which Thou, sweet Lord, didst suffer in the hour of Thy most bitter passion; the second is that I may feel in my heart,

so far as may be possible, that exceeding love whereby Thou, Son of God, was enkindled, to bear willingly such passion for us sinners.

His companions inform us:

> About two years before his death, at the approach of the Feast of the Exaltation of the Holy Cross, he was praying one morning on the slope of Mt. Alvernia. He was uplifted to God by desire and by seraphic ardor and felt himself transformed by a tender compassion for him who, in the excess of his charity, willed to be crucified. A six-winged seraph then appeared to him, bearing between his wings the form, of great beauty, of One Crucified, having the hands and feet stretched on the cross, and clearly a figure of Our Lord Jesus. Two wings were folded so as to hide his head; two others veiled the rest of his body, and the other two were extended to sustain the flight of the seraph. When the vision had disappeared, a wonderful ardor of love rested in Francis's soul; and, more wonderful still, in his body there appeared the impression of the stigmata of Our Lord Jesus Christ. The man of God hid them as much as possible until his death, not wishing to make public the mystery of the Lord; but he was not able so to conceal them from his companions, at least from those that were most familiar. But after his happy departure from this world all the brothers who were then present, and many of the laity saw his body gloriously marked with the stigmata of Christ.

A study of the life of St. Francis reveals his great love for God, the Cross, the angels in his life, for the Real Presence of Jesus Christ in Catholic churches. His awe of the priesthood was associated with the Eucharist, the power to make Jesus Christ present and to perpetuate

Eucharist

Christ's great offering in the Sacrifice on the Cross. As indicated in early chapters, the Eucharist and priesthood are associated with the reality of what the Church is. The angels who are in such awe of the Cross, through the Seraph Angel, bestowed the marks of Christ Crucified on Francis.

The good angel inspires us to say yes to whatever the Lord calls us, even for some to live a lifetime constantly on the bed of sorrow and physical sufferings to spiritually aid other members of the Mystical Body, the Church. That can be more meritorious than all other lives when united to Christ Crucified. It can be more meritorious than an active life of prayer and sacrifice for family and friends and neighbors.

A multitude of things can be adoringly held up to God while performing one's daily duty. Wherever possible, if our daily duty permits it, we should participate in the daily Holy Sacrifice of the Mass and thereby achieve union with Jesus Christ — it is there especially that our daily duties and joys, our sacrifices, and the crosses become sanctified and one with the Cross of Christ. Nothing sanctifies the day, the week, as uniting all to Christ Crucified through the Sacrifice of the Cross perpetuated at each Holy Sacrifice of the Mass.

11

The Church Is Guardian of Eucharistic Faith

Heaven comes down to earth every time the Eucharist is made present on the altar. With the Most Blessed Sacrament we have Heaven on earth, for Jesus Christ, and the entire Most Blessed Trinity, is present wherever there is the consecrated Eucharist. The Church has mightily defended and promoted this Eucharistic Faith from the earliest centuries.

In the Most Blessed Sacrament of the tabernacle, Jesus Christ is present in the fullness of His Godhead, in the majesty and splendor of His glorified humanity. This is the Sacrament of Love. It is the Sacrament of the Mystery of Divine Love. It is the Real Presence.

Pope Benedict XVI wrote in *Sacramentum Caritatis*, as previously stated: "Every great reform has in some way been linked to the rediscovery of belief in the Lord's eucharistic presence among his People." I think we could say also that every heresy has in some way been linked to a denial of the constant Faith of the Catholic Church in the Eucharist as sacrifice and sacrament.

Pope Paul VI on September 3, 1965, issued *Mysterium Fidei* (*Mystery of Faith*). It was an encyclical on the Holy Eucharist. He had a serious reason for issuing that encyclical. He explains why himself with this document:

> And so, with the aim of seeing to it that the hope to which the Council has given rise — that a new wave of Eucharistic

devotion will sweep over the Church — not be reduced to nil through the sowing of the seeds of false opinions. We have decided to use Our apostolic authority and speak Our mind to you on this subject, Venerable Brothers.

We certainly do not deny that those who are spreading these strange opinions are making a praiseworthy effort to investigate this lofty Mystery and to set forth its inexhaustible riches and to make it more understandable to the men of today; rather, We acknowledge this and We approve of it. *But We cannot approve the opinions that they set forth, and We have an obligation to warn you about the grave danger that these opinions involve for true faith.* (13–14, emphasis added)

What was happening at the time that motivated Pope Paul VI to issue this encyclical, giving strong reasons for doing so? The fourth and *final* session of the Second Vatican Council called by Pope John XXIII was about to begin. Pope John XXIII died after the Council's *first* session which concluded without any completed results. The *second* session of the Council closed on December 4, 1963, with promulgation of the Constitution on the Sacred Liturgy. While the Council called for some changes in the liturgy, there were writers and theologians promoting all kinds of strange ideas about the Mass, the Eucharist, the priesthood itself.

Many priests began to abandon their vows and vocations as they felt there was a crisis to the priesthood. Among a certain number who stayed it would have seemingly been better if they had discontinued to practice the priesthood to which they were not being loyal in their teaching. Outside the practicing priesthood they would have caused less harm to the faithful by their unorthodox doctrines concerning dogma, and also their immoral opinions concerning moral law. This was a great disaster for the Church. Jesus had warned: "You are the salt of the earth; but if salt has lost its taste, how shall its saltness be restored? It is no longer good for anything except to be thrown out and trodden under foot by men" (Matt. 5:13). Even some bishops, and an occasional cardinal, got into scrambles that confused and scandalized the faithful.

If one has studied the Church and Her long history, it is seen that it has happened before that some bishops and priests have not been loyal. Judas was the first. Yet, ultimately, the Church survives and comes out even stronger. Bishops are the keystones in the structure of the Church. There are innumerable good shepherds who fulfill their duties to God and His Church. There are also hirelings, who are guilty of the worst tribulations that can afflict the flock of Christ. The devil is always active in working against Jesus Christ and His Church and has done so since its foundation. We see this in a sermon on pastors by St. Augustine quoted below:

> *Therefore, shepherds, hear the word of the Lord: I live, says the Lord God.* Notice the beginning of this passage: it is as if God were taking an oath, giving testimony to his own life. *I live, says the Lord.* Which shepherds are dead? Those who seek what is theirs and not what is Christ's. But will there be shepherds who seek what is Christ's and not what is theirs, and will they be found? There will indeed be such shepherds, and they will indeed be found; they are not lacking, nor will they be lacking in the future. (Sermon 46, 18–19: CCL 41, 544–546)

The wonderful encyclical of Paul VI, while certainly encouraging to those loyal to the Church, and reaffirming the faith of loyal bishops, priests, religious, and the faithful in general who learned about it, yet did not succeed in ending the cancerous evil that was spreading. I recall that at the time as a young priest, I used the opportunity to preach strongly on what Paul VI said in *Mysterium Fidei*.

Almost three years later, on May 8, 1968, the same Pope Paul VI felt obligated to explain his proposal to assist at the International Eucharistic Congress that was held in Bogota, Colombia, in August of that year:

> It is not the external solemnity that draws us here, although it also has its highest value.... It is the affirmation of the Eucharistic Mystery that draws us; an affirmation that wishes to consolidate strongly and express in an unequivocal form the faith of all the Catholic Church... an actual confirmation of the Eucharistic doctrine in the face of the ineptitude, the ambiguity, and the errors from which a part of our generation suffer with regard to the Mystery of our altars.

Pope Paul VI made public an apostolic exhortation to all the bishops at Rome on January 5, 1971, on the occasion of the fifth anniversary of the closing of the Second Vatican Council. He used a forceful and demanding tone, which was not his usual character. It showed his concern that not all the bishops were fulfilling their duty:

> Many of the faithful feel themselves disturbed in their faith by an accumulation of ambiguities, uncertainties, and doubts in essential matters.... While, little by little, silence is recovering some of the fundamental mysteries of Christianity, we see a tendency to construct a Christianity derived from psychological and sociological data, a Christianity separated from the uninterrupted tradition that goes back to the faith of the Apostles. And we see a tendency to exalt a Christian life deprived of religious elements.... And from our own number — just as in the days of St. Paul — shall arise men speaking perverse things, to draw away disciples after them (Acts 20:30).

Paul VI, the successor of St. Peter, was speaking to bishops at the time. Closely linked with bishops and priests is the glorious mystery of the Holy Eucharist. If the mystery of the Real Presence of Jesus in the Eucharist, and His sacrifice perpetuated, is obscured and clouded, the less importance it will have in the lives of Catholics. This means people will be drawn farther away from Jesus Christ and His love, and closer to darkness. This was happening in broad sectors and so Paul VI was greatly concerned. The crisis of doctrine concerning the worship of the *mysterium fidei*, "mystery of faith," had broken out in different countries. Disrespect for the Real Presence of Christ in the Eucharist was shown by reserving the Most Blessed Sacrament in inappropriate places in many churches. Some churches were designed as centers of reunion, rather than as places to meet with the Lord Jesus present among us, to adore, to participate in the Divine Liturgy that perpetuated His infinite Sacrifice of the Cross. Communion rails were removed; Communion was received too often carelessly and without thanksgiving. Benediction was often eliminated, as was the Forty Hours' Devotion and processions of the Most Blessed Sacrament.

Eusebio Garcia de Pesquera, O.F.M., Cap., tells in *She Went in Haste to the Mountain* the following:

> I was waiting at a train station in Seville, speaking with a man who had begun his theological studies in a diocesan seminary. We had a friendly conversation and ... this stuck especially in my mind: "The other day several seminarians were talking about what each one wanted to do in his church as soon as he was in charge of a parish. One of them ... ended like this: 'I haven't decided yet what to do with the tabernacle. ... although perhaps, when my time comes, that won't be a problem, since it will have disappeared.'" The seminarian was certainly speaking ironically, but this illustrates the truth of

the statement: Less and less importance is being given to the Eucharist....

Pseudo-prophets with their distorted nuances ranting about renewal and liberation are attempting to discredit the ascetic and penitential way of life, as though asceticism were not an evangelical sign.... Anti-asceticism is the order of the day.

But for whom did Jesus say, "If anyone wishes to come after me, let him deny himself, and take up his cross"? (Mt 16:24). Certainly this is not for those who never mention Him except to speak about self-determination, self-fulfillment, self-advancement. And this explains many things....

The Passion of Jesus! They are not interested in this.... For them the only things that matter are actions and words that are favorable for their liberty and their life, which is very far from, "He became obedient unto death, death on a cross!"

Fortunately, the crisis that Paul VI was most concerned about has somewhat subsided. Yet its effects still linger in many instances.

About the time I was researching and writing this book, I received a long-distance call, as I've received many thousands concerning the Faith during my years as a columnist and writer of books and articles. The caller told of his brother-in-law who is known as a "Catholic who does not go to Church." He said that at the time his marriage took place he had assumed the man was a good Catholic having had much education in Catholic grade and high schools. "Recently," he said, "I was riding with him in a car and desired to approach the subject of his non-participation in the Mass and the sacraments so as to invite and encourage him to return. I begin with, 'You know what is wrong in the Catholic Church? They don't teach often enough that Jesus Christ is really present in the Eucharist.' I had hardly got those words out of my mouth when he angrily shot back at me, 'No. That is not true. I was told in a Catholic school Jesus is not present in the Eucharist.'"

The man who called was ready to blame the archbishop of his territory. But I was informed of that archbishop and knew he was a good and orthodox bishop. I asked, "How old is this brother-in-law?" The response was, "In his fifties." I informed him that unfortunately during those years (same years of grave concern to Paul VI when he wrote *Mysterium Fidei*) many teachers of religion in Catholic schools and CCD programs had swallowed the errors about which Paul VI wrote in his encyclical on the Eucharist. They were teaching falsehoods to children and teenagers in our schools, even to older students in some of our college Newman Centers. It is better that you influence this member of your extended family by good example rather than direct words."

I then suggested to him that he might someday find the occasion to hand him a simple book on the faith, such as *A Young Catholic's Apology for the Faith*, which I had written for just such people, saying, "I found this interesting. Would you like to read it?" The simple book was a prelude, hopefully, for deeper reading, such as *Protestant Fundamentalism and the Born-Again Catholic*.

On one occasion a twenty-five-year-old man phoned me long-distance to inform me how excited and happy he was after reading the book, *Protestant Fundamentalism and the Born-Again Catholic*. "That on the Holy Eucharist was especially great and touched me deeply and put me on fire for the Catholic Faith."

Then I asked the twenty-five-year-old young man, "How did you learn of this book?" His response: "My Aunt who is married to a minister, they are both anti-Catholic, came across the book and, thinking it was against the Catholic Faith, gave it to me to read. Supposedly she thought it would lead me out of the Catholic Church and I'd be born again. But it had put me on fire with the true life of authentic Catholicism."

In *Mysterium Fidei*, Pope Paul VI was most anxious to proclaim to the world the two-thousand-year-old faith of Jesus Christ in the Eucharist. The encyclical recalled how Moses made the Old Testament sacred with the blood of calves, so too Christ the Lord took the New Testament, of which He is the Mediator, and made it sacred through His own Blood, in instituting the mystery of the Eucharist. He reminded Catholics that the Evangelists narrate how it is the Eucharistic *Sacrifice* and Jesus Christ "made clear that He wanted it to be forever repeated" [the same sacrifice offered] (28). Paul VI explained that the Eucharistic Sacrifice was foreshadowed by Malachi (Mal. 1:11) and "has always been offered by the Church, in accordance with the teaching of Our Lord and the Apostles" (29).

Jesus Christ struck the New and Eternal Covenant on the Cross on the first Good Friday. The evening before at the Last Supper, He made it clear that He was already offering in the Eucharist at the Last Supper the same sacrifice to be offered on the Cross.

Theologian and biblical scholar Scott Hahn has frequently spoken and written on the meaning of covenants. It is important, he tells us, for us to have the sense of covenant as it was lived in biblical cultures. We should understand covenant, not only in the Hebrew and Christian religious cultures, but even in the Gentile and pagan societies of the ancient world. Covenant was the foundation of these societies. Individual persons were given the sense of kinship, relationship, and of belonging — to a family, a tribe, even to a nation. Hahn informs us: "The covenant oath was the foundation of family, national, and religious life."

The words *contract* and *covenant* are not the same. They are not interchangeable when we are speaking of the New Eternal Covenant established by Jesus Christ. In a mere contract people may set the terms. But God has set the terms in giving us Jesus Christ who gave us the Eucharistic Sacrifice. God's own covenant with man is not negotiable. We must live up to His terms.

Scott Hahn reminds us that contracts are not only based on the parties making the promises, but are for profit. Covenants are based on love. Contracts are for self-interest. Covenants call for self-sacrifice.

Contracts as legal devices can be negotiated, even broken. A covenant is unconditional and ongoing, and though it can be violated, it is not thereby dissolved. Contracts have limited scope. Covenants cover many, even all the areas of life. Contracts have a limited duration. Covenants last for life, even for future generations.

A covenant far surpasses the mere contract even though every covenant includes some element of contract. Covenant surpasses the mere contract and involves a personal relationship. A covenant is a sacred bonding.

A husband and wife in a true sacramental marriage enter into a sacred bond for life. Jesus has the Church for His Bride. As the New Adam, Jesus Christ strikes the Eternal Covenant for mankind on the Cross of Calvary, seals it with His Precious Blood. Where Adam failed in the first covenant into which God entered with him for mankind, Jesus Christ the New Adam enters for mankind into the New Covenant, which is final and eternal.

> The prophets heralded a new and everlasting covenant, which would be a renewal of the original covenant between God and Adam, God and humankind, God and all creation. It would, in fact, be so all-encompassing as to be a "new creation." The imagery of the prophets, which was employed in turn by Jesus Christ, was the imagery of betrothal and marriage. Thus, when Jesus came, He called Himself the "bridegroom" and those who were united to Him in baptism were called "espoused"

(see John. 3:29; Mark. 2:19; Mat. 22:1–14, 25:1–13; 1 Cor. 6:a5–a7; 2 Cor. 11:2; see Catechism of Catholic Church 796). (Scott Hahn, *Catholic for a Reason IV*).

In all of this, as we see in studying two thousand years of Church history, Jesus used judgment, enlightened by the divine wisdom of the Holy Spirit, in determining that the Church would have a pope, with the last word in teaching the Faith; that Peter should always have a successor as visible head of the Church.

12

Fire and Spirit — Heaven and Earth Unite

For fifty years I taught our holy Catholic Faith in Catholic classrooms. I started teaching before ordination and continued as a pastor for forty-eight and a half years thereafter. I loved to teach young people, even children in early grades, all the way from first grade to twelfth, each week. I'd teach them: "When we are at the Sacrifice of the Mass, it is the same as being with Mary, the Mother of Jesus, and John the Apostle beneath the Cross of Jesus on Good Friday. We are there as Jesus offers the Sacrifice of His death for our salvation."

What Jesus Christ offered at the Last Supper was a true sacrifice when He consecrated the bread and wine into Himself. What He offered on Good Friday, as He died on the Cross, was a true sacrifice. What the duly ordained Catholic priest offers at Mass today is a true sacrifice. Holy Thursday, Good Friday, the Mass today, all are one and the same true sacrifice. At Mass we are present at what Jesus did and offered Holy Thursday evening and on Calvary that first Good Friday. The Eucharist concerns not a mere representation but rather a re-presentation.

> The sacramental re-presentation of Christ's sacrifice, crowned by the resurrection, in the Mass involves a most special presence which — in the words of Paul VI — "is called *real* not as a way of excluding all other types of presence as if they were

'not real,' but because it is a presence in the fullest sense: a substantial presence whereby Christ, the God-Man, is wholly and entirely present." (*Ecclesia de Eucharistia*, 15)

The Council of Trent taught clearly that the whole substance of the bread is changed into the substance of the Body of Christ Our Lord, and the whole substance of the wine is changed into the substance of His Blood. "And the holy Catholic Church has fittingly and properly called this change *transubstantiation*."

Jesus Christ perpetuates His Sacrifice of the Cross at every Mass at which you are present whether you receive Holy Communion or not. And that sacrifice offered is of infinite value in the eyes of God. But at the same time, as *Ecclesia de Eucharistia* teaches regarding spiritual efficacy for full participation and obtaining the graces of the Eucharist, the "saving efficacy of the sacrifice is fully realized when the Lord's Body and Blood are received in Communion" (16). By this gift of Jesus Christ received in Holy Communion the effects of the gift of His Spirit are intensified, which were already poured out in Baptism and bestowed as a "seal" in the Sacrament of Confirmation.

According to *Ecclesia de Eucharistia*, Holy Communion "expresses and reinforces our communion with the Church in heaven" (19). Each time we celebrate the Eucharist and receive the Lord we have expressed and strengthened our communion with the Church in Heaven. The Communion of Saints is a reality for us here upon earth as it is for the souls in Purgatory and those saints in Heaven. Our Christian vision and celebration of the Eucharist leads us to a "new heaven" and a "new earth" (Rev. 21:1). Our citizenship is in Heaven. The Eucharist is the sacrament par excellence of the Mystical Body. It builds up the Church.

Celebrating the Eucharist with faith and understanding of its reality encompasses responsibilities to others, especially the poor, the underprivileged, the handicapped. Jesus gave us the example of the washing of the feet at the very occasion when He instituted the Holy Eucharist. St. Paul the Apostle speaks of it as "unworthy" of a Christian community to partake of the Lord's Supper amid division and indifference to the poor (see 1 Cor. 11:17–22, 27–34).

The Apostle Paul tells us that when we celebrate the Eucharist, we "proclaim the Lord's death until he comes" (1 Cor. 11:26). This of course is in reference to the Eucharist as sacrifice, and our sincere celebration of it means a commitment to change our lives so they become Eucharistic. We are thus in commitment by the Eucharist to work, not only to transform ourselves into Christ but to transform others of the world.

Each one of us first entered into covenant with Jesus Christ at Baptism. That incorporation into Christ by sacred bonding or covenant is constantly renewed and strengthened each time we conscientiously worship by faith and love in our hearts and share in the Eucharistic Sacrifice. We receive Christ. Christ receives us. He renews His friendship with us: "You are my friends" (John 15:14). "Abide in me, and I in you" (John 15:4).

The Eucharist is both the source and the summit of all evangelization. We receive spiritual power to do our part in the Church to carry out her mission, to bring others to Christ, and thus to the entire Blessed Trinity. The mission of Christ is the mission of the Church. "As the Father has sent me, even so I send you" (John 20:21). Spiritual power to evangelize comes from Jesus in the Eucharist.

We can experience the infinite love in the heart of Jesus by coming before His Eucharistic Heart. There before Jesus we can receive the power and fire of His Heart, and especially during that fifteen to twenty minutes that Jesus is sacramentally within us after receiving Holy Communion. We can thus experience His love and strength to evangelize.

Eucharist

The Real Presence of Jesus Christ under the sacred species reserved after Mass is linked to and dependent on the celebration of the Sacrifice of the Mass. We could not have the Real Presence to adore and be reserved in our tabernacles without first having the celebration of the Eucharistic Sacrifice. We should all, at times, spend time in spiritual conversation and silent adoration of Jesus Christ present in the Most Blessed Sacrament.

The practice of Eucharistic adoration is seen in the lives of many saints. Of such adoration St. Alphonsus Liguori wrote: "Of all devotions, that of adoring Jesus in the Blessed Sacrament is the greatest after the Sacraments, the one dearest to God and the one most helpful to us."

As the Church is apostolic, so the Eucharist has apostolicity. The Eucharist was entrusted by Jesus Christ to the apostles. The apostles have handed the Eucharist down to us through the centuries through their successors. Bishops of the Catholic Church today are successors to the original apostles, and they share their fullness of Jesus' priestly powers with ordained priests. Succession to the apostles is accomplished through the Sacrament of Holy Orders. There are three steps to the Orders; deacon, priest, and, finally, bishop, which involves the fullness. The existence of the Sacrament of Holy Orders does not detract from the importance of the laity, "for in the communion of the one body of Christ which is the Church this gift [the Eucharist] redounds to the benefit of all" (*Ecclesia de Eucharistia*, 30). Understanding a proper definition or explanation of the reality of what the Church is in Her fullness must include the Eucharist, the priesthood, and the papacy.

The Church lives and grows and expresses her divine institution especially in the Eucharist. The term *Communion* or *Holy Communion* is one of the names given to this sublime sacrament.

It is especially through the Eucharist that our communion with God the Father is perfected by becoming one with His only begotten

Son through the working of the Holy Spirit. It is good for Catholics to cultivate constantly a desire for the Sacrament of the Eucharist. When one cannot receive Jesus sacramentally, it is beneficial to express the desire for Jesus to come to our souls spiritually. This is known as a *spiritual communion*. It can be expressed in such words: "Jesus, since I cannot now receive you sacramentally with your Body, Blood, Soul, and Divinity, I desire that you come spiritually into my heart." or, simply, "Come to me, my Jesus, I come to Thee."

The starting point for achieving communion with the Most Holy Trinity is not the celebration of the Eucharist. Rather, celebration of the Eucharist, and especially its reception in Holy Communion, presupposes that communion to a degree already exists. The celebration of the Holy Eucharist is to give glory to God and bring our communion with Him to greater perfection, to straighten that union; to increase sanctifying grace within us. In the Eucharist there is an *invisible* dimension to communion with God and a *visible* dimension.

At least while we are upon this earth the invisible dimension involves our union in Christ with one another through the working of the Holy Spirit, who unites us among ourselves to God the Father, indeed, to the entire Most Blessed Trinity; such is the effect of Eucharistic Communion. The visible dimension for Catholics involves the actual celebration of the rite of the Mass, extraordinary or ordinary Roman Rite, and the reception of the visible species of the Sacrament, which contains Jesus Christ substantially and living.

Both rites are of equal divine power, and both contain the one same Sacrifice of Jesus Christ which is of infinite value. One rite does not contain the infinite value of Christ's sacrifice more than the other. Both can be offered with great reverence. For this visible aspect to be possible there is required union with the Church's hierarchical order, as explained above. For reverence, it requires that the priest follow the official rubrics of the Church with fidelity, whether it be the extraordinary or ordinary form. There must be a priest ordained by a bishop in true apostolic succession to effect the Eucharist. The invisible dimension of Jesus Christ is sometimes spoken of simply as "the hidden Jesus." The visible dimension involves the ordained bishop or priest, bread and wine as species, and the ceremonies of the Divine Liturgy as approved by the Church.

The invisible communion requires the life of sanctifying grace. We become "partakers of the divine nature" (2 Pet. 1:4), possessing the infused virtues of faith, hope, and love. In that way we have the indwelling of the Most Holy Trinity, the Father, the Son, and the Holy Spirit. Faith alone is not sufficient. What is required is "faith working through love" (Gal. 5:6).

Simply put, we must be in the state of sanctifying grace to receive Our Lord in a worthy manner in Holy Communion. To approach the reception of this holy sacrament in the state of mortal sin would be the serious sin of sacrilege. The Word of God so speaks through the Apostle Paul: "Let a man examine himself, and so eat of the bread and drink of the cup" (1 Cor. 11:28). St. John Chrysostom with eloquence put it this way: "I too raise my voice, I beseech, beg and implore that no one draw near to this sacred table with a sullied and corrupt conscience. Such an act, in fact, can never be called 'communion,' not even were we to touch the Lord's Body a thousand times over, but 'condemnation,' 'torment' and 'increase of punishment.'" This teaching is reiterated in *Ecclesia de Eucharistia* (36–38).

The authentic Catholic in his spiritual vision and in the manner in which he beholds the celebration of the Holy Eucharist recognizes always the universality of the Church. His sense of faith is that the Church is one, holy, catholic (universal), and apostolic (back to the apostles). Thus, the celebration of the Eucharist is never seen as simply an act of worship of this particular community. While it is offered in a particular community, it is the Eucharistic Sacrifice of the one, holy, catholic, and apostolic Church. A true Eucharistic community can never be closed in upon itself. It must believe and act in harmony with every other Catholic community of the universal Church.

The bishop is the *visible* principle and foundation of unity of the particular local Church (diocese). "The Roman Pontiff, as the successor of Peter, is the perpetual and visible source and foundation of the unity of the Bishops and of the multitude of the faithful" (*Lumen Gentium*, 23). Communion with the pope is thus intrinsically required for the celebration of the Eucharistic Sacrifice:

> Every celebration of the Eucharist is performed in union not only with the proper Bishop, but also with the Pope, with the episcopal order, with all the clergy, and with the entire people. Every valid celebration of the Eucharist expresses this universal communion with Peter and with the whole Church, or objectively calls for it, as in the case of the Christian Churches [Orthodox] separated from Rome. (*Letter to the Bishops of the Catholic Church on Some Aspects of the Church Understood as Communion*, 14)

One of the reasons for the importance of participating in Mass on the Lord's Day, Sunday, is for the promotion of communion with God and other members of the Mystical Body of Christ, the "Whole Christ." Sunday Mass is a fundamental necessity for the life of the Church and of individual believers. The faithful have a serious obligation to participate in Sunday Mass, unless they are impeded for a serious reason beyond their control.

So much is the Eucharist the Sacrament of Church Unity that it is never legitimate to celebrate the Eucharist with others who are not in full communion with our Catholic Faith. The denial of one or more truths of the Catholic Faith regarding the Sacraments of the Eucharist and Reconciliation (Penance) would render a person improperly disposed to receive them legitimately. Catholics may never receive communion in non-Catholic communities, which, at any rate, lack a valid Sacrament of Holy Orders and therefore lack the true Eucharist. As already indicated their "communion" or "Eucharist" — or whatever word they may use — is not the Real Sacramental Presence of Our Lord and Savior Jesus Christ. The Catholic Church has always emphasized the importance of great reverence and adoration toward the Holy Eucharist, which contains the Real Presence of the God-Man, Jesus Christ. That is why the genuflection is made to the Most Blessed Sacrament upon entering the Church where Jesus is present in the tabernacle, or anytime we pass before the tabernacle. It is why there burns before or near the tabernacle the sanctuary lamp as a sign of His Real Presence.

The Church through the centuries has shown her great concern to express adoration for the Eucharist, and in a proper setting with the same care the disciples had when preparing the upper room. While the expression of *banquet*, or *Eucharistic banquet*, for the Sacrifice of the Mass expresses familiarity and communion, the Church has never permitted this "intimacy" with her Spouse to be trivialized. The Church is always mindful that Jesus is her Lord. The "banquet" in Church doctrine is always presented as a sacrificial banquet and contains the same Blood of Jesus shed on Golgotha. This bread of angels (*panis angelorum*), cannot be approached or received properly and worthily except when one does so with humility, like that of the centurion in the Gospel: "Lord, I am not worthy to have you come under my roof" (Matt. 8:8).

With this faith and love of the Church for the Eucharist there has developed through the centuries *a particular form of regulating the Eucharistic Liturgy*. The Church insists that her priests follow the approved liturgy of the Church and not develop or improvise their own. The priest is not acting in his own name but *in persona Christi* on behalf of the universal Church. He cannot develop his own way or rite of offering the liturgy. The liturgy is the work of Christ and His universal Church, not simply the work of the particular priest offering; that is because the authentic Eucharist is always offered *in persona Christi*. Strictly speaking, no priest can speak of "my Mass."

Church architecture — in the way of great cathedrals of the Middle Ages — as displayed in churches — whether large or small — with their altars and tabernacles within Church interiors, seeks to express the awe, the wonder, and proper understanding of the mystery of faith, the Eucharist. The same could be said of sacred music developed through the centuries, Gregorian melodies, and the like. And when architecture, music, furnishings, vestments, and so on are secularized, faith in the Real Presence of the God-Man Jesus Christ goes down, as does remembrance of the Sacrifice of Christ perpetuated. Reverence is thus lacking, and this lack of reverence weakens or destroys faith.

Interior disposition of devotion to the Mystery of the Eucharist through the centuries has found outward forms to express and emphasize the grandeur of this central mystery of our Catholic Faith. The designs of altars, tabernacles, vestments, and church interiors, have not been simply artistic presentations but expressions of appreciation and understanding in awe of the Mystery of the Eucharist. The Eucharist and its spirituality have affected our "culture," and when faith and the sense of the Eucharistic mystery suffers, so does our culture.

The Greco–Byzantine and Slavic traditions have given the Church some of Her greatest architectural and artistic works. The sacred art of the East has been especially powerful in its sense of mystery — inspired by the Holy Spirit. The East has created artistic beauty that is a real service to the Faith and does not attempt to present mere natural beauty, but mysteries of faith — the very soul and spirit of the Person of Christ, and that of the Most Blessed Trinity, angels, and saints.

In saying the Church and the Eucharist go together because of their profound relationship, we must at the same time consider Mary, Mother and Model of the Church. Mary has a profound relationship to the Eucharist, so much so that she is called "Our Lady of the Eucharist."

While the Gospel accounts of the institution of the Holy Eucharist on Holy Thursday evening make no mention of Mary's presence at the Last Supper, still, she was present among the apostles who prayed "with one accord" (Acts 1:14) in the first recorded Christian community. It is obvious that Mary, Queen of the Apostles, gathered with that first community after the Ascension; thus she was present at Eucharistic celebrations with those first Christians devoted to "the breaking of bread" (Acts 2:42).

As Abraham was the man of faith in the Old Testament, Mary is the woman of faith in the New Testament. The Eucharist, *mysterium fidei*, central to our Faith calls forth as our model, Mary, Woman of Faith.

Our Catholic Faith tells us, as Sacred Scripture reveals, that the Eucharist contains the Sacrifice of Jesus Christ on Calvary. Mary had within her the sacrificial dimension we find in the Eucharist. She already bore the sacrifice at first of not even her husband Joseph knowing that she had conceived of the Holy Spirit. She heard the prophecy of Simeon when she brought the newborn Child Jesus to the Temple "to present him to the Lord" (Luke 2:22), that this Child would be a "sign that is spoken against" and that "sword will pierce through your own soul" (Luke 2:34–35).

Mary knew in a special way, as the Spouse of the Holy Spirit, the meaning of the prophecies concerning the suffering servant who would redeem us, and so as the Child advanced "in wisdom and in stature" (Luke 2:52), Mary too experienced a kind of anticipated Eucharist. After Easter she was able to partake of the Eucharist, living in the home of the young Apostle John and thus recalling and celebrating the memorial of the Passion of Christ, and her own passion, and also then receiving the resurrected Christ in Communion.

Picture Mary's heart as she hears one of the apostles, Peter, John, James, or one of the others, speak the words of Consecration first spoken at the Last Supper: "This is my body which is given for you" (Luke 22:19). This Body, which her faith knew brought forth in sacramental signs the Real Presence of her Son, was the same Body which she had once conceived of the Holy Spirit in her womb when she answered *fiat* to the archangel Gabriel. What must have been her thoughts as she received the Eucharist, welcoming again into herself the Son of the Most High made flesh?

When the Sacrifice of Calvary is perpetuated, there becomes present all that Christ did with regard to His Mother and for us. *Since the Church and the Eucharist are inseparable, so are Mary and the Eucharist. The Church, Eucharist, and Mary go together.* This explains why, from the beginning of Christianity, the commemoration of Mary has always been a part of the celebration of the Eucharist in the Church, both East and West.

When we receive Jesus in Holy Communion, it is therefore ideal to do so in union with the spirit of Mary, recalling the spirit with which she first received Jesus at the Annunciation and later received Him in the celebration of the Eucharist by one of the apostles.

The *Magnificat* expresses the spirituality of Mary. This spirituality helps us experience the Mystery of the Eucharist.

Jesus Christ, in speaking to those present, always spoke in the present, but always with a view to the future. When Jesus told the parable of the vineyard and how they killed the various representatives of the owner of the vineyard, and finally his son that was sent, Jesus was speaking about Himself sent by the Father. He was speaking to those present and even to us today. Pope Benedict XVI reminds us that such is the logic of the modern world. Declare God is dead and then we can make ourselves "god." The devil tempted Jesus to turn the rocks into bread, thus attempting to distort the Messiah's mission, which culminated with the institution of the Eucharist on the eve of His physical death. The transubstantiation of bread into His Sacred Body would always make present Jesus' redeeming sacrificial death and Resurrection.

We notice that Jesus used wine, the fruit of the vine, to be changed into His Precious Blood. He also spoke of Himself as the true vine and us as the branches. The parable of the vine occurs during the Last Supper. While the Apostle John, in the sixth chapter of his Gospel, gives us Jesus' long discourse on the Eucharist, he does not speak of the Church as the Body of Christ. However, the parable of the vine and branches is placed in the context of Jesus' Last Supper and thus points to the Eucharist and our union with Christ through the Eucharist.

The multiplication of bread and His speaking of the true Bread from Heaven that He would give us, speaks of the Eucharistic Bread, His Real Presence and Sacrifice to come. In speaking of the vine, Jesus is speaking also of the new wine that had been prefigured at Cana. The wine that will flow from Jesus' Passion, in His love "to the end" (John 13:1), is Jesus' own Precious Blood flowing from His own Sacred Body on the Cross. We see in this that the parable of the vine is Eucharistic. When Jesus said to His Mother at the Cana wedding banquet, "My hour has not yet come" (John 2:4), He was thinking of His institution of the Eucharist and His sacrificial death to be thereby perpetuated. It was like saying, "Mother, do you realize what you are requesting in telling me they have no wine? You too will be associated in that hour that you are asking me to prefigure and anticipate."

Jesus, the true vine, pours the blood of His true vine out on the Cross, preparing us for God's marriage feast with man, a union achieved in the Eucharist, a union perpetuated for the Church now on earth, extending into the heavenly liturgy. In Heaven, we shall forever participate in this wedding feast and banquet. The ultimate fruit of the true vine is love, the love of Jesus and the love of Christ to exist in each one of us, united as branches to the true vine.

Jesus' long discourse on Himself as the true Bread come down from Heaven is pointing to His Incarnation and to His Paschal journeying toward the Eucharist, in which His Incarnation and Easter Resurrection are always present. The Eucharist is right at the center of our Christian lives and the center of the very existence of the Church. The Eucharist is man's greatest encounter with God and with the Communion of Saints.

The Divine Liturgy of the Church par excellence is that of the Sacrifice of the Mass. In it we participate not only in something from the past, but are made contemporaries with our future life in Heaven. The Eucharist is not simply a meal. We are made contemporary with the Paschal Mystery of Jesus Christ, which He first lived. We are also caught up in Jesus' Resurrection, Ascension, and his Presence now in the sight of God the Father.

Since the past and the present penetrate each other in the Divine Liturgy of the Eucharist so that the past is a far-reaching power of what follows while being made present, thus the future, also, is present in the event of the Eucharistic Liturgy. It is an anticipation of what is to come. That is, our eventual presence in Heaven and our risen bodies also in Heaven flow from the Eucharist. It is an anticipation of Heaven on earth. The resurrected Christ ascended and now in Heaven becomes present on the altar and comes to each of us as the source of our own future resurrection.

When my mother was dying, she spoke well of the Eucharist as her death approached. After living in my rectory for sixteen years after I was assigned as administrator of my own parish, my mother participated daily in the Sacrifice of the Mass that I offered. As a part of her thanksgiving after Mass, she would make the Stations of the

Cross. During the day, among other things, she meditated on the mysteries of the Rosary. During the years she was with me she would look toward the Church from her window and informed me that she was conscious that Jesus was there in the tabernacle. When she was dying, my mother said to me: "The years I have spent with you have been like Heaven on earth."

Remembering St. Monica's words to her son, St. Augustine, as she was dying, I told my dying mother, "I'll remember you at the altar of God." During the long time of natural grieving after her death, as I would celebrate the Eucharist, I knew that my mother in Heaven was in the presence of the same Jesus Christ, together with the entire Blessed Trinity, made present at the altar before me. The liturgy is meant to make it possible for me to become contemporary with the Pasch of Christ and assimilated unto God. I knew my mother had her passover into eternity, and I could be united with her in Christ at each Eucharist.

By prayer and reflection, we need to probe deeper with our minds and hearts — into the Mystery that is the Holy Eucharist. The infinite God is present in the Eucharist; the entire Blessed Trinity is present because the Body, Blood, Soul, and Divinity of God the Son made man is present in this Most Blessed Sacrament of the altar. In my fifty-four years in Christ's holy priesthood, I am coming ever anew to a deeper understanding of the Eucharist, which shall be continued and completed only in Heaven, already begun on this earth.

I grew up on a farm in rural South Dakota. Without electricity or running water, and with very cold northern winters, it was a childhood I'd trade for no other. My father had died shortly after I turned one year of age, leaving my mother with eight children. He had been sick for a year before his death. Yet, I inherited a legacy of faith from him as well as our mother, who remained with us until shortly before her eighty-fifth birthday. She spent the last sixteen years of her life in my rectory and in parishes where I was the pastor.

Fire and Spirit — Heaven and Earth Unite

I remember one summer night, lying with my brothers on a hay pile in our yard — after complete darkness — without even the moon shining, but the sky was completely clear. The bright stars were without number to us. And we considered how great God is. There is nothing like looking at the stars at night out in the country with no other lights around to get a sense of the incredible vastness of space that reflects the infinite God. And now we know God has made billions of other galaxies. Yet, as awesome as it is, the universe is just a tiny reflection of the Creator whose presence surrounds and sustains every particle of His creation. Certainly if God's love were as visible as the moon and the Milky Way on a clear night, we would be more awed than any stargazer looking into the night sky. His love is limitless. No one falls outside its scope, not even "outsiders," like the Canaanite woman of the Gospel. The Canaanite woman reminds us that no one is an outcast when it comes to God's love.

You have heard of St. Thomas Aquinas. He became perhaps the greatest theologian of the Church since St. Augustine of an earlier century. An advisor to popes, despite his formidable intellect, Thomas remained humble and even childlike. His profound writings are studied to this day and formed the basis of my own theological formation in the seminary. He was a prolific writer. Most of his theological work survives, a total of six million words. His daily routine was one of profound prayer, lecturing, and writing, and with profound energy. It was said that he never wasted a moment. But everything changed for his daily schedule on December 6, 1273. Thomas was still hard at work on the *Summa*, but something happened at that day's morning Mass. Despite urgings, he never took up his pen again. Only to Reginald, his secretary and closest friend, did Thomas eventually reveal what happened. And Reginald revealed it only thirty years later on his own deathbed.

While celebrating Mass that December 6, St. Thomas had a vision of the Crucified Christ, who spoke to him: "You have written well of me, Thomas. What would you ask of Me?" To which Thomas could only reply, "Nothing else but you, Lord."

Compared to what he had seen and understood in this experience, Thomas explained that everything he had written seemed of no more value than straw. He could write about theology no more. He refused to take up his pen again. He then withdrew and declined physically. He had energy only for constant prayer. After that vision of Christ Crucified, as he was offering Mass, Thomas comprehended the love of God so greatly. Having been in good health until that December 6th at Mass, he was dead a few months later. He left us with a personal teaching that the best response to the mystery of God is love. Doesn't it make you think how limited is our understanding of God's love for us?

God so loved the world that He gave us His only begotten Son, and the Son so loved us that He laid down His life on the Cross for our salvation. We know these words well; we say them, but how deeply do we probe their meaning? We need a special grace of the Holy Spirit, penetrating our hearts deeply, to appreciate in any great depth their meaning. The good holy angels were already in utter awe at the divine mercy of the infinite God become man; man, a nature lower than their own. And the good holy angels behold God become man dying on the Cross for sinful creatures made in His own image and likeness. When the God-Man hung dying on the Cross for our sins, the awe of the good holy angels knew no bounds — as they were gathered by myriads about the Cross on Calvary. They saw the Precious Blood of the Lord being poured out for us; poured out so as to redeem the world.

St. Thomas Aquinas, who was recognized in his lifetime, and even today, as one of the most brilliant theologians — six million words in many volumes still in print — in an instant, during Mass that day, gained immeasurable knowledge of God's love. Seeing Jesus Christ Crucified, and that is what the Mass is, perpetuating the self-same

Sacrifice of the Cross, the Holy Spirit infused into his soul the deeper understanding of the mystery of the Cross, God's love and blood outpoured. In a moment Thomas could see that his great writings had hardly skimmed the surface of the reality of the *Real Presence of Christ and His Sacrifice of love that is the Eucharist*. The glory of the Holy Eucharist is that, as we receive the Holy Eucharist and pay attention to the way we live, we become one with Jesus Christ, filled with joy and love. Jesus said: "He who eats my flesh and drinks my blood abides in me, and I in him" (John 6:56).

We must depend on Jesus to feed and protect us, for He is the Way. Jesus is our merciful Lord and Savior. The time is coming when each of us will be seriously tested and persecuted for living the Faith. If you follow the news, you know there are many indications of persecutions coming and which have already come in many places. We will be tested and persecuted. We must come to know Jesus in a deeper way. We must receive the sacraments often so we have the grace needed to say no to the enemy. The world is becoming darker. Every day we need the help of Jesus, "the Light of the world," to do His will. We must turn to Jesus' message of love, mercy, and forgiveness. We must walk in Jesus' footsteps and carry each new cross with joy. Jesus is Truth. Jesus is Love.

Let us pray that we open our hearts to the Holy Spirit to touch us in some way, as St. Thomas Aquinas was transformed deeply in a moment. At every Sacrifice of the Mass, reflect on the infinite act of love, mercy, and adoration by the God-Man in which we participate whenever we celebrate the Eucharistic Sacrifice of the Mass.

In this book I have dealt often with the teaching that during the Divine Liturgy of the Eucharist we are united with the heavenly liturgy and that the mysteries of Christ are made present. I am more and more conscious of this as I celebrate the Eucharist daily as a senior priest. I appreciate it then when I read the following from the works of Bl. Anne Catherine Emmerich about the Three Kings who came to adore the newborn Savior, such as we celebrate at Epiphany each year:

> Oh what heavenly peace surrounds the prayers of these good men from the East! As I saw them, I said to myself: how clear and untroubled are their hearts, as full of goodness and innocence as the hearts of pious children. There is nothing violent in them, and yet they are all fire and love. I am dead, I am a spirit, otherwise I could not see it, for it is not happening now — and yet it *is* now, for it is not in time; in God is no time, in God everything is present. I am dead, I am a spirit. As these strange thoughts came to me, I heard myself being told: "What is that to thee? Be not troubled, look, and praise the Lord who is eternal and in whom are all things." (*Life of the Blessed Virgin Mary*)

Pope Benedict XVI, already as Cardinal Joseph Ratzinger, gave us much theology on covenant. His theology of covenant, it is said, gives the master key to a unified interpretation of Sacred Scripture centered on the Person and work of Jesus Christ. And Pope Benedict reminds us over and over that Jesus Christ is *God* as well as man. He tells us the theology of covenant is integral to Christian identity as given by divine revelation, and especially as recorded in the New Testament. In an article he wrote for *Communio* entitled, "The New Covenant: A Theology of Covenant in the New Testament," Ratzinger writes, "Christology thus appears as the synthesis of the covenantal theology of the New Testament, which is grounded in the unity of the entire Bible."

We have earlier written of covenant as a *sacred bonding*. Pope Benedict XVI expresses covenant as an unsought gift of God to man. We don't merit grace or union with God. It's a free gift of the merciful and loving God. "The covenant then is not a pact built on reciprocity, but rather a gift, a creative act of God's love" (Ratzinger, "New Covenant," 636). It is not simply a contract. Ratzinger noted that the Old Testament distinguished the Noahite, Abrahamic, Mosaic, and Davidic covenants, as, in salvation history, the covenants of God take multiple forms.

St. Paul wrote of "covenants" to explain God's dealing with Israel (Rom. 9:4). The most important of the covenants, as St. Paul wrote of them, were the Abrahamic and the Mosaic, both of which relate to the New Covenant. All of the covenants are part of salvation or human history, but the Abrahamic Covenant and the New Covenant have a divine permanence, whereas the Mosaic Covenant has a transitory and provisional nature. The Abrahamic Covenant is fundamental and enduring, the Mosaic covenant is intervening.

The Mosaic Law would pass as it was a transitional teaching destined to end once the goal was achieved. The goal of the Law was none other than Jesus Christ Himself (Rom. 10:4).

To say it briefly, Jesus Christ is Himself the New Covenant. He establishes it firmly in the words of the institution of the Eucharist, as He spoke over the chalice during the Last Supper. "This is my blood of the covenant" (Mark 14:24). It reminds one of the institution of the Mosaic Covenant in Exodus 24:8. What Jesus is speaking of established a blood union or kinship between its participants. God establishes a "mysterious consanguinity" between Himself and man (Ratzinger, "New Covenant," 642).

The Last Supper was the "sealing of the Covenant" and is identified with Christ's Sacrifice of the Cross and the Mass today. The Eucharist is today making present to us this covenant. The Blood of Jesus Christ is really offered to the Father in atonement (Heb. 9:11–14, 24–26).

St. Paul and St. Luke, in teaching the revelation given us by Jesus Christ, teach the same, but in a different way. It is not the "blood of the covenant," but the chalice is described as the "new covenant in my blood" (1 Cor. 11:25). This is to allude to Jeremiah's prophecy of the New Covenant (Jer. 31:31–34). This prophecy tells that the New Covenant is never to be broken. It is contrasted with the Mosaic Covenant "which they [Israel] broke" (Jer. 31:32).

In violating the Mosaic Law, Israel incurred the curses of the Deuteronomic Covenant (Deut. 28:15–68; 30:1). Jesus took these curses upon Himself on the Cross (Gal. 3:13). His death fulfilled "the perfect realization" of the Day of Atonement. In fact, Jesus took upon Himself the sins of all peoples, of all times.

Sacred Scripture presents salvation history as a dynamic unity. Seen as a whole, there is only "one covenant." This is to say the "eternally valid" covenant of Abraham is now perfectly fulfilled in Jesus Christ (Ratzinger, "New Covenant," 640). One was the promise; the New Covenant in Jesus Christ is the fulfillment.

In God's plan the Abrahamic Covenant was always intended from the beginning to be fulfilled by Jesus Christ. God confirms that the New Covenant struck with the death of His Son incarnate is indestructible, will be everlasting, eternal. And yet it is made present to us at the Sacrifice of the Mass and is present in the eternal heavenly liturgy. It is everlasting, eternal. In this New Covenant, the past, the present, and the future join in the eternal *now* of God.

St. John the Apostle, in his Gospel, presents the miracle of Jesus' multiplication of the loaves (John 6:1-15), and Jesus focused immediately thereafter on His gift of the Bread of Life. The apostle is contrasting Moses and Jesus. Jesus will become the greater Moses, the "Prophet" whom Moses foretold of at the border of the promised Holy Land. Concerning the "Prophet," God said: "I will put my words in his mouth, and he shall speak to them all that I command him" (Deut. 18:18). Moses struck the rock in the desert at God's command to bring forth water. Jesus promises the water of eternal life. The people, even years later, are impressed in memory with the gift of the manna, or bread from Heaven. But their favorable impression with the manna to fill their stomachs is misdirected. They miss its meaning, as the sign of the multiplication of the loaves was missed.

What do we see different between Moses and Jesus? True, Moses spoke face-to-face with God, "as a man speaks to his friend" (Exod. 33:11; Deut. 34:10). Moses was thus able to bring God's word to men. But Moses sees only God's back. His face "shall not be seen" (Exod. 33:18, 22–23). Even the great Moses has limitations compared to Christ.

"No one has ever seen God; the only Son, who is in the bosom of the Father, he has made him known" (John 1:18). Jesus, who is God, sees God. Jesus is one with the Father and sees God face-to-face. He came that we may have eternal life and, finally, as a result of Eucharistic union with Jesus Christ, come at last to see God "face-to-face."

Jesus had a dispute with the Jews at the synagogue at Capernaum and pointed out that they failed to understand the "sign" in the multiplication of the loaves. They were rather focused on eating their fill for their stomachs (John 6:26). They were missing the real meaning of salvation and were interpreting Jesus' words and miracles in purely material ways. The manna was not in reality heavenly bread, but earthly bread that Moses obtained for God's people. It would cease when Israel came out of the desert.

The bread of the Torah showed only God's back or was but a "shadow" of "the bread of God … which comes down from heaven, and gives life to the world" (John 6:33). Jesus' discourse on bread is pointing to the reality of the Incarnation, "the Word made flesh," and the Paschal Sacrament He instituted to make the Incarnation, Calvary, Easter all come together and be forever present. This places the Eucharist right in the center of Christian life, that of the Church and Her existence and permanency. "Unless a grain of wheat falls into the earth and dies, it remains alone; but if it dies, it bears much fruit"

(John 12:24). Jesus' teachings on the Eucharist stretch across the pages of recorded Scripture, salvation history, and divine revelation.

Jesus is "the promised shoot of Judah, who unites Israel and the nations in the kingdom of God." Members of all nations become the People of God with Israel through the acceptance of the Davidic Kingdom (Ratzinger, *Many Religions — One Covenant*, 25). It's God's rule on earth extended from Heaven (Isa. 52:7) and extended to Heaven. There is now only one true People of God, the Body of Christ, and both Jews and Gentiles of every nation are welcome. Jesus, the New Adam, was given the mission that He accomplished of uniting Jews and Gentiles in a single People of God. It is often called the Mystical Body of Christ. The Gentiles, as St. Paul explains it, have been grafted onto the Body of Christ (Rom. 11:17–24). Only those are pruned from this good olive tree, those branches that refuse faith in Jesus Christ (Rom. 11:20). The Old Testament is important to appreciate and understand faith in Jesus Christ. "There is no access to Jesus and there can be no entrance of the nations into the People of God without acceptance in faith of … the Old Testament" (Ratzinger, *Many Religions*, 28).

The sanctifying grace we have in our souls now is the same eternal life of God we shall have in Heaven. In this truth we can understand how Heaven begins already on earth, for it is a sharing in the life of God now. Our future salvation requires a way of life that is human here and empowered by Christ's grace, making us capable of living the life of God for all eternity. We must live a life of righteousness on earth and die in grace. In Jesus Christ there is the unity of God and man. And Jesus Christ lives in us by grace as an extension of His Incarnation in His Mystical Body. Eternal life is a quality of existence in our soul, which is united to our body, and is already present as we live our earthly lives. We live in grace now and by faith, not by sight, which we shall have fully only when we see God face-to-face even as

He is. "We walk by faith, not by sight" (2 Cor. 5:7). Eternal life then is not simply what comes after our life on earth. While imperfect and fragmentary in fashion, it is already present to us now on earth.

Eternal life is another level of being, and is here in the midst of time, even now as we come face-to-face with God in contemplation of the living God, while not yet living in sight. Certain rare souls, like certain mystics, experience the presence of God to the degree of ecstasy. Yet, all who live in grace with divine charity in their souls, touch Heaven even now; Heaven touches them. "This is eternal life, that they know thee the only true God, and Jesus Christ whom thou hast sent" (John 17:3). The time of Holy Communion, when we have received the Living Bread come down from Heaven, when the living Body, Blood, Soul, and Divinity of Jesus Christ is within us, is the closest union with God possible on earth, next only to our union with Him in the realm of Heaven.

The eternal life we have within us as we live our earthly life is untouched by the death of the body. Some greater conception of its reality gradually develops in us as we grow in spirituality. The beauty of eternal life within us gradually transforms us. We are liberated from self, and this is what makes sense of eternity. Not only are we gathered into the gaze of God's love, but we attain fellowship, union in God, through Jesus Christ, with all those who accept and live in that same love. "The kingdom of God is in the midst of you" (Luke 17:21). Thus God is all in all. We are one Body of Christ, and the joy of one member is the joy of all other members. When we will live in the state of being in Heaven, this communion with God here and now takes this here and now up into the great infinite expanse of the ultimate reality of God; our participation in eternal life is no longer fragmented by time. In God there is only *now*.

If the above seems overwhelming, and it does to me, especially at times, then I remember one of my favorite scriptural quotations. It seems an excellent manner in which to close our attempt at explaining the Eucharist in this book. It is to be found in the second chapter of the First Letter to the Corinthians: "What no eye has seen, nor ear heard, nor the heart of man conceived, what God has prepared for those who love him" (1 Cor. 2:9).

About the Author

Fr. Robert J. Fox (1927–2009) was ordained a priest for the Diocese of Sioux Falls, South Dakota, where he served as a parish priest for fifty-four years. He wrote more than fifty books on the Catholic Faith, including catechisms. He is renowned for his devotion to Our Lady and built three shrines in her honor. He was also the founder of the Fatima Family Apostolate, the National Marian Conference, and *Immaculate Heart Messenger*. For many years, he was a columnist for the *National Catholic Register* and a writer for *Our Sunday Visitor* and many other publications. He often appeared on EWTN and produced many educational recordings.